Lucilla Andrews was born in Suez, the second daughter of an English father and Spanish mother. Her late father was then a manager in the Eastern Telegraph Company. At three she began her education in an English private girls' boarding school in Sussex and when she was eleven she wrote her first novel – an epic of love, lust and banditry in China. Unfortunately the manuscript was discovered and ended in the school incinerator.

During World War II, Lucilla Andrews entered the Nightingale Training School at St Thomas's Hospital in London and five years later left with an S.R.N. and S.C.M. Part One. She married a doctor, had one child, and when her husband's illness necessitated that she become the family breadwinner she returned to nursing.

Her first book, *The Print Petticoat,* was written while she was working as an assistant Night Sister in a small Sussex hospital. Since that time it has never been out of print.

Over the years Lucilla Andrews has established herself as one of Britain's leading popular novelists. She created what was virtually a new genre – the hospital romance – written against an authentic and detailed medical background drawn from her own experience.

Lucilla Andrews lives in Edinburgh.

NO TIME FOR ROMANCE

An autobiographical account of a few
moments in British and personal history

Lucilla Andrews

CORGI BOOKS

NO TIME FOR ROMANCE

A CORGI BOOK   0 552 99315 8

Originally published in Great Britain
by Harrap & Co. Ltd.

PRINTING HISTORY

Harrap edition published 1977
Corgi edition published 1978
Corgi edition reissued 1988

This book is set in 10/11pt Plantin

Corgi Books are published by Transworld Publishers Ltd., 61-63 Uxbridge Road,
Ealing, London W5 5SA, in Australia by Transworld Publishers (Australia) Pty.
Ltd., 15-23 Helles Avenue, Moorebank, NSW 2170, and in New Zealand by
Transworld Publishers (N.Z.) Ltd., Cnr. Moselle and Waipareira Avenues,
Henderson, Auckland.

Printed and bound in Great Britain by
The Guernsey Press Co. Ltd., Guernsey, Channel Islands.

To all my fellow-nurses, trained and untrained,
who worked in all British hospitals,
at home or overseas, in the
Second World War.

*The reader will not credit that such things
could be — but I was there and I saw it.*
IZAAK WALTON, 1593-1683

Glossary

ack-ack	anti-aircraft gun/fire
AIF	Australian Imperial Force
A.P.C.s	Aspirin, Phenacetin, Caffeine tablets
A.R.P.	Air Raid Precautions
A.R.R.C.	Award of the Royal Red Cross
ATS	Auxiliary Territorial Service
BBC	British Broadcasting Corporation
BEF	British Expeditionary Force
BRCS	British Red Cross Society
Cpl	Corporal
C.P.O.	Chief Petty Officer
civvy street	civilian life
D.F.C.	Distinguished Flying Cross
D.I.L.	Dangerously Ill List
EMS	Emergency Medical Service(s)
ETC	Eastern Telegraph Company
F.R.C.S.	Fellow of the Royal College of Surgeons
Gnr	Gunner
G.O.C.	General Officer in Command
G.P.	General Practitioner
H.M.S.	His Majesty's Ship
Ike	General Dwight D. Eisenhower
I.T.M.A.	*It's That Man Again* (BBC radio programme)
K.R.R.s	King's Rules and Regulations
M. and B.	May and Baker (tablets)
M.O.	Medical Officer
M.O.Q.	Married Officers Quarters
multip.	Multipara (More than one pregnancy)
N.	Nurse
N.C.O.	Non-Commissioned Officer
non-coms	non-combatants
N.D.K.	No Diagnosis Known

N.Y.D.	Not Yet Diagnosed
O.B.E.	Order of the British Empire
O.R.s	Other Ranks
P.A.D.	Passive Air Defence
P and O	Penninsular and Oriental (Steamship Co.)
pro	probationer (student) nurse
Pte	Private
P.T.S.	Preliminary Training-School
QAs	Queen Alexandra's Imperial Military Nursing Service
Q-ship	Armed British merchant ship in First World War; camouflaged as unarmed until attacked
RAMC	Royal Army Medical Corps
R.A.P.	Resident Assistant Physician
R.A.S.	Resident Assistant Surgeon
RASC	Royal Army Service Corps
RN	Royal Navy
RNR	Royal Navy Reserve
RNVR	Royal Naval Volunteer Reserve
R.S.M.	Regimental Sergeant-Major
R.T.O.	Railway Transport Officer
S.C.M.	State Certified Midwife
Sgt	Sergeant
S.I.L.	Seriously Ill List
S.R.N.	State Registered Nurse
STH	St. Thomas's Hospital, London SE1
STs	Sanitary Towels
Tpr	Trooper
u/s	Unserviceable
V1	Vergeltungswaffe Eins (Revenge Weapon No. 1)
V2	Vergeltungswaffe Zwei (Revenge Weapon No. 2)
VAD	Voluntary Aid Detachment
V.E.	Victory in Europe
V.J.	Victory in Japan
WAAF	Women's Auxiliary Air Force
WRNS	Women's Royal Naval Service
WVS	Women's Voluntary Service(s)

Chapter One

As always, it was the sudden silence that woke me, but that morning in March 1945, for the last time. The silence meant the flying bomb overhead had switched off its engine and within seconds would explode on the ground. By my counting, eight seconds; others varied this from five to fifteen.

I was sleeping face downwards with a then habitual pillow over the back of my head and neck. I preferred to risk a severed spine to having my face sliced off and had nursed enough flying bomb casualties to know I could have that choice. I was sleeping in my own room on the top and fifth floor of Riddle House, which was the nurses' home on the Thames-side site of St Thomas's Hospital, London SE1. The two others, the Nightingale Home and Gassiot House, had been destroyed by enemy action years earlier in the Second World War. By that early morning in March the air attacks were tapering to their end. Our authorities no longer insisted nurses slept in the basement shelters as they had done during the blitzes and when the flying bomb attacks had started in June, 1944. For the first few weeks of the attack, between 100 and 150 flying bombs were launched on London daily. Familiarity and fatigue had bred in me not contempt but a passion for privacy. Five years wartime nursing had removed the terror from the thought of facing possible death alone. Death, as I had too often observed, seemed an inexorably lonely yet strangely unfrightening place. I remained terrified by the thought of the mutilating injuries that did not always kill.

It was that thought that triggered the conditioned reflex that jolted my body from the bed and my voice into counting aloud before my eyes were properly open. Counting, I ran from my room along the top floor and down the stairs round the liftwell. That the lift was elsewhere and out-of-bounds from 11 p.m. to 7 a.m. was immaterial as it was the last sanctuary I would have chosen in a building at risk of caving in. I reached the third landing at 'eight', and had just flung myself face down on the floor with both arms folded over the back of my head, when the explosion rattled teeth, bones, eardrums and every inch of metal in the liftwell. Riddle House swayed perceptibly then settled, unharmed. It was the only building I was ever in during air attacks to give that odd, reassuring sensation of riding with the punch. All the others had shaken, rocked, groaned, creaked, cracked, spattered glass, bricks, plaster, dust, and the omnipresent blackout screens. I was not in Riddle House during the London Blitz, but whenever I was in the building during the flying bomb and rocket attacks, I noticed that all it did was shed a few blackout screens and clouds of dust. If any plaster came down, it was not on my head.

I picked myself off the floor, sat on the stairs to get my breath and only then realized one of my set of fourth-year student nurses was sitting a few steps up. We looked at each other and grinned euphorically, triumphantly, because we were still alive. At few moments is life more worth living than in those following the one that could have been one's last.

My friend, as myself, was barefoot, but in short-sleeved cotton pyjamas instead of a nightie, with a navy nurse's uniform cloak slung over one shoulder and clutched in her hands, a lipstick and her fiancé's photograph. Over my cotton nightie was the small fur carriage rug I used on my bed. On the landing floor were my eyelash curlers and the much-mended-with-sticking-plaster red cardboard foolscap file of notes for the books I one day intended to write. I had no recollection of grabbing rug, curlers or notes on my way out; my conditioned reflexes had had good practice.

There was little time for private notes in the second half of '44 and early months of '45 in London. The flying bomb attacks started shortly after D. Day (6th June), the rockets in

September. The official name for the flying bombs was V1s. (Vergeltungswaffe Eins: Revenge Weapon No. 1.) The rockets were V2s. The RAF and London nicknamed the flying bombs 'doodlebugs', often shortened to 'doodles'. In other areas of Britain they were nicknamed 'buzzbombs', and in parts of the country well beyond their range, apparently, regarded as a joke.

These bombs were small automatic aircraft, roughly twenty-five feet long, with noses filled with explosive and tails that spat flames as they streaked jerkily across the sky. The peculiar chug-chug-chug roar of the engines in flight reminded me of the revving of an unsilenced motor-bike engine. Before it was launched each bomb was set to a chosen course and to switch off and dive at a chosen point. In flight the bombs looked evil; when they achieved their pre-set object they caused evil. London learnt to live with them as London had learnt to live with 'ordinary' bombs, high-explosive bombs, fire bombs and land mines, but whilst the flying bomb attacks lasted I never met anyone in London, including myself, who did not fear them far more than the rockets, though the latter were politically regarded as the greater menace.

'Mind you, nurse, like as I says to the wife when they fetched us out—seeing as you ain't gone, gal, and me neither, reckon we're in luck. But you ought to see the muck as is all that's left of our street, nurse. That doodle come down on the end house, see, and our whole row go down like a pack of cards—and all but the one in the row opposite and there it is sticking up like me old dad's one front tooth. Blast, that's what. Cruel the blast from them doodles—and no telling what it'll do! You take me son-in-law, nurse! Caught out, he was, when one come down Kennington way last week—not a stitch—not a stitch left on! Mother naked, wasn't he—and me daughter she didn't know where to put her face! Just atween you and me, nurse—tell you straight—can't be doing with them doodles, I can't. Different afore. Well, I mean to say, with them old H.E.s and the like you knew what was what. You knew as Jerry was up there bunging 'em down and taking his chances and—well—fair's fair as you might say. But what's he a-doing now, eh?

Sitting on his backside with them Frogs—if you'll pardon me
French, nurse—and a-pushing a button to lob 'em over! Not
right, it ain't. Oh dear me no, it ain't right! Is it right what the
warden says about your copping another on this lot, nurse?
Just come down on one of them ruined blocks? Cor! That's
alright, then, ain't it? But I can't be doing with them
doodles. . . .'

St Thomas's Hospital stands on the bank of the Thames
directly opposite the Houses of Parliament. This site, ideal in
peacetime, was rather less so when central London was the eye
of the target of enemy air attacks, which happened quite often
in the Second World War. My general training lasted from '41
to '45. From first to last day every remaining window in St
Thomas's, London, was bricked in, every balcony door at the
far end of the long wards had fixed boarding over the former
glass panels.

To work in constant artificial light, to disturbed nights, to
off-duty postponed, cut short or cancelled at the last moment
because another bomb or rocket had landed in our zone,
became for a while a normal way of life. In war as peace the
London hospitals, in general, admitted patients from their
own zones, and ours covered a heavily populated area south of
the river. With a little experience it was fairly easy to gauge
from the sound the approximate distance of any explosion and
to know that, if in our zone, within minutes the first casualties
would start coming in. In that event staff about to go off,
stayed on; staff off-duty, in hearing of the explosion, returned
automatically to their wards and departments. I neither remember, nor did I note down at the time, authority asking,
much less demanding, this of the staff or medical students. It
was something that seemed to happen as regularly as clean
aprons were ruined and clean caps wrecked by diving under
benches in Casualty, or the heavy ward tables, when a flying
bomb's switch-off overhead interrupted the writing, giving, or
receiving of ward reports. As regularly, out of the hospital, one
learnt to travel round London by Underground and to dodge
at the double between stations.

'You take my tip, miss, and get down the Piccadilly Line.

Good and deep that is.' The policeman who had flattened himself beside me on a pavement of the Waterloo Road helped me up and brushed us both down. 'As well it's not wet. You'd not want mud on that nice frock.' He replaced his helmet and scanned the long trailing silver legs of the great balloons poised like pregnant spiders all over the sky. 'Seemly, that one come down in the river, but best not to take chances. There'll be another along sharpish,' he added, as if advising on the next double-decker bus. 'Best not to wait for it.'

When working in an above-ground ward, I enjoyed sorting the dirty wet linen dumped in the large flat-covered bins kept on the ward balconies. In normal circumstances, sorting dirty linen was a junior job, but as first and second year junior nurses needed constant supervision and teaching and there was little time for either during air raids, as a general rule, after the London Blitz, only third and fourth year student nurses worked on rota in St Thomas's, London, with the permanent staff of Sisters, Charge Nurses and a few very experienced full-time VADs.

From a second floor ward balcony overlooking the Thames, in the dark early mornings and the evenings, London in the blackout was either a charcoal etching or a sepia sketch. The fading colour of the buses, trams, and very occasional light-coloured car, merged into charcoal or sepia until illuminated by the new daylight or extinguished by night. Once it was properly dark, for the first few seconds on the balcony, darkness blinded; then, after a few more seconds, London reappeared. The river running slowly and black as oil; the line of seemingly omnipresent coal barges just in front of the hospital floating with the delicacy of feathers; the traffic creeping furtively behind muffled lights, the public vehicle windows black-painted and criss-crossed with anti-blast paper to lessen the dangers of flying glass. Westminster Bridge, a drawing by da Vinci; the Houses of Parliament, a black lace frieze not against but suspended from the opposite sky; the jagged, battered skyline of the City softened in darkness, the curve of St Paul's dome just visible by leaning forward over the cold flat stone top of the balcony balustrade and peering to the far right. When there was a good moon and the skies were quiet, London looked a medieval city of uncanny serenity. The moonlight filtering palely through the black frieze, laying silver streaks on the river, white swathes on the bridges, transforming the coal barges into the oblong iced spongecakes we had at birthday parties when I was a child, moving slowly through the gaping ward windows of the empty roofless ruins and reminding me of the torchlight of a night nurse going round her sleeping patients. Occasionally one of the balloons turning into a solitary silver Japanese lantern, the legs invisible, or just the legs appearing as silver threads swaying in air that whatever the hour, after the ward air, smelt fresh and slightly of salt and tar. Always before going back into the ward I gulped in air exactly as if going back to swimming under water.

On other nights all serenity was shattered and the darkness splashed by the red glow of the arc lights of the rescue squads digging out bodies. Sometimes the bodies were still alive; sometimes the rescuers worked all the following day and still the next night the red glow was there. One night even the river between Vauxhall and Westminster bridges glowed red and the face of Big Ben was touched with pink.

One evening after an unnaturally quiet day, a Thomas's houseman and I had drinks at a pub over the river with a houseman and nurse from the Westminster Hospital. We had all been given unexpected free evenings, and, sitting round our corner table in a basement bar, we decided either the RAF had had a bumper day shooting down doodles over Kent and Sussex, or Jerry had for once got his sums wrong and was dropping them short of London. Our hospitals stood on either side of the river. We were shouting each other down as to which had the tougher job, when we heard the first distant chug-chug-chug of the day. We stopped talking as the sound grew louder and at the cut-out dived simultaneously under our table. The explosion was further off than we had expected. We surfaced chorusing joyfully, 'Bart's or U.C.H.! (University College Hospital)'. One of the men picked up our scattered glasses and asked what the other girl and myself had muttered as we went down.

'Please God, don't drop it in Westminster's!' (Zone).

'Please God, don't drop it in Thomas's!' (Zone).

The men said they were sorry for God. 'What's He supposed to do when you're both on the job for the one that's got to get one of us?'

The following Saturday afternoon a bomb exploded in mid-air and the bits landed harmlessly in the river between our hospitals. I was on-duty at the time and met the houseman on my way to tea. 'Keep it up, Lu, keep it up! I'm too young and pretty to die!'

Too many rose-coloured nights, too many days too long and too hideously similar to be remembered individually; too many times when Casualty had no time to spare for warning the wards of incoming patients and the sweating, shirt-sleeved medical students carrying the stretchers would just appear in the ward doorways. 'Another five—seven—ten—coming up. Where do you want him/her, Sister?'

The students, all male, did much of the emergency stretcher-bearing as the few, more experienced in casualty-work, porters were needed to help with the flood of casualties in Casualty Hall and for ferrying the more urgent cases to and from the temporary theatre in the basement. The proper theatre block had been blitzed years earlier.

On one evening of a hideous day, I was sent down to the theatre on a ward errand. The deep, cavernous, hospital base-ment ran roughly the half-mile length of the main ground floor corridor. The uneven ceiling and walls were lined with huge and small pipes, and off the main basement corridor were endless caves of varying sizes housing workshops, stores, laundry, physiotherapists' offices, exercise rooms, wards, and the improvised operating theatre. That evening the 'theatre proper' was partitioned from the empty 'anaesthetic room' by green curtains. Whilst waiting for attention outside the theatre curtains, through a gap I counted five operating tables in action. Each table had its own operating team and, though within touching distance of the tables on either side, each team looked in a private, apparently timeless, world. Only apparently, as a queue of casualties needing immediate operations still waited in the rabbit warren of tiny examination rooms off Casualty Hall. I learnt later the theatre that day worked non-stop for twenty hours. There were other days when the theatre worked longer.

On such days at each reappearance the students' shirts grew more begrimed with the filth of centuries that encased the grey faces and torn, matted clothes of the women and girls under the grey casualty blankets. Immediate ward treatment of air raid victims had then altered. Instead of, as earlier in the war, instantly removing the patients' clothes, washing and putting them into clean nightgowns, it had been found less shocking—where individual injuries made this possible—to leave them in their own clothes until the shock wore off. The filthy dust hung in the ward air and mingled with the smells of fresh and dried blood, of sweat, and the ugly unmistakable smell of human fear. To be buried alive, whether injured or not, can and usually does cause acute clinical shock. Once that shock began to wear off, memory and fear of repetition made beads of black sweat glisten on the still grey faces that, whatever the individual age, looked old. This was one reason why air raid casualties who could safely move were, whenever possible, moved out of London within twenty-four hours of admission. Another reason was the need to keep empty beds for the next incoming wave of casualties.

The wave slackened to a gentle ripple. Then in an hour our ward filled with old ladies and survivors of an Old People's Home damaged on the periphery of a rocket's explosion. 'Of course, had it been any closer, nurse', an air raid warden removed his no longer shiny black tin hat, mopped his brow and left a white streak on his blackened face, 'you'd still have your empty beds.'

The V2 rockets were uncanny things. They came in silence too fast to be seen, too fast for any warning or protection from coastal guns, RAF fighters, or the balloon barrage. When one landed, the first survivors knew of it was a blinding flash followed appreciably seconds later by the first almighty explosion. Then, survivors at a safe distance saw great buildings collapsing as dust into a massive crater and heard the second almighty roar of the falling buildings.

'No sense to worry about a rocket,' said the air raid warden. 'If Jerry gets you with a direct hit, you've had it and you're knocking up St Peter before your mates below've heard the one with your name on it. Don't know how Jerry thinks up these things. Got a clever mind whoever thought this one up.'

(The inventor of the V1s and V2s in Nazi Germany was Dr Werner von Braun who now (1976) and for many years has worked in the United States, mainly, I understand, in connection with the Space Programme.)

A priest connected with the Old People's Home told me: 'Many of my old folk nearly passed on when they heard the second roar. They thought a second rocket had landed on them.'

'I'd have thought the same, Padre. Considering their ages, they've been incredibly lucky.'

He was very tall, gaunt, and looked straight into my face with dark, sunken eyes. 'Not lucky, nurse. Your prayers were answered.'

Later I repeated this to Sister and added, 'I felt horribly guilty as I keep forgetting to pray off rockets and hadn't the nerve to tell him.'

Sister placidly suggested I send up a blanket prayer to keep off rockets for the duration. 'Don't you think that'll cover the situation?'

I was very angry that night. They were nice old ladies and, from what they had said, they had enjoyed their Home. 'Sister, I don't dare think on this sort of day.'

'Wise girl,' she said.

And Wilfred Owen in another war and another time: 'Happy are these who lose imagination. . . .'

There had been other times when thought had to be suspended and imagination stifled, but never had I found either mental discipline so difficult, or downright impossible, as in that time and ward. Too often to number the sight of so much grief, pain, misery and courage rekindled a terrible, silent, anger and taught me to hate screens. The ordinary screens we used to provide privacy round the beds as none then had bed-curtains. Ordinary portable screens on solid feet, not wheels, that had to be lifted into position and carried to and fro on the hip in the approved method long taught by Sister Preliminary Training School. For normal purposes—bedpans, blanket baths, dressings—two screens. For the dangerously ill, the dying, the dead—three screens. Before the removal of a dead patient, screens outstretched on either side of the ward to shut out all the beds whilst the mortuary trolley was wheeled away feet first. All live patients on stretchers, head first. And at certain times screens fixed half-open at strange angles all round the ward to save those patients with undamaged eyesight from seeing certain faces. Faces nursed unbandaged to promote better healing, and heavily dusted with the yellow penicillin powder we were using for the first time and which the artificial light made more garish: the faces of women and girls, all that I nursed, Londoners, and mostly from Lambeth—or to be accurate, what remained of their faces.

Women, generally, were good patients. Nowhere have I nursed better than in that ward at that time. Very few of those patients had had more than the minimum state education, some had begun earning at thirteen, some at eleven. Some lived and some died, but all did both with patience, courage and dignity. Some even managed—and God alone knew how in their circumstances—to meet horror with humour. When London was suffering the Great (bubonic) Plague, her citizens sang *Ring o' Roses*.

> Ring-a-ring o' roses, a pocket full of posies,
> At-tishoo—at-tishoo—we all fall down!

Amongst the symptoms of bubonic plague are a red ring round the mouth, violent sneezing, and collapse.

So that time:

'Come to put some more pretty yeller powder on one of the ruins what 'Itler knocked abaht a bit, duck?'

'Just call me Nelson, nurse! Done alright with 'is one an' only didn't 'e? An' when they 'as me up along of 'im dahn Trafalgar Square them ruddy pigeons'll 'ave to watch it!'

And:

'Nurse, before she comes round from the anaesthetic be sure to check there's no mirror in that handbag her family have just brought up. . . . Nurse, take that powder compact and put it in the desk drawer. . . . Nurse, I think we need a screen moved—down beyond the end bed to shut off the sterilizers.'

The highly polished silvered sides of the large bowl and smaller instrument sterilizers fixed to a panel at one side of the wall by the ward doorway made distorting mirrors, but still mirrors.

At times the ward entrance seemed haunted by huddled little groups of anxious, exhausted relatives. Civilians in the last war were provided with identity cards but not identity discs. Women of all ages most frequently carried their personal papers in their handbags. The rescuer's first object was to save lives, not property. Often for hours and longer our admissions were nameless.

'Sister, please—we're looking for me mum—elderly party—white hair—oh—er—maybe seventy odd—that's right isn't it, Bill—mum's passed seventy—have you got her, Sister—have you got her?'

'I can't find me wife, nurse—can't find her nowhere—oh—well—let me think—oh—red hair and blue eyes—yea, blue eyes—slim like—thirty-two but she don't like to say—is she in here?'

'For Gawd's sake, nurse, have you got a little girl? Eleven—little girl eleven—me Nora—dark hair—short like—but big for her age she is—for Gawd's sake—have you got her—please—?'

In one of the bathrooms outside the ward was a special small table holding the ward stock brandy bottle and medicine glasses on a round tray. The distraught relatives were taken first to that bathroom. 'Would this be your mother's shawl? Cardigan? . . . . Your wife's coat? Dress? . . . . Your little girl's skirt? Jumper?'

Often the clothes were stiff with dried blood; always they were impregnated with dust, soot and plaster. When there was time they were arranged in tidy bundles; when there was not they lay heaped in the empty baths.

'That's hers! Oh, thank Gawd! Can I see her, please—now? How is she?'

And after, the brandy was needed.

Or, 'Nah. Nah. She never wore them. . . .'

'Have you tried Brooke Street? (Hospital). St James', Balham? Well, why not try your nearest Warden's Post again? They may have more names by now. . . . Yes, we do hope so. . . . Yes, we are very sorry—wish we could've helped. . . .'

We gave them tea and when the brandy ran out and was down at the dispensary being refilled, amon. aromat. (Sal volatile). We tried to give them comfort but there is no comfort for those still unsure if the people they love are alive or dead.

The shawl belonged to Mrs B, a First World War widow who had supported a family and herself by dressmaking. 'Fifteen hours a day I worked until me youngest left school, nurse, and then it was only the nine or ten, dear. I've always been handy with my needle. Ever so lucky, that.' Mrs B, blinded by a flying bomb, and badly injured. A few weeks after her death her eldest married daughter came back to the ward with her mother's life savings. Ten pounds. 'Mum asked me special to see it went to her nurses here.' After it had been tactfully explained that in no circumstances could any St Thomas's nurse accept a gift of money from a patient: 'Oh no, we couldn't keep it for the family! I promised Mum special! Will it be alright then if I give it to help build again like it says on the boxes outside? Mum'll give it to old Thomas's that way and she'd want that.'

From the blitz in '40 the collecting boxes had been fixed to the wall oustide the main entrance to Casualty and labelled: ST THOMAS'S IS DOWN—BUT NOT OUT. PLEASE HELP US REBUILD.

Josie had no time to save. Josie was my age, twenty-three, had the same near-black hair and previously, from her family's description, the same very pale complexion. Her maternal grandfather had been an Italian immigrant who had settled in Lambeth and married a local girl. Even by current ward standards, Josie's injuries were gross. She had come home on leave from one of the Women's Services and a posting well out of the bombs' range and stopped to watch 'the funny little thing streaking fire turn off its engine'. That was her last sight on earth.

For several days I was her special day nurse and, as almost invariably happens when a nurse spends so many uninterrupted hours with a 'special' patient, we became great friends. She could just talk and loved talking. She talked about her friend in the Navy on the Atlantic run, her service mates, her family, but never of herself or the future. One evening as I sat by her, feeding beaten egg and milk into her gastric tube, she suddenly turned her head away. 'Ta, duck. That's me lot.'

'You've only had half, duckie. Try a little more. It'll do you good.'

She turned her head my way and slowly groped for my arm. 'Want to ask you something, N. Andrews.'

'Sure, Josie, what?'

'If you were me, duck—would you want to be done good?'

We were friends and she trusted me not to lie. I couldn't answer.

She gave my arm a tap. 'Ta, duck. You been ever so kind. You all been ever so kind. Ta. Ever so.'

In the early hours of the following morning Josie died in her sleep.

That afternoon one of her many female cousins came up to collect her few possessions. She was a youngish married woman and her pretty, sensible, face was creased with compassion. 'Poor kid. Lovely looker she was. Dottie Lamour the boys used to call her. Just as well she never knew proper what they done to her.'

I let that go. No-one had told Josie, but she had known.

The cousin continued: 'I feel badly not coming up to see her more than the once, but they said just her mum and dad when she was took that poorly—and—tell you honest, nurse—not sure I could have bring meself to come back. Don't know how you nurses and the Sister stick it in here— honest, I don't. Wouldn't have your job for a fortune, and couldn't do it, neither, if they give me a fortune. But there—like as they says—you got to be born to it to be a nurse.'

I didn't tell her, but I was not a born nurse and nor before 1939 had the idea of nursing ever occurred to me. I was made a trained nurse by the Second World War, the Nightingale Training-School, St Thomas's Hospital, and my antecedents.

Chapter Two

My father, William Henry Andrews, was born in London in 1876 and, though he never again lived there after 1896, all his life he thought of himself as a Londoner and had a deep, nostalgic affection for the city. In later life he often told us of the London of his young manhood, of music halls, Marie Lloyd, Little Titch, 'swells', 'mashers' and straw boaters worn at outrageous angles. But he said little of his childhood and of the lasting scar left by the death of his mother, Elizabeth, when he was eight. He then had two elder brothers and a younger sister and brother. Their father, a Master in the Mercantile Marine (later Merchant Navy), was mostly away at sea, the children were split between relatives; the three youngest went to one family, the two elder boys to another. Father was still a child when the family was temporarily united by their father's second marriage in which another son and daughter were born.

From the one extant photograph of my paternal grandfather, in middle age in his sea captain's uniform, he looked rather like King Edward VII at the same age, but had much harder eyes. Not long after it was taken he died after being injured on his bridge in a bad storm at sea. Of his five sons, only the eldest, Matthew, followed him to sea and became a ship's Master for many years that included the First World War. According to father, Matthew throughout the war never lost a ship because he invariably nailed the Red Ensign to his mast and confused the U-boat commanders into thinking any ship sailing so openly under the British flag could not be the unarmed merchantman she appeared and must be some form of Q-ship.

Matthew and father lived to retire and die in their beds.

Harry, the second son, and John, the fourth, were killed fighting in the First World War. John was father's great friend amongst his brothers and his death haunted father for years, though by 1914 all four brothers had gone their separate ways.

In, I think, 1894, father went into the old Eastern Telegraph Company (later Cables and Wireless). In 1896 the ETC first sent him abroad to the Seychelles, and until he retired in 1932 he spent his working life in the Company's African and Mediterranean stations. From the few yellowing, carefully posed Victorian photographs, as a young man father was thin as paper, had the face of an innocent aesthete and an enchanting smile. Age altered him little and in his sixties he weighed no more than in his twenties.

The ETC had transferred father to Gibraltar when, in 1912, at a ball at Government House he was introduced to Lucilla Quero-Béjar, the elder of the two daughters of a Spanish doctor. Mother was a very slim, attractive girl of twenty, with beautiful dark eyes and hair; then, as ever, she spoke fluent English with a strong Andalusian accent. After the ball she told her sister, 'I'm going to marry that Englishman.' Her mother was appalled. 'Who is this Englishman? What do we know of him? Nothing! He could be a nobody! No daughter of mine is marrying such a man—say no more!'

My maternal grandmother—whom we always called Grandmama with a capital G—was a strong-minded lady, but her eldest daughter and future son-in-law had equally strong minds. Father had already decided he wanted to marry that fetching little Señorita Whatsit-Whatsit and had better call on her father to ask if he could pay his respects. When he did so he found an unexpected ally.

I have always wished my maternal grandfather, who died in 1914, had lived long enough for me to know him. Luis Quero-Béjar was a man of humour, intelligence and remarkably advanced opinions and ideas for his time and social background. Born the youngest son of a duke's daughter he endured the rigid conventions of the nineteenth century Spanish aristocracy until his thirties when he shocked family and friends by entering the University of Madrid to read medicine and, after qualifying, worked as a General Practitioner for the rest of his life. He spoke little English and father as little Spanish, but the two men seem to have liked and understood each other. He told his wife, 'That Englishman is a good man who will make Lucilla a good husband.' As he was a Victorian father and Spanish husband, once his permission was given, the matter was settled. My parents were married in Gibraltar on 6th October 1913. Despite the differences in age, nationality, outlook and background, for the thirty-one years of their marriage they remained devoted lovers and each other's greatest friend.

A couple of months after the marriage father was transferred to Alexandria and from there to Mozambique. Mother never saw her father again and possibly the shock of his sudden death from a stroke, her youth and living in the tropics for the first time combined to delay her conceiving her first child for a few years. Then my elder sister, Elizabeth (Betty), was born on a Portuguese ship off the coast of Zanzibar. Betty was nine months old when father was transferred to Suez where Luis, who died in infancy, then myself (Lucilla Matthew) and then John, were born. John on the same day, 21st April 1926, as the then Princess Elizabeth.

By then Betty and I were installed in the small private boarding-school in Sussex where Betty had been sent when she was seven; I joined her at three-and-a-half. The school stood in its own fairly extensive grounds on wooded downland a few miles inland from the coast and had about sixty boarders and no day-girls, or only very rarely. As far as I know, the school had no reputation for academic merit, but amongst expatriate parents it was highly regarded as a safe and healthy sanctuary for their daughters. Whilst I was there, most pupils were the children of parents stationed in the various outposts of the still massive British Empire. The maps of the world on the classroom walls were ringed with the pink patches that marked British possessions and every new girl was thrust at a map: 'Where's your Mummy and Daddy? Ours are—here!' Then, 'What does your Daddy do? Ours is a manager in the ETC— the Hong Kong and Shanghai Bank—the Anglo-Iranian Oil

Company. . . .' The children of Empire-exiles learnt to appreciate protocol before shedding their milk teeth.

The Empire provided our fathers with jobs, reasonably good or very good incomes, large houses or bungalows, hosts of servants, active if strictly limited social lives, and for those who loved music, books and the theatre, usually years of deprivation. It provided our mothers with constant leisure that some translated into boredom, and others accepted as a natural right. It provided for both parents the ultimate prospect of retiring on restricted pensions to Britain to live out their lives amongst strangers, often the more strange for speaking a common tongue but not the same language. Many never lived to retire. Malaria, yellow fever, blackwater fever, dysentery, typhoid, rabies, tetanus, heat stroke and cirrhosed livers were just a few of the occupational hazards of Empire exiles before the discovery of penicillin and the antibiotic shield, when vaccinations and immunizations were in their medical infancy. Only the fittest survived. The thousands of children's graves in the British cemeteries that ringed the world with the pink patches were part of the price of the British Empire to the British. Very rare was the exiled parent spared the agony of watching a beloved small child die. I never saw my father in tears or ever losing his Victorian self-control. It was not until after his death that mother told me he had wept all night after Luis died.

Generally when a child was about seven the parents had to decide how the family was to be split. There were two main choices: send the child 'home' to boarding-school in Britain; send mother and child 'home' and maintain a separate long-term home there. There was no air travel. Sea voyages were long, expensive additions to the boarding-school fees, and were seldom subsidized by the father's employers. Leaves were mostly either three months every three years, or six months every five. Our parents chose the former, my husband's parents in India at the same time, the latter. Neither solution has seemed to me satisfactory, but probably there was no satisfactory solution. Either way, children and at least one parent became strangers and the younger the child at the split the wider the subsequent gap—in comparison with which the overrated modern Generation Gap is a hairline crack. Parents and children who habitually, or only in the school holidays, share the same roof, do recognize each other across a street. When parents and growing children are reunited after an interval of years, they can find each other physically unrecognizable.

I started school with fair curly hair. Two years later when I next saw our parents my hair was near-black and the dead straight it remained until my teens when the curl came back. 'Darling! What's happened to your golden curls?' I didn't know and, being shy with strangers, didn't answer.

In those two years and again a year later Betty and I, and several other children with no English-based relatives able to have them, stayed at school during the holidays. Our situation was not exceptional in that time, or in the previous hundred or so years in Britain, and many boarding-schools catered accordingly.

In the holidays our Head kept on a skeleton domestic staff, often one mistress, and always stayed herself. We were well looked after, allowed to wear 'holiday' clothes and as far as possible in any institution to have a homely rather than Home atmosphere. We were allowed to play in areas forbidden in term: on the large pink-patterned rug on the polished front hall by the open door of the Head's study; the wide back lawn cut and rolled to green velvet; or the massive rhododendron bushes backing the rose beds lining the lawn that made hide-and-seek territory and my private secret places. Beneath the bushes the ground was thick, soft and damp with old leaves, the giant purple and crimson flowers and dark green leaves shut out world and sky, but let the greenish light filter down like soft water alive with swimming insects. The insects never stung or frightened me, but if a ladybird plopped down she had instantly to be caught, carried out, placed on an external leaf and warned her house was on fire and children had flown. 'Ladybird, ladybird, fly away home—quick! And don't forget Ann's under the frying-pan!'

We were taken for occasional 'treats' to the nearest seaside town and always to the same ultra-respectable tearoom where we ate the long iced buns we called White Mice and drank lemonade through straws. Teatime music was provided by a trio on a small platform backed by a multi-coloured paperbead curtain. The lady playing the piano, the lady playing the violin and the singing lady all had short bobbed hair, heavy fringes and rows of chunky glass beads round their thin necks. I liked the way they always seemed to play the same tunes, and I learnt the words of the songs before I could read and sang them tunelessly under the rhododendrons with the singing lady's stresses, 'What-TAIR befall I STILL recall that SUNlit mountain SIDE. . . .' 'I want TO BE happy but I can't be HAPPY till I make you HAPPY toooooo. . . .' Sometimes the singing lady played another violin and then, whatever the non-vocal number, the trio played as if their lives depended on their finishing it at record speed. The fringes bounded up and down, the chunky beads swirled from side to side, and at the end we children clapped enthusiastically and even the adult customers joined in, occasionally.

If one of us had a birthday we had a party amongst ourselves, wore party dresses and clung impatiently to the backs of chairs whilst Grace was said. 'For what we are about to receive may the Lord make us—girls, please! A birthday party is no excuse for bad manners. No scraping of chairs, please. Now—for what we are about to receive. . . .'

The one long table in use in the large dining-room was transformed with crackers, paper hats, bowls of lemon and orange jelly decorated with hundreds and thousands, the plates of banana sandwiches and white mice without which no treat was complete and the iced, candled birthday cake long ordered from Suez, Singapore, Hong Kong, Madras. 'Big breath, dearie, and all out in one blow. Have you remembered to wish ?' Then the chorus, 'We wish, we wish, your wish comes true', that had to be answered, 'I wish, I wish, the same to you.' (No singing of Happy Birthday as that custom had still to cross the Atlantic.)

At Christmas a tree was set in the dining-room's great bay window. We helped with the decorations and piled round the tree's foot the parental parcels ordered from England or heavy with foreign stamps, stout string and sealing wax. 'Quiz—my Chinese stamps?' 'Ego!' 'Not fair—bags I—I said it first!' 'Didn't—' 'Snubs to you, smartie—did, did, did!' 'Children, please! This is not a nice way for little girls to talk to each other!' On Christmas Day we sang carols round the tree and some of the bigger children cried and those too young to remember Christmas with their parents could not understand why.

But I was never too young to feel or forget the bleak cloak of loneliness that settled over the shoulders on the last day of term when all that lingered in the classrooms were the empty desks, the smells of damp blackboard dusters, chalk and lead. Or to have permanently in memory the silent cluster of children looking out of a front classroom window at the 'other girls' ' luggage being loaded into the station van and watching the empty drive after the van disappeared through the gates. Or those nights in the 'babies' dormitory, one of the smallest in the school and set across the corridor from the Head's bedroom. The pines outside the windows cast flickering shadows over walls, empty white-quilted beds and dressing-table mirrors; shadows that elongated to clutching fingers or shaped unknown monsters that had to be evil as they came by night. Echoing in from the dark Sussex countryside, the hoot of a solitary owl, scream of a hunted rabbit, or unnatural swish-swoosh of a bat, evoked a sweating terror to be sweated out with the head under the blankets, the only comfort a much-forbidden sucking thumb, until the glorious moment too early to place when my mind began telling me the stories that ever after at school provided an absolute refuge from the terrors of darkness and turned the night into my friend. Every holiday morning brought nearer the golden day when 'the others' came back and the holiday-stayers watched with grim smugness the new girls' tears.

When I was five, for a few halcyon months our parents took Betty and me back to Suez and imported an English governess to teach us. In Suez was the home I had loved and forgotten until I clambered up the steps to the shaded verandah running round the house and saw our old head house-boy (we had eleven Egyptian 'house-boys') smiling and bowing in his spotless long white gown. I flung myself at him and slid instinctively into the fluent Arabic that had been my first spoken language. I never recall sprinkling my English with Arabic at school but the return to Suez produced total recall, to the profound disapproval of our new governess, Miss Y. 'Nice little girls must not gossip with servants in their heathen tongue . . . no, no, no, child! Say "Please God make me a good little girl" not—whatever it was you said!'

'In shâ Allâh, Miss Y, and that means—' (Roughly, as Allâh wills it).

'You mustn't talk of Allâh when saying your prayers to God.—'

'But Allâh means God!'

'That's enough, child! Now then, into bed and once I've tucked in your mosquito netting all round—so—no undoing it or sucking the netting or you'll get typhoid as well as malaria.'

'Imshi!' (Go away!)

'And what, pray, does that word mean?'

' "Sorry",' I lied to please her, and before she had left the bedroom I had convinced myself it was a more polite translation. She was an angular, ageless Englishwoman who wore shapeless cotton dresses and a disapproving expression. Mother's elegant, spectacularly Spanish appearance and attitudes and insistence on personally supervising the daily boiling of all drinking water, the soaking of all fresh vegetables and fruit in Condés Fluid solution, and the boiling time of all cooked food by our cook and his army of assistant relatives, upset Miss Y's notions of English suburban respectability, though it spared us all from typhoid, dysentery and even 'gippy tummy'. She equally disapproved of the heat, the flies, the sun, the sand, the Arabs, Egyptians, Soudanese and Nubians, whom she referred to as 'the natives' in tones of doom that puzzled me, as I loved our kind, gentle-voiced household staff who had spoiled and indulged me from my cradle.

When out of doors all the British wore solar topees with rounded crowns and oblong brims; lined externally with white duck, internally with dark green. Dark green, thin muslin veils were suspended over our front topee brims and tied firmly round our necks by Miss Y before any outing. The veil tasted of dirt, sand and salt.

'Stop eating your veil again, child! I don't know why you haven't got typhoid. . . .'

In shâ Allâh.

The ETC had a cablehouse in the desert and often we were driven out to picnic in the narrow shadow of the low stone building. The hot desert air was laced with oil from the great refineries at Port-Tufek, the pungency of the mis-named Sweet Water Canal, and an eternity of scorched sand. Miss Y sat bolt upright against the cablehouse wall, and surveyed with distaste the smooth, secretly shifting waves of the seemingly petrified white ocean. 'Pity this desert has so much sand, children. Quite pleasant, if only there wasn't all this messy sand.'

Other picnics within sight of the Suez Canal were magical— when we sprawled face down on the hot sand in the shade of a huge oil pipe the Canal became invisible and the ships gliding slowly up or down in single-file convoys glided on sand, silently as dreams.

One day when our parents were away until evening, despite warnings from our head house-boy that there was talk in the bazaar of a coming sandstorm, Miss Y insisted on taking us for our mid-morning walk along the fringe of the desert. Our head house-boy after further attempts to dissuade her re-treated into In shâ Allâhs. 'Lot of nonsense,' said Miss Y strid-ing out. 'Lovely clear sky. A good walk'll do us all good.' We were away from the houses and shacks and probably not more than a few hundred yards into the desert when the sun sud-denly became a red haze and a red-brown curtain unrolled from the sky and rushed towards us. Miss Y grabbed our hands. 'Run, children, run! Back to the nearest house!' But we had been long enough children of the desert to defy her, and pulled her down on the sand. 'Flat on your face, Miss Y, hang onto your topee, jam the brim into the sand and keep your eyes and mouth shut—hang onto your topee or you won't breathe!' In seconds the sandstorm reached us and slashed with hot stinging whips bare arms and legs until we were buried. When the storm rolled on we dug ourselves out, and despite topees and veils our hair, faces, nostrils, mouths and bodies were caked with sand. Betty and I thought it all very funny, but Miss Y and our parents did not. A few weeks later Miss Y returned to England. Shortly after, a dog with suspected rabies blundered into our kitchen and bit father when he caught it. Next morning he vanished to the Pasteur Institute in Cairo for treatment and not long after his return we sailed back to England and boarding-school.

I lost count of the times we sailed the Mediterranean in the 1920s in the old orange and black painted P and O liners with names echoing the British Raj—*Kaisar-i-Hind*, *Rawalpindi* and so many others. Homeward-bound the British returning from India were easily identifiable as their faces were the deepest yellow and their skins, whatever the age, the most dried-up. The mid-morning beef tea and little square dry biscuits tasted nicer in the Bay of Biscay than in the Mediterranean, unless we sailed during the equinoxes. Then old Med. hands with strong stomachs would nod to each other as the fiddles came up round the tables in the dining-saloon, and the deck-chairs and occupants vanished from the open decks. 'The Med.'s far worse than the Bay this time of the year. Typical of St Paul to sail at the equinox. Man was a born martyr.'

Being then a good sailor and already addicted to my life-long habit of listening to strangers' conversations, I glowed with smugness at knowing about St Paul and longed for our ship to be shipwrecked and give me a chance to strike water from any handy rock. But the liners pitched, rolled and creaked on through the gales. 'So here you are again, dearie,' said our Headmistress. 'And quite lost your rosy cheeks. Never mind. Soon have them back.'

She was a small, stout, Oxford M.A., with an untidy grey bun skewered to the top of her head, with outsize hairpins which she shed as the leaves in autumn. Her stern manner could reduce parents and her staff to speechless jellies; but not her pupils, as she never used sarcasm on us, was genuinely fond of children and we knew it. Apart from the pupil-teacher, all her staff were graduates and, as herself, single women. But I never remember our Head making any pretence of preparing us for anything but marriage. She was an ardent upholder of the married state, the importance of good manners, good deportment, wool next to the skin, the Church of England, the Book of Common Prayer, the New—but not the Old—Testament, and Gregory Powders all round the junior dormitories on Saturday nights.

She only taught Scripture and often devoted half the period to social education. This did not include human biology. Throughout my school years the word 'sex' was only mentioned in language classes. But by eleven I knew how essential were good shoes and gloves. 'Never forget, girls, one can always tell a lady by her gloves and shoes.' And I knew the sight of my sitting with crossed legs would inevitably mean social ruin. 'No nice girl ever crosses her legs when sitting, girls. Knees and feet together, if you please.'

'But, please—it's so uncomfortable—'

'Dearie, no lady is ever concerned with her physical comfort on social occasions. *Il faut souffrir pour être belle*—you, child, translate! Quite right. Yes?'

'Please, why is it so wrong to cross your legs?'

'That is not a nice question, child! Nice girls do not ask such questions. Now, as I was saying—at first St Paul was most reluctant to allow the young John Mark. . . .'

Probably no-one born in Britain since 1939 can properly appreciate the effect of that throttling 'nice' on my generation of middle-class British women. Every adult responsible for our formative years interminably stressed the vital necessity of being nice: the alternative was to be fast. Not only social but economic ruin awaited fast girls, since British women in the 1930s (as the 1970s) were overwhelmingly, socially and economically dependent on their husbands. No nice boy would consort with a fast girl, and if the wretched creature survived to adulthood she became a loose woman. That no gentleman would marry a loose woman we knew as surely as we knew nice girls and nice boys grew up to be ladies and gentlemen. Our

Head preferred 'gentlewomen' to 'ladies', but allowed the latter as she liked to keep abreast with changing times. That there might somewhere be a world not wholly composed of ladies and gentlemen was never mentioned. We were told how to recognize a nice boy at sight: when shaking a nice girl's gloved right hand a nice boy took off his own right glove first and looked briefly, politely ONLY at her nice face. This dictum caused considerable confusion in a dormitory of thirteen-year-olds, as then we had met boys on holiday, and observed their unaccountable preoccupation with our legs and newly bulging bosoms. As most of us had acne, we decided sadly but truthfully that our faces weren't really very nice.

We talked boys in giggling whispers in the dormitory or when changing shoes in the basement bootroom, but pregnancy and babies were such taboo-words that I recall no occasion when either were mentioned. The word 'intercourse' conveyed nothing to me until my gynaecological lectures in 1942. The official and approved description for this dangerous ignorance was 'girlish innocence'.

But as the onset of puberty and its concomitant upsurge of unmanageable emotions demanded an outlet, some girls had crushes on older girls or younger mistresses. These were officially discouraged, but as they rarely went beyond sighs, giggles, and saving chairs by the dining-room fire and hot cups of cocoa for the current beloved senior at mid-morning break (the juniors reached the dining-room first), the syndrome flourished pretty continuously amongst the elevens to thirteens. By fourteen, if not before, most of us on holidays had had our first dates with boys and, once the emotional interest was transferred to a young male, the need for a crush nearly always disappeared.

The other girls' crushes worried me until I was nearly fourteen, as I could not understand them. Father had then retired, Betty had left school and was living with our parents in the small, semi-detached house in St Leonards-on-Sea, Sussex, which father had bought on mortgage. In the holidays I had met boys and discovered I preferred them to girls. During the term I was quite happy to make do with an over-

Valley Of Kings
Visitor - Adult
Printed on:24/02/2024 12:_
Valid on :24/02/2024
Price:600.00 LE

16243RCYBQ1B19

وادي الملوك
Valley of the Kings
مقبرة الملك رمسيس السادس
Tomb of King Ramesses VI

worked set of fantasy figures I used in rota, as male leads in the
particular heroic saga evolved to suit my particular mood.
Whatever the setting and theme, every saga ended with a
climatic holocaust from which either the boy rescued me or
vice versa and we were both tremendously gallant.

At thirteen I was still desperately anxious to conform in all
respects. As to be in fashion I had to have a crush, I decided
to pretend one. First I had to find my crush. I looked the staff
over in morning prayers. They stood in order of seniority
against the wall a few feet from the music mistress at the piano,
and, with the exception of the sturdy gym mistress in navy
serge gym tunic and long brown woollen stockings, favoured
limp hand-knitted jumpers and cardigans in muted shades of
mud, sensible tweed skirts, lisle stockings and laced brogues.
After close observation I decided I was not a good enough
actress and did a second survey on the senior girls. Finally,
without enthusiasm, I picked the hockey captain for two
reasons; I wanted to get into the First Eleven and as she was
tall and thin I could pretend she was a boy in disguise. I began
working mentally on a new saga in the first verse of 'Heavenly
Father Send Thy Blessing On Thy Children Gathered Here'.
Before we were marched out to Percy Grainger's *Country
Gardens* the hockey captain was a Middle European prince
hiding out in a girls' school to save his ailing father's throne. His
regal mother had so movingly begged him to flee that my form
mistress interrupted her opening address to ask if I had a cold.
'No ? Then don't sniffle, girl! It's not nice.'

Our classroom was nearest the dining-room. At the break-
bell, I charged ahead, uptilted a chair by the fire to mark it
'bagged', collected a hot mug of cocoa and when the seniors
arrived presented both to the astonished hockey captain. I
had then to queue for my own cooling cocoa and join the
juniors masochistically shivering well away from the fire.
Suddenly reality broke through, and for the first of countless
subsequent occasions in life I decided that if others were prepared to put up with, or even enjoy, this situation, I was not.
Anyway, I brooded, any prince fool enough to take refuge
amongst giggling girls and wear navy gym slip, purple jersey,

long black stockings, navy woollen bloomers with white cotton linings, Chilprufe vest, and stays—the hockey captain being too flat-chested for that daring innovation, a brassière, recently permitted to the more developed girls—was clearly a mother's boy who deserved to lose his throne and would get no help from me when struck by fire and flood. The end-of-break bell ended my only crush and last conscious desire to conform in all respects.

In the summer term in 1934 I wrote my first full-length novel. Having no other spare paper I wrote it in my Special Drawing Book after first hiding this in my bootroom locker, reporting it as lost and being given another. Why I was put in the Special Drawing class was a mystery. I had no talent for drawing. But the Head and my parents decided I should take the extra lessons. I was the sorrow of the art mistress but enjoyed her classes as she was too good at her job to waste time trying to teach the untalented a talent and left me to sit and doodle and live in fantasy. I worked on my novel every evening during prep. period, and by using a mapping pen, purple mapping ink and both sides of the foolscap cartridge paper, managed simultaneously to cram in more words and persuade the mistress taking prep that I was working on geography. I finished the novel before it was discovered, confiscated and I was summoned to the Head's study.

Our Head was very distressed. She said never in her long experience of girls had she been so disappointed, appalled, nay saddened. First there was The Deceit. Then came the shameful misuse of preparation time and waste of my father's hard-earned money. Did I not realise the cost of my second Special Drawing Book would be placed on his bill, or was I so lost to all decent feeling to have forgotten my filial duties? Having read my disgraceful tale, our Head feared this must be so. She would not now dwell on my lamentable grammar, spelling and style, but I could depend upon her taking these matters up with my English mistress in due course. Duty, however, forced her to deal here and now with my theme. This concerned banditry, murder, lust, true love and the flooding of the Yellow River in China. I knew nothing of China, either. My theme was NOT NICE.

She gave me a Bad Conduct Mark—the school's Mark of Cain—and I never saw my manuscript again. I guessed, probably correctly, that it was burnt in the basement boilers by the elderly, lugubrious, head gardener, the only man allowed to roam unescorted in the school basement and on the ground floor, but not above stairs. I was too furious at losing my manuscript to care about my Bad Conduct Mark, though it meant no tuck for the rest of the term. Eventually I forgave the Head because, fundamentally, I was fond of her. I never forgave the gardener, nor the form mistress who found my novel in one of the unannounced inspections made in our absence on our desks and dressing-table drawers.

School life was minutely regulated and supervised for all but the much-envied seniors in the Upper Fifth, the School Certificate form. I longed to be a senior, to enjoy the wonderous privileges of not going to bed until 9 p.m. and playing gramaphone records in the gym after senior supper at seven-thirty. On summer evenings the tunes floated up to open dormitory windows . . . *Love Is The Sweetest Thing* . . . *I'll See You Again* . . . *Someday I'll Find You* . . . *Love In Bloom* . . . and the one that had the whole dormitory bouncing up in bed and miming 'Where's that tiger ?' Harry Roy's *Tiger Rag*.

Until the golden future life was organized from first waking bell at 7 a.m. to lights-out. Junior bedtime began at 6 p.m. and in each dormitory lights-out came one hour after the youngest occupant went to bed. Talking was forbidden between lights-out and waking bell, so we talked, argued, fought, made up stories, plays, poems, sang songs in whispers and took turns to guard the door and hiss 'Cave!' When, as often, the warning was too late: 'Hands up who's been talking. Miss break tomorrow and write twenty lines—"I must not talk after lights-out".'

Our very occasional midnight feasts were more successful, as better planned. We worked out a rota to ensure one girl was awake at midnight to wake the rest to churn up lemonade powder and water in toothglasses and eat the cakes, bullseyes and biscuits removed by stealth from parental tuck parcels. These were opened under supervision before being locked in the tuck cupboard and issued in rationed quantities on Saturdays and Sundays after lunch. Extra sweets, chocolate bars and the bright yellow lemonade powder were usually illicitly bought from the nearest sub-post office-cum-general stores. This stood a few yards back from a very sharp corner of the main road that was the route generally taken by returning school walks, as the pavement was wide enough for the two-abreast crocodile. Once we were round the corner, the shop was invisible. One pair would ask the walk-mistress's permission to drop out to re-tie a previously loosened shoelace and, permission granted, fiddle with the lace until the crocodile vanished round the corner, then race into the shop. Officially, money was forbidden us, but by careful joint hoarding, one shilling (5p) or two raised in pennies bought a feast. Twenty caramels cost 2d. Lemonade powder 1d. a quarter. Chocolate bars 1d. each, a Mars Bar 2d. The goods were divided in pockets and bloomer legs to be stored mostly in shoebags in bootroom lockers until the night of the feast. I remember everything always tasted of bootpolish and mud, but never one post-feast upset stomach.

When we walked in crocodile conversation was only permitted between each pair. From our junior years we learnt to talk to the pairs ahead and behind without turning our heads or moving our upper lips. Consequently, I have long been convinced the traditional stiff upper lip of the English middle classes originated in their English boarding-schools. After a decade of school walks to talk with a stiff upper lip became an ingrained mannerism I have still to lose.

Those walks, and so many other aspects of my education, would have come in very useful had I been imprisoned in Colditz. Yet, if the iron routine attempted, not necessarily successfully, to stifle individuality, it had some concrete advantages for insecure children. Rare is the child of absent parents who is not insecure. It was reassuring to know exactly what was and what was not permitted and that on either side of the authorized path were the invisible, solid walls of adult rules and conventions. If those walls limited and blinded, they also guarded. Children may not always enjoy being guarded, but almost always they sense the need for the guard as they are themselves far more conscious than many adults of the terrifying vulnerability of childhood.

There was a paradoxical security in the frustration of knowing the day of the week from the morning hymn and pudding at lunch. 'New Every Morning' and ginger sog (sponge)—Monday. 'Praise My Soul' and dead baby (plain suet roll sprinkled with brown sugar)—Friday. No prayers and mending at ten past nine with a story—Saturday. The staff took mending classes in turn and I longed for the geography mistress's turn as she read us Haggard and Stevenson in her ordinary, and not 'I'm-reading-Eng. Lit.' tones, often pausing to explain a long word, or repeat or comment on a phrase or sentence as if thinking aloud rather than instructing the young. 'One step nearer Mr Hands and I'll blow your brains out. . . . One step nearer Mr Hands and I'll blow your brains out.' Long pause. 'Yes. Jim Hawkins would have called Israel Hands "Mister" as he was a polite boy, but that wouldn't have stopped him blowing off the man's head if he'd had to. Good manners make life pleasanter all round and are a very useful way of disguising one's real feelings, but anyone stupid enough to mistake politeness for weakness is usually in for a very nasty shock.'

Outside the sheltering walls of that oasis of the long, lingering Edwardian middle-class evening, lay an unknown England. Being still an infant at school during the General Strike, all I remember of it was the later apocryphal legend of the day the bigger girls cried and refused to eat lunch because the pet rabbits had been killed and cooked. In the 1930s, neither the Depression, nor the two million unemployed, the Jarrow hunger marchers, the Dole and the Means Test, cast even small shadows over my walls. I saw no newspapers at school and the 'wireless' was a strictly rationed novelty which I only remember permitted for broadcasts involving royalty. The wedding of Prince George, newly created Duke of Kent, to Princess Marina of Greece, gathered the whole school into the dining-room to sigh romantically and enjoy a lesson-free day. The approaching death of King George V interrupted senior prep, and the announcer's measured 'The King's life is drawing peacefully to its close. . . .' sent fearful yet not unpleasant chills down the spine. The Abdication broadcast of King Edward VIII followed special history lessons on the meaning of Instruments of Abdication, the Monarch's position as Head of the Church of England, and that Church's attitude to divorce.

In the Christmas holidays just after the Abdication mother, and my friends' mothers, continued to discuss it in the hushed, dazed voices of those who have suffered shattered dreams. 'Who could have believed our nice dear Prince of Wales . . . such a charming young man . . . different if she had been a pretty gel . . . when a man of his age falls in love with a pretty gel, he's bound to lose his head, but—really! Of course, he had to go . . . my dear, if not, the end of The Home! One feels so distressed for poor Queen Mary . . . of course, the poor Duke of York is a perfect dear and so good with his Boy's Camps, but that stutter must be a trial. . . .'

I was delighted we never heard news bulletins at school. At home in the holidays our new wireless seemed perpetually tuned to the news that my parents insisted be heard in silence. Either I left the room, or mentally switched off into my fantasy world, and the few outstanding events that did penetrate did so mainly by worrying father. Germany walking out of the League of Nations, Italy invading Abyssinia, made father leave his chair and stand straight-backed at our dining-room window, to chew his pipe and stare down at our back garden. The long narrow strip of gardens, as all the gardens in our row of small semi-detached houses, sloped downhill to join those behind the row of houses on the opposite hill and form a little valley of gardens. All the houses in our row were new, the gardens rough virgin turf when the first owners moved in. Father had dug, drained and planted the heavy Sussex clay with the special love of a returned exile and passionate amateur gardener owning his first home and strip of homeland. All his retired years, always when worried, either he silently retreated to work in the garden, or as silently watched it from the dining-room window.

The outbreak of the Spanish Civil War impinged more strongly as it affected us personally. Mother was deeply anxious for her country, relatives and friends, and constantly infuriated by the BBC news readers' Spanish pronunciations: 'Aie, aie, aie! Not Andalooziar! Underluthia! Not Toeleedo—Toletho!'

Then Munich; newspaper pictures of Londoners digging trenches in Hyde Park; mother thanking God after every news bulletin that father was over sixty and John still only eleven and at prep. school; more newspaper pictures of Mr Chamberlain waving his little piece of paper and father at the dining-room window shaking his grey head in anguished incredulity. Being a transparently honest man incapable of dishonesty he never understood nor suspected it in others. 'We've broken our word to save our own skins. We won't. This is only a breathing space.'

Whilst the country had a breathing space in 1938 I had heart-block after diphtheria, and for about six months had to stay in bed at home. No-one explained why I had to stay supine until I asked our elderly G.P. the reason. He sat on the side of my bed, drew pictures of a diagrammatic heart to illustrate his detailed explanation. 'Understand, do ye?' He looked over his glasses at the blue rug in front of the dressing-table. 'Understand now that if you get up and dance on that rug when your mother's back's turned, you'll die?'

Mother was shocked and outside my room she told him so. 'You've terrified the child!'

Our G.P.'s boom echoed round the house. 'Very much doubt it. But we've got to have her co-operation. If you want the young to co-operate in illness, you must give 'em the truth. Got any whisky in the house? She can have it now and straight. Pulse is down to 32 this morning. Got to get it up.'

I loathed the taste of whisky, but once I stopped feeling choked I rather enjoyed being ill as it provided unlimited reading, thinking and mental story-telling time, and after the first two or three months I was allowed to be visited by my St Leonards' friends. That illness began the great friendship between our G.P. and myself that lasted until his death in

1969. In 1938 his fair hair was beginning to turn white, his long drooping moustache, grey, and his vivid blue eyes looked over not through the glasses propped on the end of his nose. He was a man of strong opinions, few words, and a Fellow of the Royal College of Surgeons. When he had been a house-surgeon at Guy's Hospital, Lister's carbolic spray was in use in operating theatres. 'Theatre air was thick with carbolic and we'd great sheets soaked in the stuff hanging over the doors—my god-fathers, child, how it made the fingers tingle. After a long list, tips of m'fingers were numb for hours.'

Once I began to convalesce his boom from our minute front hall dispersed my own and parental fears. 'Delicate? Non-sense! No-one's delicate! Either a bad illness kills you or it doesn't and you get well. Not delicate—well! Don't turn the child into an invalid. The illness is over and sooner she gets back to normal and forgets it, the better.

'She'll do. Well, what do you think of the news, eh? War's coming....'

Every adult seemed to be saying that last by the uneasy dawn of 1939. Waiting for the war was like waiting for a door to bang even if I could not follow why it had to bang, or why everything I had been told or read about the Great War being the war to end war, was apparently all wrong. Slowly, almost shamefully, as it involved disloyalty to my parents, I wondered what else I had been told and taught would prove to be false. I did not discuss this with my siblings or friends, partly as it worried me too much and partly as we were all exasperated by the non-stop war talk of our elders. When the subject did crop up amongst my own age group, we moaned over the madden-ing interruption it was bound to cause our lives and changed the subject.

By early summer the lives of most of the older boys and younger men in my circle were already interrupted by con-scription into the Army, or the arrival of call-up papers from Territorials, Royal Naval Volunteer Reserve, or University Air Squadrons, nearly all initially joined as a means of getting in free riding, sailing, or flying. When home on twenty-four or forty-eight hour passes, these friends called at our house to show off their new uniforms. The Army conscripts' (Militia-men) khaki were uniformly as ill-fitting and unattractive as their pudding-basin hair-cuts. 'Bloody bore,' they said when my parents were out of the room 'and bloody itchy'.

I had left school, and as Betty spent that summer visiting our relatives in Gibraltar, once John's prep. school broke up for the summer holidays, most days (after my share of the house-work) John and I spent the rest of the day on the beach. August in St Leonards was hot and dry. Throughout the month letters and cables flashed to and from Gibraltar in-sisting and promising Betty would be back for the war, as if the expected holocaust were some social season.

We always used the bit of pebbled beach just left of St Leonards' pier and, like our friends, we kept our striped canvas bathing tent in a cavern under the promenade behind that beach, in which the Corporation rented storage space to local residents during the holiday season. The small colony of coloured tents transformed 'our' beach into a summer youth club enlivened by the music blaring down from the pier's loudspeakers. Often that August someone's father brought a portable wireless onto the beach and the little picnic groups in swimsuits, beach jackets, long fading khaki shorts that were relics of Africa and India, and the bathing trunks that only a year or so back had evoked 'Well, really, it's not that one's old fashioned but what will young men wear next?' but by 1939 were worn by every male under thirty, all swung their heads towards the wireless as if they were puppets and some unseen hand had twitched their strings. The pebbles at the water's edge shimmered in a heat haze, the sun made millions of diamonds dance on a Channel blue as the Mediterranean in high summer, the black raft thirty odd yards out bobbed lazily, emptily, the lukewarm hard-boiled eggs and limp lettuce sandwiches tasted of the dried salt on the lips, the glare stung the eyes behind dark glasses, and the unemotional voice of the news reader was half-drowned by the pier music. *South of the Border . . . Roll Out The Barrel . . . The Woody-Woodpecker's Song . . . The Ferryboat Serenade.*

'I want to ride a ferry . . . where music is so merry . . . According to our Berlin correspondent, Herr Hitler . . . Mummy, can I have another ice-cream—why not ? Why should I shush, Mummy, why ? . . . South of the border . . . down Mexico way . . . Herr Hitler is reported as saying the Polish Corridor . . . Can I swim now, Daddy ? It must be an hour since I had my sandwiches . . . That's where I fell in love . . . when stars above . . . Danzig . . . Danzig . . . Herr Hitler says . . . Did you see me swim round the raft, Lucy ? Next year I'll swim right round the pier . . . There in a veil of white . . . Danzig.'

John standing on his dripping dark brown head, his long skinny boy's body tanned as a Latin and looking, as all his life, a Spaniard not an Englishman. The sun drying in minutes the new scarlet cotton decorated with large white carnations bathing suit that had cost me five shillings and my friend George had just described as 'very fetching'. John liked George as he kept him supplied with pennies for iced lollies, and every penny kept John in the lolly queue for roughly fifteen minutes.

George was one of the few local boys I knew who was not yet called-up. George was an engineer in an aircraft factory and on the reserved occupation list. He was home for his annual two-weeks' holiday. We had met in school Christmas holidays a few years earlier, when, along with most of my local friends, we had been reluctant performers in our Rector's annual Nativity Plays. We spent hours talking together on the beach and tried to avoid the war but it kept creeping in. 'Thought about joining anything, Lucy ? Or will your heart keep you out ?'

'No. The Doc. says its o-kay now. Snag is, I still want to be a journalist, but the parents won't have any. I'll probably be a VAD. The parents'll let me do that as Betty's one already.'

'Are you old enough ?'

'They'll take me in the BRCS (British Red Cross Society) if Daddy signs the consent form as I'm under age.' I watched a posse of small boys surfacing like dolphins from attempts to drown each other and vaguely recognized one of the spluttering faces as John's. 'I saw a Commandant here yesterday. She says I'll have to go to some lectures and do ninety hours at the

East Sussex (the Royal East Sussex Hospital) before I can be Mobile. Then I can nurse in military hospitals in this country but not overseas as you have to be twenty-one. Maddening! Years to wait.'

'War can't last that long. Think you'll like nursing?'

'Dunno.' I stared at, but no longer saw, the human dolphins. Instead I saw myself gallantly dodging shells on French battlefields, gliding softly, gracefully up long hospital tents laying my cool hands on fevered brows. 'Maybe.'

'Let's go in again.'

We swam out to the raft and I climbed on it laughing as I climbed blind because my hair was over my face. I never used a cap in the sea, I loved the feeling of water in my longish hair and the swish of the sea slithering by my ears. We had the raft to ourselves for a while and lay side by side on our backs squinting up at the absurdly blue sky. The gentle rocking of the raft and the warmth of the sun enveloped me in such a glorious sensation of well-being that it was rather frightening. I thought suddenly—I wonder if I'll ever do this again. I never did.

It was the last Monday in August. That evening, as usual, we took down the tent poles, furled the ancient orange-striped canvas walls, rolled our swimsuits in damp towels, and carried the tent back into the cavern under the promenade that smelt of upturned rowing boats, fishing tackle, old sandals and damp canvas. John said next year we would have to have a new tent as ours was more mends than tents. I never saw our tent again nor heard if it and the cavern survived the war. St Leonards' pier did not.

Next morning father signed my consent form and after handing it in to the Commandant of my new Detachment, (BRCS, Sussex 14), I ordered—at father's expense—full indoor and outdoor uniform for Betty and myself. Father raised his eyebrows over the bill for twenty pounds odd. 'I thought I'd agreed to fit out a couple of Red Cross nurses, not finance a hospital.' The following afternoon our family collected our civilian gas masks from our own church hall. Father was one of the churchwardens, and in that hall on countless Saturday

mornings in the holidays I had helped arrange the altar flowers
and at other times to put up and serve behind the trestle tables
in jumble sales, sales of work, or handed round trays of tea,
bridge rolls with the butter running like oil, sandwiches
decorated with sausauge-stick flags. 'Tomato on the left, fish
paste on the right—yes, such a pity the fête was rained out—
yes, jolly lucky we've got the hall. . . .'

All the early rehearsals for the Christmas Nativity Play were
held in that hall and owing to the Rector's enthusiasm for his
productions, few of his parishoners' children between ten and
sixteen managed to avoid being in the cast. Once in, by some
unwritten but fixed adult law, there was no escape until the
seventeenth birthday. Often this was then extended for the
star performers without objection, as the star parts were much
sought after. A few always remained in the same adult hands.
The Rector was St Joseph and producer; the Curate, John the
Baptist; Col . . . X (Ret.), the Centurion; and the Rector's
wife, Gabriel, as she was small, slim, elegant and the only
person in the parish to possess or fit into her long-sleeved,
high-necked gold lamé evening dress. Children started in the
crowd scenes as Children of Jerusalem. Once in the teens, the
boys rose to Extra Shepherds and later for the three with most
carrying voices, to the Three Shepherds. All the Shepherds
wore sacks with slits for heads and arms, sacks wound round
their feet, and wine bottle straw cases round their bare calves.
Ahead for the most talented Shepherds lay three of the star
parts, the Three Kings. The Kings did no speaking but were
literally in the limelight from their first appearance at the end
of the three aisles to the opening notes of 'We Three Kings' to
the final tableau on the dais in front of the rood screen. They
wore borrowed silk dressing-gowns, rows of maternal neck-
laces and bracelets, and two had gold and silver paper crowns
and the King from the East a silver lamé turban above his
blacked-up face.

For Shepherds who failed to make Kings lay the lesser glory
of marching as Roman Legionaries and being drilled in the hall
by the Centurion in his old parade-ground voice. The Legion
wore cardboard helmets, breastplates, daggers, and short stone-

coloured kilts of great antiquity—and to the younger cast, of unknown origin, but generally agreed by the off-stage crowd waiting in hall, ante-room, vestry and Lady-chapel to have been worn by Harold's army in the Battle of Hastings. 'What you mean they didn't wear no kilts then? Was you there, smartie?'

Girls, normally, progressed from Children to Angels. One couldn't, said the Rector, have too many Angels. Then he took me aside and explained very kindly why he could not make me an Angel. 'Your hair is too dark. I'm afraid we can't have black-haired Angels so I want you to be—er—a Girl of Jerusalem.'

I seethed with fury and envy. Betty, Ann, Ruth, Peggy—all the other girls had silver stars and tinsel on their miserable fair hair and long white nightdresses with silver cord belts, and all I had was a mouldy brown tent and stiff white cambric triangle hiding most of my regrettable hair. I kept pushing back the triangle and authority kept heaving it forward. 'No, no, dear, you mustn't show so much hair. No respectable Girl of Jerusalem would show so much hair. You wouldn't want the congregation to think you a fast girl, would you?'

I would. If I could not be an Angel I wanted to be Mary Magdalene—a vain want as she did not figure in the play. Then I discovered the unexpected compensation of being a non-speaking crowd of one and mostly off-stage. All my entrances, as the Shepherds, were from the vestry on the left, whilst the main crowd of adults and children came from the Lady-chapel, right. The vestry crowd had to overflow into the ante-room and the Rector did not mind where we sat to wait, so long as we kept still and quiet. Directly the organist began 'Oh Come, Oh Come, Emmanuel', someone produced cards, and to the cry 'Watchman, what of the night?' we used my tent skirt as a card table and settled down to the game. It was there, from the Shepherds, that I learnt poker, whist and vingt-et-un.

The church was newish and being the size of a young cathedral had ample room for the dais and many crowd scenes. We always had several semi-dress rehearsals before the three public performances and during the former the Rector dodged in and out keeping an eye on us and, as a fold of my voluminous skirt had been flicked over the cards, nodded approvingly. 'Good quiet youngsters—what's that Gabriel, my dear? Can't hear the Baptist from the front?' He dodged away and his voice floated back. 'Louder, dear boy, louder! Take it from— "I come as one crying in the wilderness. . . ." '

When I was sixteen, on the day of the final full-dress and make-up rehearsal, the statutory Virgin Mary caught 'flu. My tent was replaced by bright blue muslin, my cambric triangle by white georgette and after the opening minutes I was on stage in the main spotlight throughout the play. George that year was near the end of his apprenticeship, home for Christmas and as an ex-King risen from Shepherds and Crowd had refused to perform but agreed to work the spotlights. He was a very good-looking boy and in previous plays had barely acknowledged my schoolgirl existence, but after that play ended he took me to a movie, and fed me a banana split, a wild luxury that cost 1s. 3d.

On the afternoon of 30th August 1939, the trestle tables were up in the church hall, but in place of jumble, hand-made tea-cosies appliquéd with daisies, simpering crinoline dolls to hide telephones, drawn-thread tablecloths and overstuffed pin cushions, were geometrical stacks of small, square, brown cardboard boxes containing the civilian gas masks issued free to the entire civilian population. Behind the tables not efficient or fussy middle-aged women and reluctant daughters, but youngish men with neat, official, faces and older men with habitual military and naval hair-cuts and broad armbands labelled A.R.P. (Air Raid Precautions). We found the hall half-empty, but the official who dealt with us said there had been quite a rush earlier and he expected another later when people knocked off work. He demonstrated the correct use of a gas mask on himself and his muffled voice sounded as choked as he must have felt from his red face when he took it off. 'Remember to make sure the straps that go over the head are tight enough to hold the mask tautly under the chin, or the poison gas can seep in.'

John asked what happened if it was mustard gas. 'Our

science master says civilian gas masks aren't any good for mustard gas.'

The official said that was a most interesting question, young man, and rootled amongst the boxes for masks for mother and myself as if searching the right size in shoes. 'How about this for you, madam? And for the young lady?' Mother did not think it mattered what size she had as she knew she would stifle if she ever had to wear one as she never could stand anything over her face. 'Remember how I objected to my veil in Egypt, Billee—and when I was a girl and veils were very fashionable and becoming always I removed mine.' Father and the official clucked soothingly and the latter said of course we couldn't be sure but would all hope no gas would be used. John surfaced from a mask. 'Old Stinks says it will. Old Stinks says the Germans'll drop lots of gas on us and if we aren't all burnt and blistered with mustard gas we'll get the sort that'll make us sort of drown in our lungs in a green sort of froth glug-glug-glug—no, honestly, Daddy he did and he says. . . .'

I stopped listening having noticed the ante-room door was open. On the chairs the Shepherds and I had used when playing cards and waiting for cues, young women waited and beside them babies in prams. Another official was carefully demonstrating the bulky tent-like apparatus provided by the Government to protect infants too small to wear masks in gas attacks. When packed away the apparatus needed a square cardboard box large enough to take up half the pram.

The door between ante-room and vestry was shut. The church sounded empty, but not to me. Watchman, what of the night? . . . I come as one crying in the wilderness . . . And there were shepherds watching their flocks by night . . . Behold I bring you tidings of comfort and joy . . . 'Now then, choir and Children only, "Away In A Manger"! . . . Thank you, Children! Very nicely sung! Back to your places in the Lady-chapel.' In the Children's Corner in the Lady-chapel in blue letters on gold: 'Suffer the little children to come unto me.'

Mesmerized, I watched those obscene boxes being loaded onto prams and felt I had been kicked in the stomach and ashamed to be a member of the human race. I thought; no wonder Jesus wept. Two thousand years later—suffer the little children to come and get the gas masks that in a concentrated attack might, with luck, keep them alive for ten minutes. Long enough, it was said, to run to the nearest gas-proof shelters. (I presume there were gas-proof shelters in south-east England in the Second World War, but I never saw one. Nor did I see the bomb that destroyed our church but left the steeple standing, a few years later. Our G.P. and his daughter, my great girlhood friend Ann, were in their house, roughly two hundred yards down hill from the church and heard the bomb fall, but no immediate explosion. Once the sound of diving aircraft faded they went into the road and looked up the hill. 'We saw the church give a little shake and then all but the steeple cave in. We waited watching from across the road until the huge dust cloud settled and then saw the whole body of St John's had vanished. Luckily it was a weekday and empty.')

St Leonards stands on a series of hills. When we walked back up our own hill from the church, a crocodile of small children passed us on their way down. The crocodile moved slowly, raggedly, and the children clung to each other's hands as if so unsure of the ground under their feet as to be in active danger of falling through. Their hair was untidy, their faces unusually pale and pinched, knees thin and bare, socks crinkled, and they had gas mask boxes slung with string over their shoulders, small obviously new and cheap suitcases, large white labels tied to the lapels of their coats and jackets. The expression in all their faces took me straight back to my first years at boarding-school when I too had felt lost and scared without understanding why and had secretly feared it must somehow be my fault that I had been sent away from home.

Father said the children were evacuees from London being taken to their new billets. 'Madness and thoughtless!'

'But, Daddy, shouldn't they be out of London if it's going to be bombed?'

'Of course, but not brought for refuge to the East Sussex coast. If we have air raids the enemy'll be bound to fly in over Sussex and Kent as that's the shortest route to London. Bad enough for those poor youngsters being shifted from home without the prospect of being shifted on again.'

John asked if his school would be shifted. 'Last term some boys said this time next year the school would be in Devon or somewhere.' Our parents were silent. 'I think this war's going to be jolly exciting. I say—you don't suppose we won't have it?'

Father said that remained to be seen and we finished our walk in silence.

Two days later, on 1st September 1939, in a borrowed BRCS nurse's uniform, in a men's acute surgical ward in the Royal East Sussex Hospital, Hastings, I started the first of my ninety hours' basic nursing training. Before that first shift ended, one of the many patients listening intently pushed up his wireless headphones. 'There we are then, nurse. Old Hitler's marched his lads into Poland.'

Not recognizing the title, I looked round to see the nurse he was addressing, then realized this was myself and what else he had said.

Chapter Three

WHEN the train stopped at Southampton, the only civilian in our crowded carriage woke abruptly, clicked back his teeth and leapt onto the platform. Two minutes later he was back with a sausage roll balanced on the teaspoon in the saucer of his cup of Southern Railway tea. It was February 1940 and the war had not yet removed saucers from the railway buffets of southern England nor chained to buffet counters the solitary teaspoon for communal use.

The nine sailors who had rearranged themselves and their kit to give Betty and me window seats when we changed trains at Brighton reached under the seats for the small brown attaché cases that for that day alone seemed an incongrous appendage to bell-bottoms, flapping collars, round caps that defied gravity and bore only the ambiguous H.M.S. on the name ribbons. From then on I associated those cases with the Royal Navy as never once in the entire war did I see a seaman of any rank travelling without one.

The sailors' cases were stacked with packets of crusted sandwiches and pork pies. In a large biscuit tin at six that morning Mother had packed enough food for Betty and I to survive a week in the train should one of the still unmaterialized major air-raids so delay our journey to Hampshire. We shared the twelve bananas with the sailors as the elderly civilian said he was much obliged but if there was one thing he couldn't touch it was a banana or he'd know it for days. The war must have helped him there, as those were the last bananas I saw whilst it lasted.

The sunlight filtering through the anti-blast brown paper strips criss-crossing the windows was surprisingly and unseasonably warm. January had been extra cold and for weeks every branch and twig on the bare trees had been encased in ice that transformed the evergreens into glittering emeralds. To find myself travelling on a summer's day in February enhanced the sensations of unreality, and my mind's lifelong facility for framing personal situations with newspaper headlines, framed, 'journey to a war'. Not that I believed it. The large suitcase on the rack over my head might be filled with grey-blue nurses' dresses, white aprons with large red crosses on the bibs, white caps with smaller red crosses on the front turn-up, but I felt exactly as if going back to school. My new outdoor uniform coat and skirt were still navy blue serge, and if my white man's shirt and black tie were some variation, the double-breasted navy greatcoat on the rack was as bulky and ill-fitting as my old school coat. When I protested, 'It doesn't fit me anywhere!' the tailor half-strangled himself with his tape-measure in embarrassment: 'Ladies' uniforms are not —er—meant to—er—follow a lady's form, miss. The coats and jackets are meant to hang loosely from the shoulders and the skirts from the waist.' I had had to accept this and the thick grey woollen stockings but regarded the last as the ultimate sacrifice as I was proud of my legs.

Our third-class travel warrants had arrived with our call-up papers a few days earlier. Warrants and papers were heavily stamped, Mobile. At our next change the sailors heaved out our cases, holdalls, rugs and the carrier bag with the remains of the picnic and said we must give them a shout anytime we weren't shipping Mobile and they'd muster their ships' companies to carry our bags.

That station in peacetime served a small market town. 'Clapham Junction of Southern Command now, ladies,' said the harassed R.T.O. (Railway Transport Officer). 'Any chap who doesn't know what to do with his chaps shoves 'em off on a forty-eight, they end up here and we're supposed to shove 'em on—but in what?' The question seemed rhetorical since the station was nearly as alive with trains as with men. Big trains, little trains, trains without engines, engines without trains, engines pushing other engines, shunted to and fro, stopped and started, without apparently leaving the station. Every visible carriage was jammed with troops, every inch of platform, buffet and waiting rooms a solid sea of khaki. The R.T.O. sighed over our warrants, two Military Policemen loaded themselves with out luggage, the ranks squeezed themselves apart to give us a path to a train of three coaches and an engine waiting in a siding. We were put into a first-class carriage. 'Matter your warrants are thirds? Not the slightest, ladies! All the chaps are trying to get away from your camp, not go there. Probably have this to yourselves. Cheerio!'

We had the carriage to ourselves for all that remained of our meandering eight-hour journey from Warrior Square Station, St Leonards. We had been posted to a large military hospital in a permanent army camp near Salisbury Plain, but as our final approach was from the north-west, there was no sign of the Plain. The little train ambled across arable farmland, the spring ploughing had started, every field was thick with birds picking over the reddish-brown soil, every cottage and farm garden festooned with washing lines. The war seemed so alien that we wondered if the R.T.O. had sent us west by mistake until the train suddenly hiccuped to a stop in a tiny station and we found we had arrived.

Several soldiers got off with us and with no officer in sight to act as a deterrent our appearance evoked the immediate verbal barrage that we shortly learnt was the British Army's conditioned reflex to the sight of a uniformed nurse whatever her age, figure and face. From first to last year of the war, always in my experience, the barrage was good-humoured, even affectionate, and never impolite or sprinkled with the mildest epithets. 'Oy, Charlie—over there—there's the reason why I left home!' 'Oh, Nursie, I do feel queer—come and take me pulse, Nursie!' 'Oh, Nursie, me mother told me to find a girl like you—oh, Nursie, you're smashing!' Still bellowing they climbed into the back of a waiting van and were driven off chorusing a recently popular song that began: 'Nursie, come over here and hold my hand. . . .'

Being totally uninitiated it never occurred to us to expect official transport. The driver of the one taxi on the rank was a tall, straight man with cropped white hair, a civilian suit neat enough for a uniform, and brilliantly polished shoes. 'Military hospital, ladies? Oh dear me no, you don't want the hospital. What you want is the Officers' Club.'

'But, driver, it says here—'

He checked our warrants. 'No offence, ladies, but seeing as I've had the forty-two years service you'll not mind my saying as you don't want to set too much store by what it says there. There aren't no nurses quartered up the hospital. What you want is the Officers' Club. That's where all you young Red Cross nursing ladies got your billets. I'll see you're all right.'

Once away from the station and over the crest of a hill, a harsh lined mosaic of red brick opened out below. Behind the red brick were low hills fringed with low trees and beyond were glimpses of an empty, undulating faded green carpet stretching to the eastern horizon. The driver jerked a thumb at a row of neat, glass-fronted wooden shacks at the foot of the hill. 'The shops.' Another thumb jerk. 'Blocks start here. Just remember they're all alphabetical and you'll not get lost.'

Block after block of the same red brick built to the same pattern with the same white barrack squares, sentry boxes, khaki figures, all of the same sex. Men everywhere, marching, drilling, running, strolling, crawling on their stomachs, taking guns to pieces, loading larger guns onto carriers, driving cars, vans, lorries, tanks, motor-bikes and ambulances with large red crosses painted on their roofs and khaki sides. Our driver said the hospital had great red crosses painted on its flat roofs, 'Could come in handy, but then—as you might say—could not.'

He turned the car away from the red brick and drove past tennis courts, playing fields, and a row of largish semi-detached houses with blank curtainless windows and neglected front gardens. 'M.O.Q.—beg pardon, miss? Married Officers Quarters that'll be, but empty now as all the officers' ladies got moved out. Only ladies we got left in the camp now are the Sisters, you Red Cross ladies and the ATS. Not much more than the five hundred of you in all, they tell me. What's that, miss? Well, now, hard to say how many of the lads—but I don't reckon it'll be less than the hundred thousand and could be more than a mite more.'

The road widened into a long avenue lined with leafless trees. The broad grass verges were thick with broken branches and logs. 'Come down in last month's cold snap, miss. Couldn't drive down here for 'em falling. Had half a tree across the bonnet one night.' He slowed into a short, gateless drive and drew up at the pillared porch littered with women's bicycles. The bell did not work. The driver said not to worry as it had gone u/s since the ladies took over. He carried in our luggage, accepted the 1s. 6d. (7½p) fare but politely returned the tip as he said he never took more than the fare from nursing ladies. 'You want to go on through those double doors and find one of your lady officers.'

The doors opened into a large dining-room furnished with scrubbed deal tables, benches, and a long serving counter. The only occupant, a girl in a white silk shirt, navy skirt and black silk stockings, was sitting by the log fire at the far end painting her nails with colourless varnish. She advanced spraying the air with the scent of pear-drops 'Hallo! New girls! How'd you do? Terribly sorry, hands are wet—my half-day—just had to repair the damage after last night's party. God what a party! Where are you from? SUSSEX? Why the hell've they sent you to Hampshire? We've no-one from Sussex here—but Madam'll know—she send someone to meet you? Oh—can't have known you were coming. Not to worry. She'll be back from the Office in a jiff. Come and sit down and get warm. Anything you want to know?'

I asked, 'Are we allowed to wear black silk stockings?'

'Not officially but most of our age do. Of course, Madam narks, but she has to nark being our Commandant—here she is.'

The small spruce BRCS Commandant strode in with a purposeful air and impressive line of First World War medal ribbons on the breast of her jacket. 'New Members? Why wasn't I informed?' She studied our papers and National

Identity Cards. (We were not issued with Army Books 64, or BRCS Identity Cards until some months later.) 'I'll hang onto these for the present, m'dears. They appear in order, but there must be some mistake. We never get Members from Sussex this far west.' From her tone Sussex adjoined the Polish not the Hampshire border. 'I'll have a pow-wow at the Office. Probably find yourselves posted on in the morning—don't unpack too much.' She turned to a youngish, pretty woman with greying hair who had followed her in and wore an indoor uniform dress, black tie and belt, and no apron or cap. 'Find these new gels beds for the night, m'dear. Andrews, E., Andrews, L., from Sussex! And this, new Members, is our invaluable Home VAD!'

Three years earlier Betty had started nursing in Guy's Hospital, enjoyed the Preliminary Training-School but left at the end of her first month in the wards. 'Kind of Home Sister,' she translated privately. 'School matron.'

The Home VAD led us away sadly muttering 'Sussex'. In the stone-floored chilly storeroom still heady with wine fumes she explained what really worried her was German Measles. 'Suppose you haven't had it? You have! Both! Recently—oh, bless you! I can put you in infectious beds—or should it be contagious? I never knew—do you?' We didn't. 'We're having an epidemic.' She piled rough grey blankets and oblong bolsters seemingly stuffed with sand into our arms. 'Those are pillows. Now, biscuits.'

'Biscuits—?'

'That's what the Army calls these.' She slapped a stack of thin mattresses roughly two-foot square. 'Did you bring sheets? Oh, dear. I'll try and find you one each, but do write home for some and bikes if you're going to stay. There's no transport to the hospital, it's over a mile away and once on the wards your feet won't stand up to all the foot-slogging. Let's find you beds.'

Just like being back at school. Betty, my senior, went into the senior dorm.—the former Bar now occupied by only fourteen beds. I went into the junior dorm.—the twenty-bedded former ballroom.

It was a room of lovely proportions. Three walls were lined
with mirrors and, in the fourth, a row of giant french windows
opened onto the garden path and two tennis courts directly
beyond. From the high ceiling decorated with gold leaf, four
massive glass chandeliers hung serenely over chaos. The twenty
Army bedsteads and twenty wooden orange boxes that served
as dressing-tables, bookshelves, lockers, larders and dirty linen
closets were so arranged as to make movement between the
beds difficult and crossing the room in a straight line in any
direction, impossible. Spare blankets, rugs, dirty caps, dirty
aprons, cigarette ash, cosmetic jars, spilled face powder, half-
eaten ginger-nuts, suitcases, portable wirelesses, tennis
racquets and photographs of young men in uniform were
strewn as by a hurricane.

The Home VAD sighed, 'Sorry about the squalor. You
won't believe it, but this gets tidied every day. Madam'll raise
the roof if she walks in now.'

I lacked the courage to say I liked the mess as it had caused
the first real crack in my back-to-school armour. Supper,
temporarily, repaired this.

'I say, would you mind frightfully passing the salt? Thanks
most awfully! . . . I say, aren't you one of the new girls from
somewhere too peculiar? Sussex? How quaint! I say, Mary,
have you heard—the new girls are from Sussex!'

There were variations: instead of what Miss X said it was
what Sister said; some of the faces round the tables were
middle aged and pale with fatigue; and all the hands were red
and roughened as all present were amateur nurses. (Professional nurses even in wartime, from their first day in P.T.S.,
were taught to care for their hands since cracked roughened
skin more readily harboured germs.)

I was expecting a mistress to walk in and clap her hands,
'Girls, please! Less noise!', when the Commandant walked in
and clapped her hands. She addressed us, invariably col-
lectively, as 'Members!' Individually it was either 'm'dear' or
by the surname and where necessary plus an identifying initial.
It took me several days to identify myself as Andrews, L.

The Commandant announced the Company Office to be

temporarily unable to explain the postings of the two new Members from Sussex, but owing to the Rubella stalking the camp—'German Measles' murmured the girl beside me guessing, rightly, I had taken this for some form of Fifth Column—as the hospital was so short-staffed, Matron had decided to post Andrews, E. to A Block, Andrews, L. to Lower C for day-duty from tomorrow at 07.30 hours. Purely pro tem.

'Your sister's lucky,' said my neighbour. 'Acute surgical and real nursing. She had any training? Guy's P.T.S.? No wonder.'

'What's mine?'

She grinned. 'N.D.K.—No Diagnosis Known. Could be worse. Could be SKINS.'

She was a large friendly girl with the face of a cheerful horse but much better teeth. After supper she advised us to unpack properly. 'War'll be over before the bods in the Company Office have sorted out your posting.'

As far as I ever knew, she was right.

At some period, I think before the house became an Officer's Club, a long conservatory had been added. By our arrival the glass had been painted black and a row of partitioned bathrooms installed, but as the partitions fell considerably short of the conservatory roof, conversations in any bathroom were audible to all. In the bath that night I heard another high-pitched 'Too extraordinary, darling—I mean why Sussex here?'

Adrenalin and country pride rose together. I sang loudly the first verse of *Sussex By The Sea*, Betty in a neighbouring bath joined in and at the tops of our voices we repeated several times the chorus:

> Good old Sussex by the sea, by the sea,
> Good old Sussex by the sea,
> You can tell them all that we stand or fall
> For Sussex by the sea.

It could have been coincidence, but never again did I hear anyone express surprise at our coming from Sussex.

That night in the ballroom was hot and stuffy until the

Commandant was judged safely in bed in her room at the opposite end of the house and someone illicitly opened the heavy shutters blacking out the french windows and left open two of the doors. It took me a long time to get to sleep as the hard biscuits kept slipping apart. I was asleep when something shook my bed. I was blinded by a torchlight and inhaled gin fumes. 'Terribly sorry, darling—wrong bed. Mine's next. Just back. God what a party!' The torch went out.

'For God's sake shut up! Some of us', hissed another voice 'want to sleep.'

'Sorry, darlings.' Fumbling hands groped round my bed, knocked something off an orange box, then returned to shake my shoulder. 'I say, you on in the morning? Give me a shake if I'm not awake as I've got to leave at seven to walk it as my bloody bike's got two flats.'

In the dark I heard her throwing off clothes, the soft methodical clink-clink of a comb against metal curlers and fell asleep to the slap-slap of her patting cream on her face.

It seemed only five minutes later that a chandelier was switched on. It was 5.30 a.m. and the four VAD cooks sharing the room with sixteen nurses had to be on-duty at the hospital at six and were wearily climbing into uniform. Half an hour later all the chandeliers were on and everyone but the late-comer was awake. Each time I shook her, she grunted, 'I want to die,' and hauled the sheet higher over the small arms factory in her blonde hair. The other girls told me not to flap. 'At five to seven she'll explode into life, grab a bacon sandwich, eat it walking to the hospital and be on-duty in time.'

At exactly five to seven she erupted, flinging off bedclothes and pyjamas, flung on bra and pants, raced for the bathroom and on returning sat on the side of her bed, did her face and put on her cap before donning stockings, suspender-belt and uniform. I had already noticed most of the others got into uniform in that order and in a day or two and ever after did so myself. It was the quickest way of getting into uniform, as stockings could be hitched to back suspenders, dresses buttoned, apron bibs pinned en route to dining-room or ward, but a cap needed precision and a mirror.

Day-duty for VAD nurses began at 7.30 a.m., and ended at 8 p.m. During the day we had three hours off either from 10 a.m. to 1 p.m.; 2 p.m. to 5 p.m.; or the most popular, 5 p.m. to 8 p.m. We had one half-day a week and this was either a free morning to 1.30 p.m., or free afternoon from 2 p.m. Generally those who lived near enough to get home for the afternoon, chose or were given afternoon half-days, and those living too far off had the free mornings and glorious luxury of lying in bed watching the rest leave for work and sleeping on until noon. On days we had one day off per month. On night-duty, one free night awarded for every week worked, and these free nights had to be taken together at the end of the full night shift of twenty-eight nights. Night hours were from 8 p.m. to 8 a.m. Our pay in 1940 was one pound per week.

The military hospital at first sight looked like the other barracks. According to the old soldiers, it had been used as barracks until converted into a hospital between the Boer and First World War. According to some of the Sisters—known as QAs—newly recruited from the great voluntary teaching hospitals—the conversion was more likely to have happened between the American War of Independence and the Crimean War. 'Personally, I date it just after Agincourt.'

The harsh-lined ward blocks were ranged round a great square and the main entrance to square and hospital lay under a flat-roofed arch. Until the air raids started, every fine day the arch roof was lined with sick men in beds covered with scarlet blankets, or in wheelchairs with scarlet over their knees and the multi-coloured crochet shawls provided by the combined Red Cross and St John Ambulance Societies over their shoulders.

The blocks all had two floors, ground and upper, and the acute wards and operating theatres were on the latter. My first block was non-acute and from my first day onwards I knew it as the N.D.K. Block.

N.D.K. lay across the square from the arch and consisted of seven large ten-bedded barrack-room wards, three ablutions annexes, a minute scullery with a window overlooking the Ordnance railway line, and a vast reception room that served as Sister's duty-room, M.O.'s office, surgical dressing-room and ward kitchen. At one end of the hall a door opened into the square, and at the other was the doorway to the first of the seven wards. 'No bathrooms, no sterilizers—not even a fish-kettle on a primus.' The block's senior VAD ticked the missing objects off on her fingers. She had nursed as a VAD in France in the first war and wore her old and old-fashioned long-sleeved, dog-collared BRCS uniform. 'So we sterilize by flaming. Quite simple. We use this huge enamel bowl, put in the instruments—so—pour on raw meths to cover—so—stand well back—back a bit more—' she struck a match 'and so!'

When the soaring blue flame subsided—'Excuse me, Mrs S, but does it work?'

'Must do as we get very little cross infection. Of course, that could be the M. and B.'

'I'm sorry, but—what's that?'

'M. and B. 693. Short for May and Baker, I think 693 because it took them 693 times to get the combination right. They're tablets. Marvellous things. Don't know how the stuff works, but we hand 'em out for everything from septic fingers to meningitis. The boys say it makes 'em feel like the Wrath of God, but whatever it does, does the trick. When I remember all the sepsis and gangrene we had last time—Oh Lord, mustn't whoffle as we've masses to do. But there's something I must tell you about M. and B.—it clashes with onions and Epsom salts and then turns people blue. Don't forget when-ever you're sent to dole out M. and B.s to ask if anyone's eaten onions or Epsom salts that day and if so tell Sister on the double.'

That warning worried me for months and any of my patients on M. and B. 693, I daily badgered, 'You're positive you haven't eaten onions or Epsom salts?' 'Not me, miss! Cross me heart and hope to die!' But having discovered that soldier-patients were bound to admit only what they thought I wanted to hear, I watched covertly, anxiously, for signs of their turning blue. I never saw this happen.

The wards had white-quilted beds, white deal open lockers,

and a few hard chairs. Beds and lockers had to be arranged in the approved military order, chairs to stand in fixed places against the walls, the patients' greatcoats and caps had to hang from the brass hook on the wall just above each bedhead, the greatcoats in the approved folds, the cap arranged to show clearly the cap badge. The only soldiers I knew to object to the last were the sick military policemen who used to remove the outer red covers from their caps within minutes of admission. In the acute blocks the patients were issued with pyjamas or hospital nightgowns. In N.D.K. (an Other Ranks Block) any bed-patients then wore the white shirts issued with Hospital 'blues'. These much-washed and stoved bright blue woollen jackets and trousers tended to be ill-fitting and crumpled unless worn by up-patients in the Brigade of Guards. I never nursed a Guardsman up-patient who did not remove the creases from his blues jacket and put them correctly in the trousers, by flattening both under his mattress every night.

In the early morning before the C.O.'s weekly inspection of the block, whilst VADs and up-patients swept and polished floors, scrubbed lockers, burnished every inch of brass in sight, the bed-patients carefully spread their red handkerchiefs on their top pillows to protect the pristine whiteness from last-minute cigarette ash and Brylcreem. Immediately the official party was spotted crossing the square, cigarettes and handkerchiefs vanished. During those inspections, and for my first few weeks in the hospital during all medical rounds, in N.D.K. the up-patients had throughout to stand to attention by their beds and the bed-patients to lie to attention. In private, quite a few of the new and younger M.O.s admitted to sharing my fury at this iniquitous absurdity. The troops' philosophical attitude astonished me. 'You got to look at it this way, miss. If you goes on sick parade in the army, you puts yourself on a charge.'

'You mean it's a crime to be sick or injured?'

'You've said it, miss!'

On our block diagnosis list, against name after name: N.D.K. Against others: tonsillitis, septic finger, Vincent's Angina, fractured finger, query incipient gastric ulcer, backache, ring worm, dermatitis too mild for SKINS. What precisely went into SKINS I was never thankfully to learn but always secretly feared from the strange linen masks I glimpsed on the faces of the men leaning over the permanently cordoned-off area of the long, narrow iron-railed balcony connecting all the upper floors and overlooking the square.

An amazing—to me—number of our patients in N.D.K. had injured fingers and one arm in a sling. The men blamed their new tanks and enjoyed curdling the blood of new VADs with the horrors that awaited newly mechanized troopers. From their accounts, there was not a tank crew in the British Army with a full quota of fingers and thumbs. Invariably they re-told their cherished, apocryphal, story of the sergeant-instructor who pressed the wrong button in a demonstration. 'There he stood, miss—I tell you no lie—there he stood with nothing but the two stumps. Talk about surprised! Blood everywhere! Swimming in it, the lads were!'

At first in N.D.K. roughly every half-hour I had to put down some broom, scrubbing-brush, or brass-polishing rag and wash my hands to re-tie a sling. In desperation I asked my mentor, Mrs S, for help. 'I must be doing them wrong as mine keep coming undone.'

She laughed. 'Nothing wrong with your slings. The boys are undoing them. They're just trying it on as you're young and new. You can stop this easily if you tell the next to try it that Sister'll have you on the mat if she catches more of your slings coming adrift. These boys are exactly like their fathers last time—they like their bit of fun but they'll risk perjury and the glass house to save a VAD being put on the mat by a Sister.'

Her advice worked instantly, which astounded me, but not so much as the soldiers' habit of regarding admission to N.D.K. as admission to paradise. 'Been telling me mate, miss —all right in here!' Up went a thumb. 'All right, it is!'

On admission almost every patient was escorted in by his special mate from his unit. I learnt to identify the mate as the soldier who jumped first from the ambulance or van, looked the most worried and carried the small kit. 'Small kit' comprised razor, brush, comb, haircream, occasionally tooth-brush, and other personal possessions small enough to pack in a knitted khaki scarf with one of the double-sided ends pushed into the other to make an open-ended bag. At visiting times the mate coaxed, bullied or bribed comrades to stand-to for him and arrived to stand or sit by his friend's bed, often with-out either exchanging a word and sharing pages of the *Daily Mirror* or *Razzle*. When, as happened very rarely, a really ill or injured man was temporarily admitted to N.D.K. to await a bed in an acute block, his mate haunted our side exits to the square, dodged M.O.s, Sisters and N.C.O.s and waylaid VADs. 'Excuse me, miss—just a word about me mate—how's he doing? You'll—er—you'll tell him I was asking and —tell him chin-up.'

From the N.D.K. patients I first learnt the military art of scrounging. Later I met a battalion of expert scroungers, but none surpassed the scrounging talent of one Cpl C in N.D.K. Cpl C was a regular soldier with five years' service, a small sturdy man with dark hair, calm eyes and already an old soldier's rigidity in his young face. He was an up-patient with one arm in a sling and it was the constant dread of the block VADs that one day he would be discharged back to barracks. If we ran short of floor polish, scouring powder, coal for the only and open fire on which we boiled eggs, re-heated porridge, heated kaolin poultices, and when Sister was not around brewed-up instead of boiling the water for her mid-morning tea, the cry went up, 'Corp! Please!' The Cpl would silently don his cap, straighten his red tie, amble out into the square and return within minutes with the essential commodity either hidden in his sling, or when this was coal, in a fire bucket beneath a thin layer of sand. That we were always kept short of essentials ceased to surprise me after my first month in the Army as I then accepted, if never understood, authority's habit of never replenishing such stores in full or in time.

Our block Sister was then an elderly, elegant QA Reservist, with First World War medal ribbons, black silk stockings and high-heeled black court shoes. One evening someone dis-covered the following day was her birthday. Next morning, ten minutes before Sister came on at eight, Cpl C came into the reception hall with a large bunch of daffodils for Sister's desk. A cookhouse orderly lugging in the porridge buckets told me he had spotted the Cpl in the night helping himself from the C.O.'s garden. Whether or not this was true, I could believe it, but denied it firmly as a scurrilous rumour.

Never in N.D.K. did the Cpl scrounge for any but the communal or the nursing staff's good. When the front inner tube of the aged bicycle I had bought from another VAD for ten shillings was ruined by my habit of riding on flats, the Cpl produced and organized the fitting of a new tube. I was grateful but concerned. 'Corp, you're an angel, but—er—did you get this from one of the other VADs' bikes?'

'Miss Andrews, are you suggesting I'd scrounge from a nurse? What do you think I am?' He was so incensed that despite my abject apology he sulked for two days. Luckily he overheard my explosion when a broom fell apart. 'I don't mind sweeping this entire block with tea-leaves, a broom with three hairs and a handle two foot long, but if this miserable head falls off again I'm going to re-muster to the ATS! If the Army wants us to keep this block clean, why can't they give us decent brooms?'

'Let's have it.' The Cpl strolled over, jammed the head back on the pole. 'Face it, Miss Andrews. The Army'll never replace anything just because it falls to pieces. Got to crumble to dust first.' He glanced out of a window and at a medical orderly leisurely pushing dust along one of the acute block balconies. 'Seems they've had an issue of new brooms over there.'

'They have.' I was bitter. 'Trust the acutes to get first pick.'

'That's right.' He kicked off the head he had just repaired. 'This needs a nail. I'll take a walk—'

'Hey, Corp—please! The acute orderlies'll lynch you—if you're thinking—?'

He gave me a long, expressionless look. 'I got five years' service, Miss Andrews. I never think.'

I never saw that wrecked broom again nor asked how the much longer pole of the brand new broom with which I was presented twenty minutes later had been deeply charred round the point used for the block identification letters. Sister raised plucked eyebrows. 'Someone has been using that broom as a poker. You VADs must be more careful. I cannot permit such misuse of army equipment.'

'No, Sister. I'm sorry, Sister.'

The patients did not mind us sweeping floors, but objected strongly to the sight of a VAD 'swinging a bumper'. A bumper was a very long handled, heavy, flat and oblong-shaped at the polishing face, floor polisher that had to be used daily on all ward floors. In the acute blocks, generally, as these still had medical orderlies, bumpering was done by men. In blocks without orderlies, by VADs. The best results were achieved by first slinging down a handful of wax polish then one-handedly swinging the heavy bumper to and fro. But as few female wrists and arms had the necessary muscular strength for this, most VADs, as myself, used both hands. Seldom for more than thirty seconds. 'That's no job for you, miss! Let's have that bumper! Oy—Andy—Taff—Bert—stand by to take over. . . .'

In N.D.K. the patients only began calling VADs 'nurse' instead of 'miss' after Dunkirk, as it was really only then that we properly nursed them. In those earlier months we served their meals, made their beds, scrubbed their lockers, swept their ward floors always twice and often three times daily, polished brass coathooks, doorknobs, keyholes, emptied and washed thrice-daily the collection of tin lids they used as ash-trays, lit and tended the one coal fire mainly with bare hands as we had no coal-tongs and the provided shovel and poker were large enough to stoke an express engine. Our 'nursing' seldom involved more than dabbing gentian violet on ring-worm, aquaflavine emulsion on cuts and scratches, lead lotion on bruises and sprains, taking and charting temperatures, very occasionally doing a minor surgical dressing or removing a few stitches, sticking on and removing strapping plaster, and handing out doses of Gee's Linctus by the gallon, M. and B. tablets by the dozen, and the troops' beloved A.P.C. tablets by the gross.

We had a few lead-swingers (malingerers), and two or three genuine hypochondriacs who kept re-appearing when yet another newly qualified M.O. straight from teaching hospital was sent to cut his military teeth in N.D.K. The gravity of Pte X's, Tpr Y's or Gnr Z's alarming symptoms worried these young men. 'You say the pain catches you here?'

'You've got it, sir! Catches me cruel, sir—hot knife in me belly it is, sir, then down it goes into me right leg and can I move it? Helpless, sir—see? Like a log, that's what.'

'The numbness affects the right leg? But in these notes from your own M.O. the numbness is stated as affecting the left leg.'

The aggrieved note in the patient's expression and tone were perfectly judged. 'I says it was the right to the M.O. back at the unit, sir. Can't say I'm sure how he got it wrong, sir.'

'Oh, well, yes. Er—admit for observation, please.' And against the diagnosis: No diagnosis known.

The conscripts and the volunteer soldiers approved of the new M.O.s. The regulars smiled lugubriously, 'Give 'em a couple of months to forget civvy street and all you'll get then me lads is the old Aspro and iodine.'

'Excuse me, Sgt, but why Aspro and iodine?'

'This way, miss. If you feels bad in the Army, your M.O. he gives you a couple of Aspro: if you're hurt bad, he bungs on iodine. Don't reckon he knows no more but if he do he'll not let on, not if he wants his promotion.'

In those first, deceptively halcyon few months of 1940 most weekday evenings, and specially on Fridays and Saturdays, the green baize notice-board in our Mess was festooned with open invitations to parties in the many Officers, Warrant Officers and Sergeants Messes in and around the camp. The Sergeants gave the best parties. I did not go to many, as a few weeks after our arrival I met Desmond, a cavalry subaltern who also wanted to be a writer and we preferred talking to parties.

Desmond, very tall, thin and nineteen, had joined his county yeomanry as a Territorial. He loathed the Army but loved his cavalry breeches, boots and the high cap still worn by cavalry officers. On the evening when he arrived wearing the

new battledress his gloom was tragic. He owned an old Baby
Austin and as either he, or his batman—I was never sure
which—had a talent for scrounging petrol, often we drove to
Salisbury, Marlborough, and around and over Salisbury
Plain.

I loved the Plain. Double-summer-time had begun, and on
the long, light, evenings a blue haze shimmered over the
empty miles of green-brown turf. The occasional lines of low
trees made dark green fringes against the bluer sky and the
unset sun that had barely touched the horizon when I had to
be back at our Mess for nightly roll-call at 10 p.m., enhanced
the conviction that daylight and youth must last for ever.
Sometimes we regressed to childhood, drove off the road and
over the undulating turf pretending the car was a tank and
ignoring the possibility of mines. We talked of the books and
plays we would write and the books only Desmond had read.
'My God, girl! You mean you've never read Evelyn Waugh?
Christ, you must!' We sang duets, endlessly. Our favourites
were *Begin The Beguine* and *A Nightingale Sang In Berkeley
Square*. 'Come on, Lucille—you be my Anne Zeigler and I'll
be your Webster Booth. On the fourth—da da da da—That
certain night, that night we met, there was magic abroad in
the air . . .'

And magic at Stonehenge one night.

We had both been free at five, driven to Salisbury, gone
round the Cathedral and forgotten the time and the war until
blackout screens went up in the restaurant. 'Desmond! I've
missed roll-call!'

'Christ, so you have! Be on a charge?'

'If I am, I'll be the first VAD in history to be put on one.
Oh, woe. Madam'll flap like mad.'

'Tell her we've had a puncture.'

'No-one'll swallow that obvious line.'

'Any bod who knows anything about my tyres'll swallow it.
Always having punctures. Anyway, it's more likely to be
swallowed because it is so bloody obvious. Bods'll think if it
really was a line you'd think up a much better story.'

'Maybe. Should I ring Madam?'

'Don't be so wet. How could you ring up when stuck out on the Plain with a puncture? But if you're going to be hung, why not for a sheep? Then we can go and look at Stonehenge in moonlight. My batman's mate says there'll be a good moon tonight and he should know. Chap was a fisherman in civvy street.'

'Then why's he a trooper?'

'God only knows. Chap swears blind he joined the navy.'

It was dark when we left the restaurant and in the blackout Salisbury had slid back into the Middle Ages. The refined lines of the Georgian houses, the soaring elegance of the Cathedral spire, were hidden, but the jumbled outlines of the medieval buildings leaning against each other or companionably towards the opposite rows in the narrow streets, were still darkly etched against the low, dark sky. As we left the city Old Sarum loomed above, a massive black shadow fortified by the unseen ghosts of Iron Age men, of Romans, of Normans. We wondered how those alien soldiers had thought and felt when they looked down from the ramparts over the hostile miles of the Plain, and we grew so engrossed we lost our way.

After about an hour of crawling in the thin rays filtering through our black-papered headlights, I unwound my window. 'Your batman's mate's slipped up. Dark as the inside of a cow's stomach.'

'At least it doesn't smell of cheese. Where the hell's that bastard of a moon?'

As if on cue the low sky suddenly lifted and the moon broke through. A three-quarter moon that hung low over the land and to our shout of disbelief illuminated the great stones standing alone and unguarded only a few hundred yards from our road. Desmond eased the car onto a grass verge, switched off the lights and in a near-trance got out to remove the rotor-arm from the engine. He looked around. 'Can't see any chaps around wanting to shoot us. Let's go closer.'

The moonlight grew stronger as we walked over the dark springy turf and with every step the strange stones grew larger, clearer, and beyond the outer ring supporting the great lintels, the paired uprights of the inner horseshoe framed weird shadows on the grass. In silence we slithered into them up the guarding ditch and walked amongst the stones. The silence was so absolute that it seemed almost possible to hear the earth's rotation. Hand-in-hand we wove in and out of the uprights, first the outer then the inner, with the compulsion of children weaving round a maypole. Whatever ancient human tragedies and pagan rites had taken place within those stones, if only for that hour, the unquiet spirits of the past were at rest. A tranquillity as tangible as our handclasps transported the war and all the rest of mankind to another planet. We did not talk until we were in the car and nearly back at the camp.

Desmond switched off lights and engine for the final few yards and coasted to a stop well away from our Mess drive. I crept in through the garden and one of the open french windows of the darkened ballroom. My particular friend Joan was awake. 'Thank God. Thought you'd had an accident. Roll-call was o-kay. I answered for you and said you were in the bath. Good party?', she whispered.

Party was the wrong word but served. 'Glorious. Thanks a lot.'

Someone overheard us and later told Betty. A few evenings later she stormed into the ballroom before going on night-duty. 'You stupid kid! What do you think you're doing letting that wretched boy keep you out half the night? Harmless—don't kid me! Cavalry, isn't he? Everyone knows what the cavalry are like! Have you told Mummy and Daddy about all these dates? Then I'm jolly well telling them as I can't be responsible. . . .'

Her anxiety was misplaced. Being only nineteen—and whether or not he liked it I never knew—Desmond accepted outwardly as automatically as myself the invisible strait-jackets imposed on us when alone together by our engrained moral conventions. These allowed a few chaste kisses and hand-holding, but very little more and nothing below the waist. If this was a strain on the very young, it was also a fairly reassuring social armour when current mores laid on the young no burden of guilt for suffering from inhibitions. When too emotionally immature to know how to handle one's sexual emotions, it was often a great relief to know that all one was expected to do was control them. Desmond would have been furious had he known I described him to my parents as 'a very nice boy'. I was never in love with him, but was very sorry when, a few days after I wrote home about him, he was posted north.

The trees in the avenue shook out new leaves and around the camp the young oaks glowed briefly golden before turning green; the may trees and the elders flowered together and as the serene spring weather slid into a serener early summer, trees and hedges were white with blossom. Cow parsley fringed every ditch and grass verge, red and white candles burnt triumphantly in the chestnuts. In our Mess garden, in the flower beds between the paths and tennis courts, the lilacs were in bloom and the camellia bushes were Victorian bouquets of white waxen flowers. On free evenings from five, or after duty finished at eight, aching feet and backs were forgotten as the weather was perfect for tennis and a 'confined to camp' order had come into force.

The camp's officers were still allowed to use the tennis courts and grounds, and for a short, timeless spell, every evening from about six onwards, the young men strolled up to our Mess singly, or in pairs. They wore uniform jackets over white flannels or white shorts, carried racquets in one hand, trailed tin hats, respirators and loaded revolver cases in the other. All officers had then to be armed at all times, and officially all VADs had always to carry respirators and tin hats. But still, unless our Commandant was present or it was the C.O.'s inspection day in our hospital blocks, most of our respirators and tin hats resided in our bicycle baskets or under our beds.

One of the roads into the camp ran parallel with the two tennis courts outside the ballroom. The outer court was divided from the road by a low, hedgeless green bank, as the iron railings formerly edging the grounds had long gone to make scrap metal. Often in those evenings a Dispatch Rider would roar to a stop in the road, hitch his motor-bike to the edge of the bank and stomp over to interrupt a game either with a message or by removing a player. 'So sorry, partner! I say—Nigel—carry on for me? Fifteen-thirty, two-one, your serve.'

The little groups sitting watching and chatting on the green between the path and first tennis court, or on the steps of the french windows would mutter, 'Jolly bad luck. Just getting his serve in.' From a portable wireless inside the ballroom or on the path, tuned softly not to disturb the players, Vera Lynn singing *Yours*, or the BBC Dance Orchestra playing *Scatterbrain*, *Somewhere In France*, *I Wonder Who's Kissing Her Now*, or the everlasting *South Of The Border*. Gentle tunes that matched the local tennis club mood and fulfilled the urgent need to cling—as small children cling to parents on the first day of school—to the pretence of normality in 'Who's on next?' in white plimsols playing discreet 'footy', in young eyes exchanging discreet 'come hithers'. Behind the pretence the recent memory of the disaster at Narvik, the growing number of British men and ships lost at sea, the strange, disquieting rumours trickling back from the BEF (British Expeditionary Force). Rumours that buzzed round the camp grapevine within hours, if not minutes, of some regular soldier's return from France on an instructor's or other specialized course and dropping in for a chat with the lads in his old unit, or the chaps in his former Mess.

Behind the soft thuds, twangs, 'Good shot, Partner!' on the courts, the distant rattle of carrier convoys, rumbles of tanks, the staccato barking of machine guns, the ugly deep-throated belch of heavy artillery. 'Not to worry—just practising!' On the green sward, men with short back and sides hair-cuts, girls with permanent waves, or rows of tight curls over the forehead, or for those with hair as long as mine, tucked up in ribbons or bootlaces to frame the face with a massive roll. All the faces blank with youth, all the conversations carefully avoiding two subjects; the war and the future. And at our feet, scattered on the green grass, tennis racquets, boxes of spare balls, khaki jackets, tin hats, service respirators, and loaded revolvers in polished leather holsters.

Almost imperceptibly, another sound became a remorseless thread in the background of our lives. The sound of the military band that always escorted regiments moving out to Active Service in France. I dreaded the hearty martial music and thought of Danny Deever. I knew the men being marched out had not come from a hanging, but every time I heard a military band that summer, unsought, unwanted, the final lines of the poem ran through my mind:

> For they're done with Danny Deever, you can 'ear the
> quickstep play,
> The regiment's in column, an' they're marchin' us away;
> Ho! the young recruits are shakin', an' they'll want their
> beer to-day,
> After hangin' Danny Deever in the mornin'.

Chapter Four

THE rumours from France became a sea that from the second week in May 1940 was composed of rogue waves each one too bizarre for credulity.

'My dear, get this gen! Jerry's crossed the Dutch and Belgian frontiers. . . .'

'You've got it, miss, nuns! Thousands! All paratroops togged up as nuns and raining down on them Dutch, but them Dutch pulled their thumbs out their dykes and drowned the lot!'

'Lucilla, this is pukka gen. Jerry's flattened Rotterdam. The Dutch have had to pack it in.'

'From what the lads are saying, miss, that Leopold's turning yellow. . . .'

'Heard the latest, Miss Andrews? Froggie's thinking of asking for his cards.'

'The French want to pack it in? Staff-Sergeant, no! Can't be gen—is it?'

'No telling seeing the wireless and papers don't tell us nothing. No surprise to me if the lads are right. Froggie mutinied in the last do, didn't he?'

'He did? I never knew that. Of course, you were in the last war.'

'That's right. And a right mucky do it were—if you'll pardon my French.'

'And you think the French'll pack up. Staff, if they do, what —what about the BEF?'

'Reckon the Navy'll be busy, like. Very busy, like.'

I thought of the men I knew in France, and the thousands

I did not know but had seen marching away to Danny Deever. Normally, as the official war news in the newspapers and on the wireless seemed days behind camp news, I seldom bothered to listen to the BBC news, or glance at more in the papers than the headlines and Jane in the *Daily Mirror*. (Jane, an engaging, nubile blonde, figured in the enormously popular strip-cartoon that bore her name, daily had difficulty keeping on her clothes and at intervals lost the lot. As the war progressed it was another cherished soldier-patients' legend that on any day Jane appeared starkers the entire British Army advanced on all fronts.) But that evening after talking to the Staff-Sergeant, when I got back to our Mess I collected all the daily papers lying about, read the war reports in detail and noticed the constant repetition of 'strategic withdrawals to previously prepared positions'. Momentarily, I stopped reading, thinking I could hear a distant drum. Later that night, in one of the growing store of threepenny exercise books I kept in the suit-case under my bed, I wrote, 'It wasn't a drum, it was my pulse banging against my ears.'

Some evenings later I was off five to eight but late getting away as the afternoon had been unusually hectic in my block Just after lunch our M.O. had returned unexpectedly, done a second complete medical round with Sister and precipitately either transferred to other blocks or discharged back to barracks two-thirds of our patients. Mrs. S and I had been alone with Sister, and whilst the latter and our M.O. had spent the rest of the afternoon at the dutyroom desk submerged by the sea of forms that had to be filled in, in triplicate, for every man being moved, Mrs. S and I had crossed and re-crossed the square to the Pack Store, returned blues, reclaimed service uniforms, stripped vacated beds, carbolized the bedsteads with carbolic solution, re-made the beds, scrubbed all the empty lockers and swept the whole block twice as once was not enough to remove the blanket fluff. No-one had explained to us or our patients the reason for the exodus. The patients were convinced they were moving to make room for casualties from some unreported big battle in France. Mrs. S told me privately she doubted this. 'For a major inrush of serious casualties they'd empty the acute blocks, not us. Probably just another almighty flap.'

It was after six when I got back to our Mess. The ballroom was deserted and the only four girls off with me were playing doubles on the nearest court. The other court was empty, the net lowered, and no watchers sat on the green sward, or young men strolled up the path. It was another glorious summer evening. The sun was still too high for the dance of the midges in the open french window doorways or the birds' evening chorus, but somewhere near, a blackbird was singing like a nightingale. I kicked off my shoes and too tired to remove limp cap or crumpled apron flopped full length on my bed and fell asleep listening to the blackbird. About twenty minutes or so later, I was woken by repeated shouts from the tennis players. Reluctantly, I yawned my way to one of the french windows. 'What's up? I'm having a kip.'

They had stopped playing and were sitting on the low bank by the road. From the fading rumble a convoy had just gone by and into the camp. 'Come over here! Come and see! Here comes another!'

I smoothed my hair and cap perfunctorily and joined the girls on the bank as the first lorry in the second convoy rattled by. 'Why the flap—' my voice stopped abruptly. I said no more for quite some time.

That convoy of heavy lorries was followed by others, and all were unnaturally identical. Army lorries and Army drivers, but all crammed with airmen. Airmen slumped like old sacks, with grey, unshaven faces, with Army greatcoats, red hospital blankets, multi-coloured crochet shawls, draped over sagging shoulders, with what was visible of their RAF uniform filthy, untidy and torn. As each lorry went by, the men in the back stared at us, dumbly as sacks. Four girls in white Aertex shirts and white tennis shorts, one in a nurse's indoor uniform, but instead of the normal shouts, cat-calls and wolf-whistles from any passing load of young servicemen, only silence. Exhaustion made the airmen's faces look old, but the faces belonged to young men.

The summer dust at last settled back on the road and remained undisturbed. We sat on, waiting, but the road stayed empty. None of us spoke. In the silence I heard the blackbird still singing. Having a mind that thrusts up lines of poetry as easily as it frames newspaper headlines, I found myself mentally quoting a verse from Julian Grenfell's *Into Battle*.

> The blackbird sings to him, 'Brother, brother,
> If this be the last song you shall sing
> Sing well, for you may not sing another;
> Brother, sing.'

That night was very hot even when all french windows were open. The sky was navy blue and starlit, the tennis nets were cobwebs floating across the courts. The clean country night air was scented with warm grass, hay and lilacs, until another in-coming convoy rumbled by and the smell of petrol, exhaust fumes and hot tyres drowned the warm grass, the hay, and the lilacs. In the morning there were no military patients left in N.D.K., every one of the seven wards had doubled its number of beds, and a disgruntled cookhouse orderly, dumping down double rations of porridge and eggs for boiling, told me his lot had had to turn out at midnight to make room for two hundred airmen.

In our wards, sitting or sprawling on every bed, unshaven airmen with wary, tired, eyes and faces painted by fatigue with the pallor of fungi. 'No, nurse, we ain't Scotch Mist. Just a surprise packet for you.'

It was their guns that most shocked me. All weapons were forbidden in military wards, yet every man seemed to have one. The greater majority had rifles, but more than a few, astonishingly, had officers' revolvers. 'How've we kept 'em, nurse? Not patients, see. When you got to pull out you got to let the rest of your kit go, but you holds on to your weapons.'

'You—er—you mean the RAF's pulled out of France?'

A crowd of men had come in from the other wards. Momentarily, the crowd was quiet and the quiet, deafening. Then, 'You've said it, nurse.' Then for the first time the words I heard over and over and at each time as if dragged from the speaker's throat. 'May as well know it, nurse—we've been on the run.' After another pause. 'Six days we had of it. We'd start building a runway in this field, see, but before we'd half the job done, along comes Jerry dropping his load, so we moved back, starts another in another field—and back comes Jerry. Days, nights, we kept at it, and Jerry kept on dropping his loads and wherever we was, Jerry knew and he was there. We got shoved so far back we run out of fields, and seeing as you can't build runways on the sea, here we are. What you got to say to that, eh nurse?'

I did not know what to say to those angry, weary, men, hugging their damaged pride as plainly as they hugged their weapons. Instinctively, as always when emotionally shocked, I took refuge in trivialities. 'That all of you obviously need good breakfasts and to get off those beards and have baths—if we can swing it with the block Sister upstairs as we haven't baths down here, but I expect you've discovered that. By the way, I suppose none of you are any good at lighting fires with green twigs—that wretch in the duty-room's just died and we haven't any other firelighters.'

In one of the most extraordinary moments of my life, the crowd gaped at me. Suddenly the whole atmosphere altered. Within minutes the fire-lighting party was at work in the duty-room, whilst other self-organized parties dealt with washing and bath queues, beds, sweeping, bumpering, lockers and brasses. N.D.K. rang with, 'Give us that bit of shammy you scrounged off that dead Jerry, Bert . . . Spit on it, mate! Only way to get a proper shine . . . So it's a cut-throat not a safety! All right? Not asking you to cut your throat with it, am I? . . . Now you listen to me, mate, you can have it soft-boiled hard or hard-boiled hard—can I say fairer?'

Two hours later the block was spruce enough for a C.O.'s inspection, one hundred and forty men loaded the nursing staff with souvenirs in the form of cap badges, buttons, bits of shrapnel and empty cartridge cases, and paraded in the square, shaven, clean and tidy airmen.

An army N.C.O. on crutches winked without humour as we watched the airmen march away. 'Trust the Brylcreem Boys to save their skins first. You know why they've been shifted smartish, don't you?'

'To make room for the Army?'

'From what I hear more like to stop our lads having a go at 'em.'

I heard much the same in the days that followed from the first of the returned, and mostly walking-wounded, soldiers. 'You say you had the RAF here, nurse? You mean we GOT a RAF? Get away! Oy! Bill, Tom, Shorty, Jock—you hear what the nurse says? We GOT a RAF!'

'You're having us on, nurse! You got to be having us on! Aren't the RAF the lads as meant to fly planes? No kidding, nurse, only planes we've seen are Jerry's—and he's got enough of 'em, he has. Them Stukas—wheeeeeeeeeee—' the scream of a dive-bombing Stuka was endlessly mimicked and invariably followed by 'rat-tat-tat-tat-tat—you should've seen the b-basket, nurse! You'd not credit how he'd spray them refugees. All along the roads they were, see—every road—miles and miles of 'em—old women, mums with nippers in prams, kids on bikes—and Jerry, he'd come down low on the lot and you couldn't get along the road in battle order (single file) for the arms and legs and heads all over the shop.'

In the last few days of May and first few of June the river of returning soldiers burst both banks, swamped hospital and camp. Impossible to remember names and numbers within seconds of copying them from sweat, sea-stained and often blood-stained identity tags strung on dirty cords, tapes, or metal chains round sleep-sagged necks. Tags that in another time in those same beds had been happily exhibited by untried civilian soldiers. 'This 'un don't burn and this 'un don't sink. Army's making sure it'll not lose me, eh, miss?'

Now: 'Sorry to wake you, soldier. What's your unit?'

'Huh?'

'Your unit. What unit were you with, soldier?'

The answers, a roll-call of the British Army. Guardsmen, privates, troopers, gunners, sappers, drivers, medical orderlies: names of great regiments that echoed Corunna, Lucknow, Waterloo, Balaclava: names of county regiments that covered the map of Britain. Englishmen, Scotsmen, Welshmen, Irishmen, and all oblivious in sleep to the oil and grime on their bodies and the relatively minor wounds that brought them into our block. Until the dirt and beards were scraped off, all the sleeping faces looked the same: all on waking briefly asked the same, 'Froggie got his cards yet, nurse?'

'Haven't heard. Have a little of this soup before you go back to sleep. I'll hold the mug and your head. Sip it, soldier—swallow it, soldier—sip, swallow—fine. . . .'

Men too tired to remember to swallow a mouthful of soup or keep their eyes open, but not to mumble, 'Thanks, nurse . . . ta, duck . . . that's great, hen . . . grand, luv . . . I say thanks awfully.'

Off-duty rotas forgotten or ignored when remembered. Day after day of washing from the bodies of exhausted men the sand of Dunkirk, the grime of St Malo, of Brest, of Cherbourg, the oil of wrecked ships, the salt from the Channel. Often the hot water in my washing bowl needed three changes before the ether soap dislodged the oil glued into pores. When the soap exposed the flesh wounds hidden beneath the filth, beads of black oil bubbled on the mens' upper lips and foreheads. Not infrequently after lathering with the soap, the colours of the men's hairs altered dramatically. Dark brown turned flaxen, or sandy, or the ubiquitous pale English brown. The hair of one very tall young Scottish Highlander under my hands changed from black to bright red. He told me his unit had spent some days on the beaches at Dunkirk, but could not remember the exact number as one day was so like another. 'It was the noise that was being the worst.'

'Under air attack all that time?'

'It was seeming so. But some of the noise was coming from the exploding mines.'

In a first-aid post on the beach the wound made by the bullet that had gone through his left leg and grazed his hip had been dressed. That was his only reported wound. After I bathed him I found twenty-three shrapnel splinters embedded fairly superficially in his flesh. We counted them together as I removed them with forceps. The deepest and largest was in his right thigh. It looked small until I began to take it out. It measured just under five inches and at its widest, half an inch.

When all were out, I nearly had to use force to get him to swallow an ounce of stock brandy. 'It is you that should be having this, nurse, not me.'

In the few scribbled notes I made that night, I added, 'I didn't dare tell him I had thrown up in the scullery before getting his brandy from Sister, or he would have poured it down me. God, he needed it. When I tugged out that big one he hung on to the bedhead so hard his knuckles were white, but he didn't make a sound till I got it out and then he said, "I am thanking you very much, nurse." '

We had a few French soldier-patients. When possible they were put in neighbouring beds; they were as exhausted and be-grimed as the British, and as they began to recover mainly talked in French amongst themselves. As only one or two spoke much English, nursing them enlarged my limited French vocabulary, and particularly with, 'Les avions allemands . . . les bombardements . . . les dive-bombers—zut alors! Aieeeeeeeeeeeee!'

Once our own men had slept off the exhaustion and long before they had energy for reading or listening more than absently to the wireless intercom now installed throughout the block, they talked. They talked in a variety of voices and accents of a variety of experiences of the massive retreat into the sea. Some of the voices were angry, some peevish, some incredulous, some almost amused, some expressionless, some deeply hurt. Not once did I hear, or expect to hear, one British soldier sound, or even hint, that he felt defeated.

For nights I was too tired to add even a couple of words to my notes, but on one night in the third week of June, fatigue was secondary to my need for the safety-valve.

I wrote: 'This morning was horrible. M (another VAD) and I had to walk as both our bikes had two flats, but it was lovely and sunny and the walk rather fun. M was in terrific form as her fiancé rang last night from somewhere in Scotland saying the Navy had just landed him in one piece. We got to the hospital by twenty past (seven) and there was a queue of ambulances waiting outside the arch. When we got through the arch we just stood still. The square was covered in stretchers, rows and rows of stretchers, loaded with men lying so still that at first we thought they were all dead. They were all covered with grey blankets and their faces were dreadful— far worse than those other men's faces. These men's were greying-black and sort of slimy, but caked. Then we noticed some of the men had their eyes open and could move their lips, so we knew they weren't dead but they didn't look living. We stopped a stretcher-bearer to ask where the men had come from. Sweat was dripping off his face and he mopped it with his stained gown before he answered. He said, 'Navy just fished this lot out the Channel. All wounded and the hospital ship they was on bought it. This lot was in luck as their stretchers was stacked on the decks. Rest of the lads gone down with her. Thousands, they say.' He didn't know the ship's name but thought it began with an L and was something like *Lucasta*. He said, 'Gawd knows where we'll put this lot. Be shoving the lads up on the roof next.'

'To get to our blocks M and I had to step over some of the stretchers. Everytime we saw a man with his eyes open we sort of smiled and said "good morning" and it sounded ghastly as it wasn't good, it was like walking through hell and I hated the sun for shining and hurting their eyes as, being nearer, I could see all the open eyes were hideously bloodshot. None of them spoke to us, but several gave us queer grimaces. I thought they were in pain and then realized they were trying to smile and the oil and salt burns on their faces made their smiles grimaces. But most didn't try to smile and just stared at us with eyes that looked dead.'

There had been no mention on the BBC news or in the newspapers of the sinking of a hospital ship, either that day or in the following days. Owing, apparently, to some governmental desire to spare the country more bad news, the event was only announced some weeks later. On 17th June 1940, the hospital ship *Lancastria* was torpedoed off St Nazaire. She was heavily laden with wounded from France. Two thousand five hundred lives were lost when she went down.

I was handing round mugs of cocoa to the patients in N.D.K. when the news of the French capitulation came over the ward wireless, first in English, then in French. A British N.C.O. murmured 'Let's hope as our lads still left behind can swim, nurse.'

Two of the three Frenchmen in that ward lay back and stared at the ceiling. The third, in a corner bed, began sobbing. To a man, the British patients buried themselves in *Razzle*, *Blighty*, the *Daily Mirror* and one young L/Cpl in *Far From The Madding Crowd*. I had never seen a man sob before and was appalled for him, the other men and myself. I did not know what to do, but only that I must do something. I put two screens round his bed and awkwardly patted his shaking shoulder. As he ignored me, I guessed he wanted to be alone, and I removed myself and his cooling cocoa. After a space I took him a fresh mug. He was drying his face with a red bandana. 'Merci, mademoiselle. Merci bien.'

Our French patients were given the choice of repatriation, or staying in Britain. All ours chose to return to France. Once this was block knowledge, for the only time in my nursing career, the inter-patients atmosphere turned icily electric until the time of transfer. Then hands were shaken, thumbs jerked up, cries of 'Bonne chance, Tommee!' and 'Good luck, mate!' exchanged, and more cap badges, buttons, and the revolting bits of shrapnel so inexplicably—to me—treasured by fighting men, were heaped on the nursing staff.

One middle-aged French artilleryman who spoke English found me washing-up mugs alone in the tiny scullery. He closed and leant against the door. 'I wished to speak with you,' he said slowly. 'I wished before returning to my country to say goodbye to the young English Miss who when I was very tired, washed and fed me as a baby with much gentleness. This I will not forget when I return to my country. This also I will not forget—that I return without honour and without hope. Possibly, with the help of the Good God, you English [*sic*] will win this war. But certainly it will be impossible for you to win without. But if you win—in France we will be happy—but also, I think we must be ashamed. If you do not win—', he shrugged, 'then you do not win.' He was silent for some seconds. 'I must tell you of my family. In France I have my wife, my two little children. One boy, one girl. My wife she is many years younger than I, myself—she is a very good wife, good mother. Now, my wife, my children, live under the Boche. If we had not surrendered to the Boche, it is possible that one day, I myself, would fire the gun to kill my wife, my children. To win a war one must forget humanity, one must think only of the victory. But I am not of such a nature. Always I must remember my family. You understand ?'

'I think so.'

'No.' He shook his bullet-shaped head. The very short brown hair was grey at the roots. 'I do not think so. You are too young to have a family. You cannot understand. You wonder, I think, what of La Patrie ? This also I tell you. I love my country—La France—La Belle France—yes—but as I would love a weak but amiable member of my family. I have no wish to die for this weak but amiable member. Possibly, life under the Boche will not be pleasant—but fighting the Boche was not pleasant. I am a baker. Men must eat bread— even the Boche. In France I return to be a baker. To remain always in England always I must be a Bombardier of the conquered French Army. I have some spirit, Miss. I prefer the contempt of an enemy I despise to the contempt of a friend I admire.'

Outside the scullery window one of the two engines used by the Ordnance Depot—the one called *Molly*—shunted to and fro twice whilst he was speaking. *Molly* shunted back again as we shook hands. 'Au revoir et bonne chance, M. . . .'

He shook his bullet head again. 'Pas au'voir, Mdlle. Je me suis fâché mais je suis bien sûr, c'est adieu.' He had served in the Maginot Line and gave me his brooch.

That night I wrote all he had said in an exercise book, then copied in the words engraved on his brooch. Words once the slogan of Maginot Line Units: Ils ne passeront pas. And I added, 'Not bloody likely.'

Once France fell, daily we expected the German invasion of Britain; on and off duty, the atmosphere changed again. Every British voice I heard said much the same: 'Much better now we're on our own. Now we know where we are. So Jerry's coming over to have a bash, eh? Right! Let the bastard try it on!'

At that time, that general attitude seemed neither arrogant nor illogical in a Britain that had just faced a massive military defeat and left most of her heavy war equipment behind in France. When discussing the situation—and it was endlessly discussed—with patients, colleagues, friends, acquaintances, strangers, always we all agreed that it was only common sense to prefer to be shot of allies who had been knocked out one by one and were more trouble than they were worth. Not that anyone to whom I spoke, or myself, by then underestimated the mighty German war-machine. 'So old Hitler missed the bus, eh, nurse? Gawd! Old Whatshisname with his umbrella should've pulled the other one! It's got the bells! Mind you, nurse, you got to hand it to Jerry—knows how to fight Jerry does, and he don't mind taking his chances.' A wounded R.A.M.C. stretcher-bearer locked his hands behind his head and smiled reluctantly. 'That's how I copped this packet in me leg. Our M.O.'d bought it, see, and we'd been told to shift the lads back to the next post as we got an ambulance and there was still the three of us on the job. We'd shifted all the lads' stretchers into the ambulance and was just shutting the doors to scarpa fast, when two lads in Froggie uniform with a stretcher between 'em comes running over the field towards us. They hollers so we waits. When they gets in range they dumps down the stretcher and the Jerry under the blanket lets us have it with a tommy (Gun). But what he doesn't know is that me mate's got another tommy—which he didn't ought to seeing as the three of us is Non-Coms. So me mate he finishes off the Jerry and his mates.'

'Were they Frogs or Jerries?'

'Not knowing can't say. Me mate hauls me in and the lad at the wheel didn't hang about asking no questions. Reckon they was Jerries. Knows all the tricks, Jerry does, like I says, he knows how to fight.'

None of us wasted energy wondering how we would win the war. Simply, we knew we had to win and so believed we would. And if that belief was unreasoned—as it was—since it was shared by the overwhelming majority of the British then in Britain, it resulted in one of the most glorious triumphs of the human spirit over disaster in recorded history. It was also unconquerable.

On another blue unclouded day when our three hours off daily had been re-instated, Joan and I rode straight from duty to the shops as we had heard that a new stock of black artificial silk stockings had arrived. We were in indoor uniform with our navy serge scarlet-lined cloaks floating from our shoulders and cap-tails flying on downhill runs as neither of our bicycles had functioning brakes. Turning one downhill corner we had to run off the road, up a bank and leap off in motion to avoid running down an army.

For a few seconds, despite the vociferous cheers, I thought I was seeing a mirage. Ambling rather than marching by were contingent after contingent of soldiers carrying full packs, casually toting rifles, and wearing broad-brimmed khaki hats upturned at one side that stirred the forgotten memory of some old first-war movie.

'Are you Australians?'

A roar came back, 'Too right, Sister! The Aussies are here! War'll be over soon! Good to see ye, gals!'

They were part of the Australian Imperial Force that had reached England too late for service in France. 'France, Sister? Bloody fair cow.'

For a short while before returning overseas the AIF was encamped on sites at opposite ends of our camp's perimeter. One of these sites was in parkland roughly half-a-mile from our Mess. The AIF patients said thirty thousand men were camped at the bottom of our garden. Never, to my knowledge, was our Mess guarded by more than our Commandant, her deputy and the Home VAD. Every night after roll-call, generally our Commandant did a solitary round of our grounds by torchlight. I think the front porch door was locked at night, but neither our seniors, K.R.R.s, the daily threats of invasion, nor nightly anticipated arrival of German paratroopers disguised as nuns, succeeded in keeping shut all night the french windows whilst I was in the ballroom. But I never heard of any AIF or British soldier, drunk or sober, at any hour trying to trespass in our Mess, or attempting an assault on a VAD in or around the camp during the seven months of my posting there. Singly, in pairs, or small groups, we walked and bicycled amongst men by the thousand, and not improbably hundred thousand, in absolute safety. Our uniforms were an inviolate armour for reasons that went far deeper than military discipline and current conventions.

In the event I took this safety for granted and only much later realized how much of it we owed to the legacy of affection and respect we had inherited from the VADs in the First World War. A legacy that lingered on in barrack rooms, and went back beyond the First World War to the women who nursed our Army in the Boer War and had themselves inherited it from its original source, the woman who, single-handed, revolutionized military and civilian nursing throughout the world, Florence Nightingale. The sick and injured British soldiers in the gangrene, diarrhoea and lice-infested wards of Scutari Hospital in the Crimea may not have realized that Miss Nightingale, by her own efforts, reduced their death rate from forty to two per cent, but they appreciated her care, practical kindness and ruthless integrity. The soldiers remembered from old soldiers' tales, the British Army remembered, and so in 1940, young nurses in their midst needed no guards. We were 'their' nurses; they were 'our' soldiers.

Within days of the AIF's arrival N.D.K. resounded with Australian voices. I wrote home: 'I'll bet before Agincourt, Crécy, Hastings, Waterloo, instead of rubbing up their long bows and muskets, the troops were flocking on sick parade with that splinter you can't see but's festering cruel, that scratch that's turned real nasty, them horrible headaches that come on, so help me, like a clap of thunder, and that real queer feeling what you can't put your finger on but leaves you all of a tremble.'

The AIF felt not 'queer' but 'crook'. And instead of the spasmodic case of German Measles which some British soldier still produced in our wards, the AIF produced mumps. This was an aftermath of the mumps that had appeared during their voyage from Australia in the *Queen Mary*, which had been converted to a troop-carrier. 'Oh my word, Sister, hit the bloody Mary like a bloody bushfire. Ain't that Gawd's truth, cobber?'

'Too right, cobber!'

One of their own M.O.s, a slight, youngish man with a clipped voice and amused eyes, had qualified in London. 'Bilingual yet, N. Andrews?'

'Fairly, thank you, Major.'

'I'll give you a few translation tips: "bloody" is the Australian soldier's term of endearment, "Sister" applies to any uniformed nurse, "cobber" is a mate, "a bloke" is a man, and a "dinkum Aussie" is a man who washes his fice in a bison. Have they taught you how to play two-up?'

'Yes, Major.' In view of his rank I did not add that this form of gambling on two coins flicked up simultaneously only stopped at the approach of medical or our QA's rounds, since all gambling was strictly forbidden in military wards. I had the impression he knew this better than myself.

'Have they offered to sell you Sydney Bridge and walking-stick farms?'

'Constantly. Bonzer deals, I gather.'

He smiled quietly and the conversation there ended as our block Sister returned from lunch and, as he was an experienced M.O., in her presence he behaved as if VADs were invisible. In that, and similar circumstances, experienced VADs behaved as if M.O.s were invisible.

I never knew, but suspected, that it was on his private advice to Sister that a new, temporary rule obtained for all our AIF bed-patients.

'Miss Andrews, those P.U.O.s must stay in bed!' (P.U.O.—Pyrexia of Unknown Origin—was, with N.Y.D.—Not Yet Diagnosed—a variation on N.D.K.) Sister handed me a list of names. 'Collect from these men, bring them to me and I'll lock them away.'

In the ward: 'You can't do this to a bloke, Sister! You can't pinch me bloody pants!'

'Sorry, but the block Sister says I must. And she says please when you go out to ablutions will you wear your greatcoats as if you will wander about in pyjamas, you'll have to hand in your pyjama trousers.'

'You wouldn't pinch a bloke's pyjama pants, Sister! Not a bonzer gal like you!'

'Sorry, but if I must—too right, I would, cobber!'

A chorus from the ward, 'Good on ye, Sister! Dinkum Aussie!'

Snaps by the score. Snaps of the wife, the kids, mum, dad, the kid sister, the kid brother, the girl back home. Not sheilas then, nor, in my hearing, poms or pommy bastards. Snaps of neat little bungalows, of untidy bungalows, of shacks with corrugated-iron roofs and round water drums propping up what looked like peeling cardboard walls, of solid English houses that could have been in St Leonards, Tunbridge Wells, or Wimbledon. And so many of the names of the bungalows, shacks and houses were more immediately identifiable to me than to the men unstacking the much-fingered contents of wallets. 'Crammond', 'Truro', 'Iden', 'Luckhurst', 'Gower', 'Jedburgh', 'Durham'.

All the AIF I nursed were the Australian-born sons of first and second generation British emigrants on their first visit to an England they uniformly called Home or the Old Country. They were as uniformly cheerful patients and convinced, for a reason known only to themselves, that no English girl would accept a date unless she had first a proposal of marriage. At the end of their first week, the three other VADs on day-duty and myself compared notes and found between us we had collected twenty-six marriage proposals. We agreed this made a change from the usual opening gambit of a box of Naafi chocolates and was much better for the figure.

When discharged back to camp our AIF patients gave us their hat and shoulder badges, uniform buttons, picture postcards of Sydney, Melbourne, Canberra, Perth, Brisbane, or spare snaps of little towns with British or Aboriginal names. They said anytime we stopped over we must be sure to look them up and meet the folks. They did not give us bits of shrapnel or empty cartridge cases as they had yet to collect either from enemy guns or talk of the war as anything but a bonzer spree. I liked meeting them and the very little nursing I did for them, but always in their presence was conscious of a new anxiety niggling at the back of my mind. It was an anxiety later to haunt me whenever nursing servicemen, but with the AIF I experienced it for the first time. I kept wondering if this was how their fathers had talked and laughed before the Dardanelles and if as many of the sons, as the fathers, would die before reaching home again. I had not yet seen death, but I had heard from Betty and other VADs working in the acute blocks, of the wounded men who had died since the retreat. I knew, as we all knew, of the many more men who had been killed in that retreat. Slowly I had come to realize war was a killing business and that those most likely to be killed in war were the young men in uniform. Looking around at the amiable and so often long-jawed AIF faces that even on the slightly older men looked to my considerably younger eyes, touchingly youthful, it was only too easy for my imagination to cloak them with the fatigue, grime and oil of just a week or so back. But the great majority of the men I had washed clean had been our own men, fighting, as they and I knew now, if not before, for the life of our own country. The AIF were so far from home and, as I had just discovered, in a strange country. I found their generosity in coming so far to help that strange country as disturbing as the thought of the possible, and still apparently totally unexpected, cost to themselves.

The banshee rising and falling wails of the air-raid Alert sirens had become daily events, mainly, said rumour, because the G.O.C. took a sadistic joy in precipitating us all into another P.A.D. drill. The only enemy aircraft yet to appear in our sky had been either reconnaissance planes, or some off-course bomber flying too high for our ack-ack guns. 'Jerry', said the patients, 'wasn't nobody's fool and wouldn't stick his neck out bashing a military target what'd hand it back to him, when he could have it nice and easy blitzing civvies.' Sometimes our otherwise uneventful Alerts were enlivened by short, violent bursts of ack-ack fire. 'Ah well,' said the patients,

'Gunners got to earn their pay.'

A gunner Cpl and former schoolmaster suffering from Vincent's Angina, and with cotton wool surrounding the kaolin poultice round his neck framing his long pale English face with an Elizabethan ruff, languidly raised himself on his pillows. 'The Gentlemen of the Artillery', he croaked, 'never fail to earn the pittance awarded them by an ungrateful nation.'

'You know why Lofty's got that poorly throat, don't you, nurse ?', said the other patients. 'Swallowed a dictionary, he has.'

One morning early in August my half-day in bed was disturbed at noon by the banshee wails. A few other girls were off with me, still in their beds, and as we knew our Commandant was out, when the Home VAD rushed into the ballroom blowing a whistle, we chorused 'Sure we'll shutter the french windows on the double!' and as she rushed out settled back in our beds leaving the windows open and our tin hats and respirators under our beds. The sound of distant aircraft and bursts of ack-ack fire followed the expected pattern. After a longish silence there was a sudden explosion from the ack-acks, then another silence. One very pretty Irish girl, a newly joined VAD cook, sauntered in her nightie to one of the french windows, and gazed upwards. 'Will you tell me something girls ? What does a plane with a big black cross on it mean, as there's one without an engine trying to land in the garden.'

I never knew whose rugger tackle floored her. The heap of girls in nighties and pyjamas leapt up and watched in mesmerized horror the crippled German bomber hit and explode in an empty field across the road. Momentarily blinded by the sheet of white flame, when I next looked the flame was red, the smoke black. Someone muttered, 'Hope to God the poor bods were dead before they roasted.' I managed to hold my vomit until in the nearest lavatory and was still retching when the single-noted All Clear siren sounded. When I got back to the ballroom the Irish girl was drifting around demanding in a daze, 'Will someone just tell me how our ack-ack missed that Jerry ? Will someone just tell me, please ?'

A few days later, in early afternoon, again as most days, the banshee wailed. I was stacking tea-mugs on a large wooden trolley and groaned with the patients, 'Why does the G.O.C. always pick on mealtimes?'

In the hospital from Alert to All Clear, all patients and staff had to wear tin hats and their respirators at the alert—i.e., strapped to the chest. In every block, Sisters, VADs and RAMC medical orderlies—where these existed—had their appointed P.A.D. jobs practised, it had seemed, ad nauseam in the many earlier drills and recent false alarms. That afternoon, our block was ready in about three minutes. Tin hats and respirators were on, blackout screens were up in all the windows as a protection against flying glass, all the outer doors were shut, electric lights on, all the beds pulled away from the walls and arranged in two rows down the ward centres, and dumped at the foot of the bed-patients' beds were the turned back spare mattresses waiting to be heaved over the patients' bodies should the hospital be the target of, or directly involved in, a direct air attack. If this happened, the up-patients had to lie on the floor under their beds, since bed-springs and mattresses provided useful extra protection.

During Alerts in our block Sister allotted two wards to the senior VAD and herself, respectively, and gave the rest of us responsibility for individual wards. We still had no orderlies on the permanent block staff. In that and every hospital in which I worked during the war, throughout air-raids the nursing staff on duty remained with their appointed patients. And in any hospital that possessed air raid shelters, it was always the most junior nurses who were sent to the shelters with those patients who could be moved and the seniors who remained in the wards, almost invariably, by the bedsides of their illest patients.

My only bed-patients then were four with Vincent's Angina and one P.U.O. with a dramatically swinging temperature that made his chart the pride of the ward and despair of our latest, newly recruited M.O. The P.U.O.'s face ran sweat under the tin hat tilted over his nose. 'Why don't they fetch the G.O.C. his char and wad so we can have ours?'

Before anyone could answer, the air was split with the whine of diving aircraft. The supine bed-patients, galvanized into life, heaved the spare mattresses over themselves before I could reach one, and as I crouched between the beds of the gunner Cpl and P.U.O., my two illest men, the up-patients flattened themselves under their beds like falling playing cards. In those and the following seconds it sounded as if every gun in the great camp had opened up, simultaneously. The sustained cacophony did more than deafen, it hurt the teeth, the ears, the facial sinuses, it made the bones ache, the bedsteads vibrate under my gripping hands and drinking glasses and tin ashtrays fall soundlessly off lockers, droplets in an ocean of noise. Yet because they were our own guns, and perhaps because heard for the first time at full roar, I found their thunderous voices extraordinarily exhilarating.

When the uproar subsided to staccato barks and hearing returned to normal, we could hear growling aircraft and explosions, some little way off. Then the guns fell silent. A second or so later the silence was splintered by the higher-pitched whines of wheeling fighter planes. One up-patient crawled to peer through a chink in a blackout screen. 'One Jerry's got two Spits on his tail! Get at him, mates!' He shouted with triumph. 'They got him!'

The bed-patients shoved off their spare mattresses, the up-patients bobbed up, all grinning euphorically. By the All Clear, our entire block was jubilant. 'Jerry got a taste of his own medicine, didn't he, nurse? Knows what to expect, don't he, when he starts his invasion. And he's welcome to try it on. Any time!'

The euphoria lasted roughly fifteen minutes. Then the ambulances began to arrive and the telephone to ring. 'A' block (acute surgical-cum-theatre) needed all available junior Sisters and VADs. Our Sister being in sole charge could not leave her block, and sent another VAD and myself. 'Take your cloaks and spare clean aprons as I don't know how long you'll be needed in "A".' The other VAD returned to N.D.K. some days later. I never worked there again.

'A' being acute was on the upper floor and had at one end

the operating theatre, anaesthetic room and proper Sister's duty-room, and at the other, five wards equipped as hospital wards and not, as N.D.K., barely converted barrack rooms. The block was the busiest and heaviest in the hospital and for both reasons the most popular amongst the VADs since the patients needed what was known to nurses, amateur and professional, as 'real nursing'.

In normal circumstances, all the patients were 'acute surgicals' and in those medical times only rarely was a patient allowed out of bed after an abdominal operation until the stitches or clips were out. Usually the acute appendices staggered to their unsteady feet on the tenth day after operation; haemorrhoids around the fourteenth; and hernias more often had twenty-one days in bed. The innumerable Dispatch and other motor-bike riders injured in crashes, if sufficiently injured to rate admission to the block, could be warded as bed-patients for weeks. Generally once an acute surgical patient was fit to be up for a few hours daily, he was transferred to the semi-convalescent surgical hut recently added to the ground floor. Post-operative physiotherapy, as the sulfa drugs, were very recent innovations.

Having never been in 'A' before I could not judge how it looked normally. That afternoon the block so closely resembled a scene of a front-line casualty clearing station in an old war movie, that my immediate reaction was disbelief. Reality began to penetrate owing to the scene not being in black and white but in colour, with the two predominating colours varying shades of red and grey.

Scarlet on the pinned-back shoulder capes of the QA Regulars, scarlet edging the grey capes of the QA Reservists; all the Sisters with grey dresses beneath white aprons, white masks on their faces and their sleeves up. It was the first time I had seen the elbows of so many army Sisters exposed, or the Sisters themselves moving at the astonishing speed that takes years of training to acquire and once acquired is never wholly forgotten. Scarlet and crimson splashing the long white overalls of the medical orderlies and the pale khaki shirts of the jacket-less M.O.s, also all masked and with sleeves rolled up and working as physicians, surgeons, anaesthetists, and stretcher-bearers. Scarlet and crimson seeping through the grey blankets covering the huddled bundles on the incoming stretchers being unloaded from the one lift with the monotony of some nightmare factory-belt. Scarlet blankets over the bed-patients being carried out to provide ward beds for the incomers, by pairs of amateur stretcher-bearers. Each pair, a regimental chaplain and a VAD as the orderlies were all needed by the newly wounded. I had never seen so many padres and had no chance or time to ask how they came to be there. I later heard that when news of the number of air-raid casualties had flashed round the camp, chaplains of every denomination had rushed to the hospital to offer help.

I found myself paired with a stout, youngish, padre, whose name and denomination I never learnt. He was in shirt-sleeves and insisted on taking the heavier head of each stretcher and repeating his terrible little jokes. 'This'll shift my spare tyre, eh, lad? . . . How's the weather up your end, nurse? . . . If you feel sea-sick, lad, remember the wind's blowing my way! . . . And who's the next lucky lad for the joy-ride?'

The patients obligingly grinned, winked, jerked-up thumbs. 'Bring on the dancing girls, eh, nurse?'

Having neither breath for speech nor free hands, I winked back. It was my first and only experience as a stretcher-bearer for men. The weight and unwieldiness of those stretchers left me with a lifelong respect for all ambulance teams in peace and war. I never knew how the padre and I safely delivered six bed-patients from one of the upstairs wards to the convalescent hut. We had to use the balcony and outer iron staircase to leave the lift for the incomers. Every time we tilted a stretcher down the iron stairs I expected the sweating little padre to collapse under the extra weight, and stretcher, patient and myself to collapse on top of him.

On one of our breathless return gallops up with the empty stretcher, I asked if he knew where the casualties were from and how many involved. Briefly, the jocular mask fell off. 'I heard the lads at the RASC Driving School got it just as they were bringing their training lorries back for tea. Not sure how many. Too many. Bad show. Very bad show. . . . So here we are! And who's the next lucky lad for the joy ride?'

'Can you find another partner, padre? I need this girl.' A Sister drew me aside. 'Find the linen cupboard. Bring to me in this ward any remaining blankets, any colour, fast.'

My hands were so shaking from the weight of the stretchers that in the linen cupboard I dropped all my armload of blankets on the floor. After I delivered them: 'I must have hot water bottles. Bring me all you can find. Fill them in pairs.'

After the first dozen I stopped counting hot water bottles, and lost count of the still incoming casualties. There was no time for properly re-making the emptied beds. Once the old bedclothes were stripped off, the long red mackintosh sheet was replaced on the mattress, covered with a grey, tucked in, blanket, onto which was lifted the crumpled figure under the sodden grey stretcher blankets. When there were no more beds, the stretchers were laid on the floor, one beside each bed, so that stretcher and bed-patient could share one of the tall, white metal and mobile, transfusion-cum-infusion stands. (The stand attached to, or incorporated in, the bedhead was still in the future.) To my untrained eyes the speed at which the injured were connected to the crimson vacolitres of whole blood and yellow bottles of plasma hanging from the stands was incredible rather than impressive. It took training to appreciate the difficulty of getting a transfusion needle into a shock-collapsed vein and then keeping, particularly the blood, flowing into the vein at the correct—and vitally important—un-interrupted rate.

Another Sister stopped me. 'Where are you taking those hotties?'

'That Sister over there told me to put them under the feet of the first two men on the left in the next ward, Sister.'

'Do it, then come back to me. And be careful not to put the bottles close enough to touch feet or legs. The shocked are easily burnt.'

In the next ward, again the stretchers and beds were paired. I crouched first by the stretcher-patient. He had dried blood on his face, but no visible injuries and his eyes were open. He stared at me, but not as if he saw me and fearfully I wondered if he has been blinded, as I was too inexperienced to recognize acute clinical shock.

A padre kneeling by the bed-patient glanced up and slightly shook his head as I put the second bottle in place. Again I failed to recognize a patient's condition. 'Take it to a man it can still help, nurse,' said the padre quietly as he covered the patient's face with the top blanket. Then he sat back on his heels and wrote something in a little notebook. Someone, I never knew who, switched the hot bottle from my hands and said, 'Padre, the soldier three down right is asking for you.'

Up to that moment I had not grasped I was in the presence of death and the dying. I stood and stared in horror at the figure covered by the blanket. Then the Sister who had told me to return to her, re-appeared. 'I want you next door.' She swept me to the ward entrance. 'You see that man with a bandaged head in the far corner bed up right? I want you to find a chair, quickly, put it by him, then sit down and hold his hand. If anyone tells you to do anything else, say I have told you to stay with him.' She gave me her name. She was a very senior QA Regular. 'He's not in pain now, and whilst he can still talk, if he wants to, let him. All you've got to do is sit by him, hold his hand, and stay there until I tell you to go. Understand?'

She was slightly taller than myself and had a centre parting and neat grey wings of hair just visible beneath the turn-up of her huge, triangular army cap and very dark lined eyes above her white mask. 'Yes, Sister,' I lied automatically, and a memory of a forgotten Red Cross lecture on acute surgical nursing pushed its way up. 'Sister, should I put on a mask?'

She looked at my face and shook her head. And she said something I remembered to the end of my nursing career. 'When patients aren't used to hospitals and are a little frightened, a mask can frighten them still more. Go to him now.'

The soldier's head and the right half of his face were not, as I had thought, bandaged, but covered with thick white sterile towels held in place with broad strips of gauze bandage tied in three large bows. The bows seemed to me indecently frivolous as I did not understand that the bigger the bow, the easier and the less disturbing for the patient it was to untie. The one visible eye was badly bloodshot and the exposed surrounding skin purple with the contused blood beneath the surface. From the smoothness of the jaw the soldier was not a man but a boy about my own age.

He blinked dreamily with his one eye. 'Hallo, nurse.'

'Hallo, soldier.' I tried to force a smile and hoped it did not look the grimace it felt. I was hollow with fear that re-doubled when I touched his icy and oddly stiff hand. Only because I knew that senior Sister was watching, was I able to hold it. I felt I should explain my presence and, not knowing how, told him the truth. 'Sister says I can sit and natter with you.'

'I say—jolly decent of her.'

'What's your name?'

He began mechanically repeating his surname and number. I stopped him, 'I meant your Christian name?'

Suddenly shyly he told me and asked mine as if we were meeting at a party. I did not answer immediately. From my Red Cross lectures and Training Manual I had learnt that never, in any circumstances, should a nurse reveal her Christian name to a patient. Neither lectures nor Manual had taught me what to say now. 'Awful mouthful. Lucilla. Awful bind at school.'

The exposed half of his face twisted. It was a smile. 'Get called Lulu?'

'Yep. And Lucy, Lu and Lucilita. I sometimes get called that at home as it means "little Lucilla" in Spanish. My mother's called Lucilla. She's Spanish. She'd call you Juanito.'

His face twisted again. 'Rather fun. My sister's got a long name—rather pretty like yours—odd—can't remember her name.'

I said I kept forgetting names and then he began talking about his school and some master who never remembered the boys' names. His voice sounded peculiar, seemed to come from his chest not his throat and had an odd rattling note. As he went on talking he started talking nonsense, at first only occasionally, then most of the time. He kept asking my name, if I knew his sister and sometimes he thought I was his sister. Sometimes, for a few seconds, he was quite coherent. In one lucid spell I asked if he was comfortable.

'Yes, thanks, except for this bandage thing over my face. Bit sort of tight. Could you sort of loosen it?'

I looked round for advice but all the Sisters in sight were busy with other patients and the senior Sister seemed to have vanished. I could not see a VAD in the ward and the two M.O.s present were dealing with blood transfusions. Then, as I did not think it would do any damage to loosen the gauze bows, I let go of his hand, stood up, undid the first and, as the sterile towel beneath slid off and jerked aside the towel above, very nearly fainted on his bed. The right half of his face and some of his head was missing. I had consciously to fight down waves of nausea and swallow bile, wait until my hands stopped shaking and dry them on my back before I could retie the bow. Mercifully, he had slid back into confusion before I flopped back onto my chair.

The confusion increased, his breathing grew louder, more laboured and sometimes rattled as his voice earlier. But he seemed to know I was holding his hand, as whenever I slightly altered the position of my cramped fingers, his cold, stiff fingers as slightly tightened their grip. His eye had been closed for some while when it suddenly opened and stared at me. Before I realized what he was about to do, with a tremendous effort he flung himself upwards from the waist and towards me. I had to wrench free my hand as I leapt up and caught him in my arms to stop him falling out of bed. He was so heavy that to keep my balance I sat instinctively on the side of his bed. He dropped his head on my shoulder and sighed. I thought he was unconscious and was relieved for his sake, but too frightened to lay him back in case the towels fell off and I had to see his wounds again. I wholly forgot I was committing the unforgiveable nursing crime of sitting on a patient's bed.

As suddenly the senior Sister was beside me. She said nothing about my sitting on the bed, but gently uptilted his head from my shoulder. 'Poor boy. Put him down, nurse.'

I only understood when she closed his one eye. An M.O. had

appeared. He helped her straighten the boy's arms and legs, roll his body in a grey blanket and lift the roll onto the waiting stretcher that had appeared on the floor. The M.O. took one end, an orderly the other, and before they were out of the ward the Sister had whisked off the under blanket, straightened the long red mackintosh sheet, tucked on a cleaner under blanket. Then she noticed me standing behind the chair. 'Go and wash that blood off your face and neck, at once, girl! It'll upset the patients. Move, nurse! Can't you see how busy we are?'

All I saw through the curtain of shock was a hideous forest of dead, white leafless trees heavy with repulsive crimson and yellow fruit and long thin red tentacles reaching down to uneven grey mounds that reeked with the sickly-sour smell of fresh blood. I wanted to run away from the ward, the hospital, the Red Cross, and nursing for ever, but I could not run as my legs were stuffed with heavy cotton wool. It was not like one of those nightmares where one wants to run from danger and cannot, it was far worse, as I knew I was awake and this nightmare was present reality.

Somehow I got out of the ward and into the nearest sluice in time. Several minutes later as I washed my face under a cold tap, one of the younger Sisters came in. 'Been throwing up? Poor kid. Always used to when I was a pro.' She chucked me a clean hand-towel. 'You'll feel better now. Anyone using you? Then I am. I've got to have some more hotties. It's no use your going round the other blocks as they've sent us all their spares. I'll be two wards down. Have a rootle round and find me some —and don't forget all the dead haven't been moved out. Look round their feet.' She read my expression and added briskly but not callously, 'Stiffs don't need hotties, kid. The living do. Get weaving!'

Unable to sleep that night, in the small hours I went out into the garden and as there was a moon and I might be seen from a window, spread my grandfather's carriage rug in the shelter of the camellia bushes. I was glad the camellias had stopped flowering as the moon was bright enough to transform even the roses into waxen flowers for the dead. The night was very quiet but I waited, tensed, for the rumble of the next convoy, the next duet of guns and aircraft. None came, but every few minutes the long fingers of the searchlights swung over the sky like some fussy housewife searching for invisible cobwebs. The night air was warm and probably scented with warm earth, grass and roses. All I smelt was blood. The smell clung to the back of my nose and throat and no amount of washing had got it off my hands. I wondered, as I was so often to wonder as a nurse, how ever again I would eat anything touched by my bare hands. At the very late supper no-one around me had wanted to eat, all I had managed to swallow was some bread and cheese eaten with a knife and fork. I thought of the bread and cheese, and only then, very slowly, of the men who had died since lunchtime and the boy who died in my arms. I wished I could weep. Usually I wept easily. I learnt then, for the first time in my life, how it felt to be too sad for tears. The feeling was agony.

As was the necessary routine:

'Nurse, get all these into orderly packs, check and then label each name and number against this list.'

I did not know how to make an orderly pack out of the torn and bloodsoaked uniforms removed from the dead. I made each set into a bundle tied with string. 'Do I take them to the Pack Store, Sister?'

'Not now. Their C.O.'ll need to see them. He'll be back, shortly. Just stack them in a tidy row on one of the metal stretcher-trolleys—or you may need two trolleys.'

I did.

Chapter Five

MY stay in 'A' was short. On one of the C.O.'s weekly inspection mornings I forgot the time. The C.O.'s party arrived in my allotted ward to find all the beds out of line and away from the walls, one of the two orderlies new that morning, bumpering, the other shaving one of the three patients on the Dangerously Ill List, two other patients shaving themselves and myself standing on a locker-top washing a lampshade. The following night I started the first of my twenty-eight consecutive nights as sole VAD on the night staff in the camp's Military Families Hospital. The Battle of Britain was then at its height though to me merely of nuisance value as, when any of the neighbouring airfields to our camp were under attack, we had air-raid Alerts that put me behind with my ward routine work. But shortly after I went on nights the night air attacks started and on many nights on another long metal stretcher trolley I stacked new-born babies bundled in shawls and cot blankets.

Families stood across the Ordnance railway line from the men's hospital. It was an independent establishment, built, I think, as a hospital, and had three floors. Maternity on the top; general medical and surgical wards in the middle; and on the ground various offices I never saw used at night, the one kitchen for the hospital, and an operating theatre only used at night during my shift as an air-raid shelter.

Every night before beginning my pre-midnight routine— i.e., hot drinks and bedpans all round; helping the two Sisters on nights to settle the patients; changing and feeding babies; I 'set for raids'. First I checked that an empty stretcher-trolley, unlit hurricane lamp in good order and box of matches, waited against the wall by the nursery door opening into the top corridor. Further along that corridor were the stairs, one lift-well, and doors to the labour and maternity wards. Always I dumped my tin hat and respirator on the empty trolley before charging down the stairs to transform the theatre into a shelter. The operating table, anaesthetic machine and other equipment trolleys had to be covered with clean sheets, a pile of cushions heaped on the floor against one wall, a line of portable canvas cots set up against another, folded blankets stacked on the covered operating table, three more hurricane lamps set in specified places on the floor, each with a box of matches, and near the cushions, a stack of women's magazines. The strongly built, windowless theatre made a good shelter and its outer walls were sandbagged. It had its own portable self-powered lights, but at night we took these up to the labour ward. Often during, or immediately after, raids our electricity failed for minutes or longer. Consequently, habitually, I carried a small torch in one dress pocket, spare matches and two candles in the other. I never needed the candles. In 1940, in normal circumstances, seventy-five per cent of all British babies were born at night. Every wartime midwife and obstetrician I met agreed that nothing so swiftly induced a baby as the sound of a falling bomb.

One morning as I pushed my bicycle back to our Mess for breakfast, I was stopped by Mrs. S. 'What's up with your bike? Tyres don't look flat.'

'They're fine. But I keep falling asleep and falling off.'

'Poor girl. Not surprised you're whacked. Nights are tough enough without Jerry making extra work.'

I leant on my handlebars. 'At least he wakes me up.'

'Expect he does. How're you liking it amongst the women and babies?'

'Much more than I expected. The women are jolly nice, the babies cute, and the two Sisters are so sort of normal I keep forgetting they're QAs.'

'Who've you got? . . . Oh, those two glamour girls! Aren't they both newish in from their teaching hospitals? Who's your

M.O. ? . . . Old—who—my child ? Kindly remember he's ten years younger than myself! Still, as well he's old enough to keep his head with the beauty chorus on the Families night staff. Trust the Army always to cloister the youngest and best-looking Sisters and VADs behind Families' convent walls. Quite a compliment being posted there.'

'Not for me, it wasn't, Mrs S. I suppose you've heard of the black I put up in 'A' ?'

She smiled not unkindly, 'I can't pretend the story hasn't gone all round with improvements. I suppose one of your patients didn't actually chuck his shaving brush at the C.O. ?'

'No.' I had to smile though still very perturbed by the episode. Betty, Joan, and other girls had tried to console me with reminders of the blacks they had put up, or invented putting up, if not under the eyes of the top brass. I had pretended to shrug it off, but sensed uneasily that my error was important. (Instinct, as always in my experience, was right. For good and bad, that posting to Families was later to alter the entire course of my life.) 'No,' I repeated. 'I think he dropped his shaving brush on the floor in horror and someone —I think the R.S.M.—picked it up, but I was too petrified to be sure. Think I'll ever live it down ?'

She looked up at the sky. 'The Army's got one or two things on its mind to keep it from being too browned-off with you. Not again ?' The Alert was sounding. 'I'll ride back with you and see you don't fall off.'

The guns had started before we reached the Mess. It was late for breakfast and most of the other night VADs had already left for the Night Home. Whistles were blowing, shutters being slammed, and I stretched out unnoticed on one of the long benches in the nearby empty dining-room, my respirator on my chest, tin hat over my face and that was the last I heard of that or any other daylight raid whilst on nights. A couple of hours later someone shook me and said I should be in bed. 'All Clear ? Went ages ago.'

The VAD Night Home was some way off and for a reason I never fathomed presided over by a youngish woman civilian whom I loved for giving me my first bedroom to myself and as this was an attic, for always calling me last in the evenings. The attic was tiny, had a sloping roof, dormer windows, bare floorboards, and the only provided furniture an army bedstead, biscuits and bedding. I turned my suitcase into a dressing-table, made a hanging cupboard by sticking two nails into one sloping wall and connecting them with strong twine. Such luxury was my delight and the envy of my friends. 'How'd you swing this, Lu?' I did not know and had been long enough in the Army not to ask in case it was a mistake. My only regret was that I spent too much time asleep properly to enjoy the privacy.

I had been tired before in hospital, but never before reached and remained at the pitch of fatigue consequent on working twelve-hour nights, seven nights a week. In the mornings I fell into bed as if pole-axed and stayed unconscious until violently shaken. 'Wakey, wakey! Rise and shine! Ten past seven and it's the second time. Third and I strips your bed! Show a leg there!'

Then came the conscious fight to surface through the smothering waves of sleep. A fight that had to be continued in the bath, getting into uniform, riding to the Mess for supper, on to the hospital, and for the first few hours on-duty. A fight that made sense of the strict rule forbidding us to sit down on-duty at night, unless feeding or special-nursing a patient, or in our half-hour night meal break. Whenever I broke the rule when alone in Families kitchen and sat on the lid of the huge bread-bin, instantly I went to sleep, fell onto the floor and only then woke as I was so scared of the kitchen cockroaches. My lowest ebb came around midnight—this ebb varied for other night nurses—but once midnight was over I breathed out, knowing ahead lay the clearheadedness of the small hours, then the pre-dawn euphoria that seemed to hit all night nurses alike before exhaustion returned with the rising sun.

As far as I had become concerned, the war only happened at night. I had no clear idea of what was actually happening to that war. I was sufficiently aware other parts of southern and eastern England were having air raids, that the RAF was being kept pretty busy, that everyone seemed to assume the raids were the opening gambit of the long-awaited invasion, to be very relieved our parents, John, and our dog Dopey moved temporarily to stay with relatives in Yorkshire at the end of July.

After the fall of France, Government posters appeared in towns on the Channel coast asking all non-essential civilian residents, particularly all schoolchildren, mothers with young children, the aged and infirm, pensioners, and the retired on private incomes, to arrange to move themselves (at their own expense) to other parts of the country, but not to East Anglia, Kent or Sussex. From father I heard the voluntary evacuation had reduced the combined population of Hastings and St Leonards from sixty thousand to approximately twelve thousand, the beach in front of both towns was mined for its length, the promenades covered with rolls of barbed wire, and the activity of the 'tip and run' raiders had caused a growing rash of boarded-up windows and ruined houses. The 'tip and runs' were German planes that flew over in the five minutes or so it took from the French coast, dropped a load of bombs and flew back immediately and generally too low over the sea for the coastal ack-acks. Our parents wrote regularly, but as letters were often delayed days, or lost, or destroyed by enemy bombs in the post, and civilian trunk calls either meant hours of waiting or could not be put through, frequently in that August and September our parents in Yorkshire seemed as distant as when they were in Suez.

One early afternoon I heard there had been an unexpected, temporary lull in the daylight raids, from a St Leonards girl who shook me awake. She was a VAD in one of the smaller camps several miles away and had hitched a lift in an ambulance sent to collect medical stores. She had called at our Mess, and as Betty was on-duty, borrowed a bicycle and ridden up to the Night Home. She said the dame downstairs had said she could come up and she was sorry to wake me, but no-one at her dump had a clue what was going on and why had Jerry packed in the daylight raids and did it mean he'd changed his mind about invading or had he arrived ?

'If he has, no-one's told me.' I was very peeved at being

woken and too sleepy to care had she said Jerry had just surrounded the Night Home.

She was peeved. 'I thought you'd have the gen! You do
have your troops in bed long enough for a natter. If ours need
more than a couple of A.P.C.s or lick of flavine, our M.O.
shoves them into you.'

'Not me. I'm in Families.'

'How's your family?'

'O-kay, P.G. Haven't had a letter—oh—about ten days.
Maybe more. How's yours?'

She thought her parents were all right as she had managed
to speak to her mother on the telephone yesterday. Her parents
were still in St Leonards and knew all the local news. Peter,
Martin, Ronald, all RAF pilots and all dead before their
twenty-first birthdays. She said, and kept on saying, 'I can't
believe those boys are dead, Lucy. I just can't believe they've
died.'

Though stunned by the triple tragedy, in a kind of frozen
distress I discovered I could believe it. Before I saw and felt
death, even my anxiety for the AIF and the marching men
earlier had been cushioned with her present incredulity. Still,
death had been an unmentionable mystery that happened to
the old, to my unknown elder brother and relatives, to millions
in the war before I was born and whom I had tried unsuccess-
fully to visualize when buying poppies, and singing 'Oh God
Our Help In Ages Past', or trying not to shuffle my feet in the
Two Minutes' Silence on Armistice Day (11th November). I
had wept over *Journey's End*, *Tell England*, and Hollywood war
films, without genuinely believing the dead had died, because
through the gauze filter over my imagination's lens I saw death
as sleep. That poets and prayer books labelled the sleep
eternal, had never convinced me as I believed literally in the
resurrection of the dead, had learnt neither biology nor
chemistry, and thought of decomposition only in connection
with garden compost heaps. There had been no resemblance
to sleep in the harsh, cold, stiffening reality of those dead
soldiers in 'A'; no later answer to the nagging thought, how
could a man with half his face and head missing, literally, rise

from the dead'. In one afternoon that particular cushion of ignorance had been removed for life.

She asked if there was more news of Betty's special boy-friend at home, now posted 'missing' in France.

'None.'

'He's not "believed killed"?'

'Just missing.'

'Poor Tony. Nice bod. Could be a prisoner. Poor Betty. Were they actually engaged?'

'Not officially. They meant to fix it on his next leave.'

'Hope to God he's all right, somewhere.'

'Hope so.' I sounded casual and knew it, but knew not whether she realized this was in self-defence. From hearing the news, I had tried to avoid thinking about Tony and Betty as it hurt so much. Yet there were moments when intentionally I reminded myself he was 'missing'; these were the moments when I squirmed anew over the arrival of the C.O.'s party in my ward in 'A'. The reminder served to illustrate the triviality of that anxiety and to sow the first seeds of the realization that one of the few advantages of having to face tragic problems is the way this ever after reduces the lesser to their right proportions.

'Wakey, wakey! Third time!' My top bedclothes were stripped off. 'Gone half-past! Get your skates on!'

No space for shock and sadness in a two-minute bath, frenzied race into uniform, to the Mess to swallow congealed baked beans on soggy toast and lukewarm tea, ride to the hospital. No second for recalling father on the first day of Tony's last leave, 'Betty, I've just answered the door to a tin-hatted young soldier who hasn't yet been issued with a service cap, looks about ten foot tall in his new boots and is asking to see you. I dimly recognize him as that nice young fellow Tony . . . who used to work in the City.' Or playing poker in the ante-room with Peter and Martin in their Shepherds' sacks and bottle straws and the three of us moaning about our School Cert. exams the next summer. Or Ronald calling to show off his new Acting Pilot Officer's uniform, embryo RAF moustache, and, puce with pleasurable embarrassment, rotating on our sitting-room hearthrug, 'I say, Lucilla, do you think if I asked your parents that they'd let you meet me in town sometime? Ever been to the Café de Paris? Nor've I. Shall—er—shall we try it?'

No time for that either.

The memories had to wait and in the waiting be imprinted for life. The sick, the pregnant nearing labour, the newly delivered mothers, the newly born babies, could not wait. 'Get a move on, Andrews! Get those first drinks out all round fast as you can. If our poor women can't get in some sleep early, they'll get even less than last night. Moon's on the wane.' When the moon went in, then, the bombers came out. Later, when instruments and aircraft improved, we loathed the moon. Later still when the bombing planes had no human pilots, the moon was unimportant

The senior of the two Night Sisters was an S.C.M. as well as S.R.N. and in overall charge with particular responsibility for the maternity floor. Her junior, an S.R.N. (as all QAs), was responsible for the general wards. (For convenience here only, Sister Maternity and Sister General). Sister Maternity was a tall, slim, attractive brunette of twenty-six. Sister General was a few months younger, and an unusually pretty, slender, blonde. Both were from separate London teaching hospital, much-liked by their patients, and treated me more as a junior pro than as a VAD. Since junior probationers in large teaching hospitals were expected to be ignorant and needed to be taught how to nurse, they made reasonable allowances for the former and, whenever possible, practised the latter. At first I rather resented this, being so accustomed to being told by a Sister to do a job and get on with it as best I could, but slowly I began to appreciate that nursing was a skilled, complex occupation about which I knew next to nothing and they knew a great deal. I liked working with them and the way the night, and above all the raids, lowered the normally insurmountable barrier hospital etiquette raised between the trained and untrained.

The London Blitz had started in the late afternoon on 7th September. That first attack lasted until just before dawn. It was a Saturday night that at first seemed to me the same as any other night on duty. At supper I had heard London had been attacked and assumed only by a short, sharp, daylight raid. That night, as usual, our M.O., Major X, arrived for his medical round. Normally, I barely registered his appearance as he was purely the Sisters' concern, but that night, though it was warm, I noticed he had on a British Warm (short officers' greatcoat) and looked as if he needed it. After he had gone Sister Maternity told me in the nursery that London was still under attack. 'Don't say anything to the patients until they have to know. Some are bound to have relatives or friends in London.'

I was bottle-feeding a baby. 'All this time, Sister?'

'Yes. Jerry's sending in wave after wave of Heinkels.'

'Not Stukas?'

'Just Heinkels. The Major says Jerry's stopped using Stukas. Don't know why.'

'Maybe he's run out of 'em?'

'Maybe.' She filled a basket with dried nappies from the airing-cupboard and methodically folded each before adding it to the depleted pile on the changing-table. 'For the first time in my life I wish my training hospital wasn't so handy for Central London.'

'Central London getting the worst?'

She shrugged. 'Sounds like Jerry's trying another Rotterdam. At least my hospital's not slap on the river opposite Westminster. Jerry's bound to aim at Westminster. Goebbels'll have a field-day if he can boast about flattening the Houses of Parliament. The Major's a Tommy's man. Tommy's is sitting in the bullseye tonight. Your lass finished? I'll change her whilst you get on with the next feed.'

We were still in the nursery when, just after eleven, my ultra-acute ears first picked up the most disturbing sound I could have imagined at that hour of the night in a military camp. 'Sister! That's the reveille!'

We went into a sluice, closed the door, switched off the lights, removed a blackout screen and opened a window. And from the surrounding barracks we heard the bugles sounding the reveille. 'Suppose Jerry's landed, Sister?'

'Maybe. Or just another flap. Or someone thinks it a good idea to have the camp standing-to because of what's happening in London. If anyone tells me what all this is about, I'll let you know.'

If she ever heard, she forgot to tell me and I forgot to ask her about it. Night life in Families became even busier, as the night Alerts increased; whether they were false alarms, enemy planes that had become isolated from their main force and had bombs to unload before returning to Germany, or the rare direct attack caused, rumour insisted, by the enemy pilots mistaking the camp for a small town—until the All Clear sounded the Alerts meant upheaval for patients and staff. All patients who could be moved were either taken, or took themselves, down to the shelter. The Sisters moved out the women and I moved all the babies except those actually born during the specific Alert. I never discovered if this was an official rule, but it was one on which Sister Maternity was adamant. 'Men make wars and men make air raids, Andrews, but no man is making me part mum and babe within minutes of birth. At that stage they're still a part of each other and as mum can't be moved either junior stays in her arms or in a cot close enough for mum to see and feel her babe. They'll live, or die, together.' She did not add—and so will I, with them—as it was 'raid routine' that she should stay on the top floor with any immovable maternity patients and Sister General do the same for the general patients. When the Sisters were absent, I was in charge in the shelter.

The responsibility would have alarmed me had I had time to dwell on it and had the patients in my charge not been so sensible, helpful and brave. They never screamed, grew hysterical, or even grumbled. If one wept, it was invariably quietly and as invariably she was comforted by the others. They wore their own or hospital dressing-gowns over night-gowns and pyjamas and sat on cushions on the floor with the blankets spread over their legs. Beside them—aside from the few ATS patients' service respirators and tin hats—were civilian gas-masks in cardboard boxes and knitting bundles. Night after night, sometimes more than once a night, they

The author's mother and father on their wedding day in Gibraltar
th October, 1913

(above) Elizabeth 'Betty' Andrews (left) and WAAF friends, 1942

Lucilla Andrews—photograph taken for
BRCS Identity Card, December 1940

(*above*) John Andrews in the RAF, 1944

This morning I sewed on my first war service stripe. It signifies that I, M.N. L.A. b/640714 have nursed with the Army for one year of active service. Actually it's 14 months since I first officially wore the brassard of a Mobile member but like most things in the Army my stripe has late in arriving. Still I'm awfully fond of it. It looks like an enormous D.F.C. medal worn high on the left arm. But they have not yet become common owing to the delay I've already mentioned & it's rather pleasant to be one of the chosen few & I hope it'll impress people as much as it does myself. But after what I have seen of the R.A.M.C's opinion — & that includes Q.A. sisters as well — I'm inclined to doubt it. Even had one to wear at F.M. Goering's decorations I'm much afraid their attitude would remain the same. It's a strange fact...

March 1941 entry—typical of notes from which this book was writt[en]

Victoria Ward, St. Thomas's Hospital, London after one of the innumerable air-raids of the blitz 1940

St. Thomas's Church S.E.1 just after blitz Sept. 1940

The Nightingale house, St. Thomas's Hospital London, 1940

Lucilla Andrews with Young 'Vee' (Veronica), and carrying the manuscript of *Print Petticoat* in a bag. St. Leonards-on-Sea, summer 1952

(*below*) Mother and daughter, Edinburgh, Christmas 1976

knitted and chatted and I felt as if presiding over an extended Women's Institute meeting. The needles clicked on, the conversations ran on, from husbands, children, boy-friend, in-laws, to the difficulties of married quarters, the move from those quarters they all expected very shortly, (rightly), to dressmaking, cooking, making one penny do the job of two, to the many-sided job of one parent doing the job of two when dad was a serving soldier, or already for some, a prisoner-of-war, or dead.

Listening to, and watching, those women provided me with an insight into my own sex and an oasis of sanity badly needed when the anger of the guns, the whines of diving aircraft, the ugly shuddering roars of exploding bombs convinced me our shelter was the bombers' target-for-tonight. The twitter of voices stopped abruptly when a bomb fell close enough for us to hear it whistle on the way down. The grey, black, brown, English mouse, peroxide blonde heads in curlers, tousled, or newly combed, swayed forward into their laps as some corps de ballet making a final curtsey. The patients recovering from abdominal operations instinctively flattened both hands over their wounds. 'That was a near one, eh, nurse? Know what they say—nearly never killed a man! There now, lovey! Did the nasty bangs wake you up, then? Never you mind! Nurse has got a nice drinkie for you—loves his glucose water doesn't he, nurse? Oh, it's a her—your little love, dear? Your first is she, dear? There. That's nice. Now when I had my first. . . .'

Every night Sister Maternity prepared the babies' individual 'shelter bottles'. Only nine on that occasion as only nine babies to go down. Other nights there were more, others less. The most I moved on one night was fourteen babies. 'Only use the glucose drinks if you must, Andrews, as their mums won't thank us for sending them out addicted to nocturnal tipples. But if you must use 'em, use 'em.'

Those women, the first I had nursed, in a very few nights demolished all my pre-conceived ideas of women as patients. I had expected to find them fussy, nervous, tearful, demanding. They only fussed on my behalf. 'Not like that, dear, or you'll have the Sister after you. You nip down for a tray, then collect the empties. Sister Maternity's ever so kind, but she'll not have you carrying nothing but on a tray.'

I should have remembered. The previous night Sister Maternity had stopped me on the stairs as I rushed back to the kitchen with four empty cups strung from my left hand and the four saucers in my right. 'Miss Andrews, where is your tray?' She always addressed me formally when I was at fault. 'How many more times must I tell you, crockery in a hospital must only be carried on a proper crockery tray. A war is no excuse for slovenly nursing!'

Certainly in the maternity ward, at some period, most of the patients wept. Sister Maternity said this was perfectly natural. 'All women get a bit weepy after giving birth and why not, as it's the most tremendous hard labour—I'm not punning, I'm being literal.'

The women on both floors appeared far less nervous about their health than the troops in the men's hospital, and with very rare exceptions, astonishingly undemanding. Next to their courage, what most surprised me was their humour. When the maternity ward, especially, was not briefly subdued by a perfectly natural weep, it resounded with yells of laughter and jokes too Rabelaisian for my understanding. I asked Sister Maternity for explanations as we fed bottle babies in the nursery. She censored some. 'You didn't get that bit about it being a man's bike? I should hope not at your age! Skip that one. I don't expect old Mother P knew you were listening. Maybe you should shove cotton wool in your ears when up the far end amongst the multips. When they get down to it, they'd make the bluest Garrison Theatre comic blush. How's he getting on with that bottle?'

'Bit slow, I'm afraid, Sister.'

She tucked her baby under one arm and stood by me. 'Your poor lad hasn't good sucking pads and he's tired. Put your thumb under his chin, so—that'll help him and he must have more as his mum's dried up. No wonder after last night. Dry my milk if I'd to stagger up and down these stairs like a yo-yo within hours of my milk coming in. When he's finished, don't disturb him with a change unless he's dirty. Put him down to get some kip whilst he can.'

I loved feeding the babies. It meant I could sit down, without risk of falling asleep, as they were so interesting, and provided another surprise by being such fun. I had not met babies before, and had not thought I would like them as I had never consciously wanted a baby, or clucked over prams. It took only a couple of nights in the nursery to rid me of the fear that either the babies would fall apart in my hands or I would drop them, and to turn me into an ardent clucker over cots, nappy changes, feeding bottles, and nursery Alerts. I was rather worried the first time I heard myself talking when alone with them in the nursery. Sister Maternity overheard. 'Don't flap, Andrews, you're not daft. Babies like being talked to and even this young once they get used to a voice, most'll stop bellowing to listen. I'll show you.' It was just before the 10 p.m. feed time and two-thirds of the nursery was shouting. She stood in the middle and clapped her hands. 'Pipe down, you lot! Grub's coming!' The shouts subsided to hiccups.

'Sister, how can they possibly understand?'

'How do you, or anyone, know they can't? They told you? All I know is, if you hit the right tone, you can get through from the first week of life.' She glanced at the clock on the wall. 'Get out of that nursery apron, nip away those last three beeps, and then I'll start bringing in the hungry.'

The only thing I really disliked about nursing women was the fact that they had to have bedpans. I loathed the bedpans and bombs alike and would probably have hated both, had not all my hatred been concentrated on the kitchen cockroaches. On my first night when I switched on the light and the black floor scuttled towards me, for the only occasion in the war I screamed in terror. From then on, as I had to be in and out of the kitchen all night and despite constant complaints to and onslaughts from the Sanitary Squads, and pounds of killer-powder I put down nightly, the cockroaches not merely survived but flourished. I maintained a private war in the kitchen. When swatting them I encouraged myself by singing:

> Christian, dost thou see them
> On the holy ground,
> How the troops of Midian,
> Prowl and prowl around ?
> Christian, up and smite them. . . .

I scattered so much killer-powder that only by a miracle did none get into the adult patients' milk (the babies' artificial feeds were prepared in the cockroach-free nursery), and the scrambled eggs and cheese toast I cooked on alternate nights for the meals the Sisters and I ate together, deliveries and raids permitting, between 1 and 2 a.m. Whatever was in that powder, though I inhaled quantities, it did me no more harm than the cockroaches. Every time I replugged their holes they staggered out again, shook themselves free of white and advanced as before in good battle order. 'Sister, unless this kitchen has a direct hit, I'll bet they're here for the duration.'

'If they can survive your hymn-singing blitzes, they can survive anything. From the row just now, I thought you'd got a Jerry in here.' Sister General kicked aside corpses. 'Come up and give me a hand with old Mrs H. She's too low in bed. I didn't ring not to wake the others.'

Mrs H, in her late forties, was the wife of a regular soldier back from Dunkirk and posted elsewhere. She was an amiable grey-haired woman with three chins, weighed fourteen stones and had recently been operated on during the day for a strangulated hernia. Sister General had taught me the rudiments of lifting and, being the more experienced lifter, gripped my wrists. 'Dig your heels in, Mrs H, and go floppy. Ready, Andrews ? Up we go. Fine. More comfortable, Mrs H ?'

Mrs H said she was lovely and she didn't know she was sure how two slips of girls could toss her about lovely. 'Time I turned me ankle last year took hubby and two of his mates to get me off me kitchen floor.' She reached for the largish piece of white tissue paper I had removed from her bedtable and was about to scrumble. 'Don't want to waste that, dear. Cut up lovely, it will, and I'll fetch it home seeing you've enough here. Hubby', she added cryptically, 'won't let me use newspaper. Not nice, hubby says.'

Outside the ward I asked, 'Sister, what did she mean?'

'Sergeant H doesn't hold with using newspaper as lavatory paper.'

'That's why she wants to save it—Sister! You can buy lav. paper for 3*d*. and 6*d*. in Woolworths!'

'If you don't need that money to feed your family. You can get half-a-pound of stewing steak for 6*d*.—more if you'll take scraps, or a pound of beef sausages. If you'd a family of hungry kids, would you give 'em bread-and-scrape for supper because you'd spent the money on a luxury like lav. paper? You do know what bread-and-scrape is?'

'Sorry. No, Sister.'

'Bread with a scrape of margarine.'

'That's—supper?'

'For thousands of kids. Maybe hundreds of thousands or more.'

'I didn't know.'

'But you must've come across enough troops by now to have noticed how much bigger the majority of the ex-public school conscripts and civvy soldiers are than the others. I wasn't thought tall at school or in training and you're my height, but we tower over most of these soldiers' wives. Know why?'

'Not really. Isn't it something to do with heredity? Or just luck?'

'It's luck, all right. The luck of having parents who could afford to give us enough protein and milk as kids and to have been born to mothers who could afford to have enough of both when we were in utero. That's why we're bigger—and why we'll eat army rissoles but none of the women here or most of the troops'll touch 'em. You must've noticed that?'

'I did in N.D.K. I couldn't think why not. The men's cookhouse makes jolly good rissoles.'

'If you thought the rissoles were made of minced dog-meat, would you eat them?'

'Yeugh! Sister, they aren't—are they?'

'Of course not, but try telling that to any troops who come from homes where often that was the only kind of meat mum could afford and so she minced it, and as you're a girl they'll tell you politely to tell that to the Marines. If you were a civvy soldier, they'd tell you what you could do with them.'

'Please, Sister, what does that mean?'

She explained clinically. My still very literal mind was more puzzled than shocked as the exercise struck me as even more pointless than uncomfortable.

The war was unnervingly quiet that night. At 4 a.m. in the kitchen, before making the tea the night staff drank standing at four-thirty prior to 'starting work' at a quarter to five, for once I had time to make a few notes on the back of an old temperature chart, and have an extra cockroach blitz. In the grip of pre-dawn euphoria, in place of my hymn I sang Noël Coward's *The Party's Over Now.* '. . . . Night is over dawn is breaking,' swat 'Everywhere the town is waking,' swat 'Just as we are on our way—' swat 'to sleep,' swat, swat.

'Andrews, stop this ungodly row at once!' Sister General swept in crackling starch. 'I heard you from my landing!'

'Sorry, Sister. Just didn't want them to think the war's over because Jerry's taken a night off.'

'Don't tempt providence!' She rapped the wooden dresser. 'Mrs Y's actually having some sleep tonight.'

Mrs Y was a cardiac patient who always wore a green rubber oxygen mask and was too ill for me to be allowed to touch her on my own. 'Sister, what's wrong with her heart?'

'What isn't? Gone into failure, plus.'

'What does that mean?'

She said slowly, 'I keep forgetting how little you know. I can't hang around to explain now as it's too complicated. If Jerry lays off again tomorrow night, I'll try and fit in a class. Very briefly now—her heart's packing up, fast.'

'She's going to die soon—but she's much younger than Mrs H.'

'Mrs H didn't have bad rheumatic fever as a kid. That's what did for Mrs Y's heart.'

'How did she get rheumatic fever?'

'Not sure. At a guess, poor feeding, poor, damp, living conditions and probably some fool somewhere said it was just growing pains.'

'Some fool—? You mean a doctor, Sister?'

She smiled faintly. 'No names, no pack drill, Andrews. If you want to go on believing no doctors can ever be fools, whatever you do, don't do a general training. You going to?'

'Oh, no, Sister. No point. I want to be a writer not a nurse when the war ends.'

'Seems to have ended—God, you've got me doing it!' She slapped the dresser. 'I must get back up. Tea nearly ready? Good. I'm dehydrated, plus!'

The war quiet was still unbroken when I cooked our scrambled eggs the next night and carried the tray up to the maternity duty-room. Mrs N, a girl having her first baby, was in the first stage of labour and Sister Maternity wanted to eat within hearing distance. Both Sisters were already in the duty-room. Sister General was seated at the small table by the electric fire, with her sleeves buttoned, cuffs on, tin hat hanging from the back of her chair. Sister Maternity was perched on the desk buttoning her sleeves. As all the ex-trainees of the voluntary hospitals I met, neither would sit down to a night meal in ward duty-room, kitchen or corridor, or drink a mug of tea standing, with their sleeves up and cuffs off. As I put the tray on the table the Alert sounded.

'Blast Jerry! He'll wake Mrs Y and I hate cold scrambled eggs!' Sister General hauled off her cap, slammed on her tin hat and vanished. Sister Maternity damned all Germans. 'My poor kid in first-stage is scared enough without Jerry.' She flung her cap on the desk, grabbed her tin hat and fled for her women. I cursed under my breath, kicked off the electric fire switch, slapped the empty side plates over the three plates of scrambled eggs and fled for my babies.

I exchanged my cap for a tin hat as I pushed the empty trolley into the sleeping nursery. I no longer put on my respirator in Alerts as it got in the way when I carried a baby under each arm, or soothed, or fed in my arms, fretful babies in the shelter. Only very occasionally did the Sisters notice and tell me to put it on properly as they were too occupied looking after their own patients.

The gunfire and growls of approaching aircraft were louder,

but none of the ten babies woke as I scooped them from their cots in pairs, and laid them on their sides, as that took less space and whenever possible I tried to move all on one trip. Back in the corridor, I hung the unlit hurricane lamp on one stretcher pole, my respirator on another and pushed onto the lift as Sister Maternity galloped back up the stairs, her tin hat a halo behind her neat dark head. 'I've had to keep up Mrs P as well, Andrews. She's just started and being her fifth junior won't hang about. Got them all? Good. Get 'em down. This sounds more than a couple of strays with bombs to unload on the way home.' She closed the lift gates for me. 'Rest of mine are all down.'

In the shelter Sister General was fixing cushions behind and spreading rugs over the women sitting on the floor. She had to go back to her floor as neither Mrs H nor Mrs Y could be moved. She told me she intended wheeling Mrs H's bed into Mrs Y's ward. 'Company for each other and I can keep an eye on both.'

The move into the portable cots woke three babies. When the babies cried it upset their mothers and as that upset the other women and the raid was already making enough noise to upset the serenity of the Archangel Gabriel, I hitched a theatre stool up to the cots and settled down to feed glucose water to the three awake. The women settled down to their knitting and hopes that young Mrs N wouldn't have too hard a time and Mrs P would have the girl she wanted after the four boys. 'Nasty night for 'em, mind you. Don't like to think of 'em all up there and the Sisters. Can't be doing that poor soul with the poorly heart no good. Thought this quiet too good to last.'

One of the general patients asked me how the two women's labours were progressing. Before I could explain my ignorance, the maternity patients did it for me. 'N. Andrews isn't allowed to go into the labour ward when Sister Maternity's delivering, dear. Under age, aren't you, dear, and not a proper hospital nurse like the Sisters. Nursery and ward only, aren't you, dear?'

'That's me!' And mentally, as when Sister Maternity had told me of this official rule on my first night, I thanked God and preferred not to dwell on her rider: 'Now you know the rule, listen to this.' She rang three short, sharp, rings on the nearest electric bell. 'Get that? Don't forget it, because that is the labour ward SOS. I hope I'll never have to ring it for you, but if I do, whatever you are doing, drop it, and beat it at the double to me in the labour ward.'

About twenty minutes later, for the only time I heard those three short, sharp, rings. Momentarily I was numbed as by an electric shock. But the patients, as patients everywhere, instantly recognized the inter-staff secret code. 'Sister Maternity needs you quick, dear—yes, we'll be all right—we'll watch the little loves—we'll not move till the All Clear—off you go, dear —God bless. . . .'

Once clear of the thick theatre walls and sandbags, the noise was literally staggering. When I was half-way up the stairs the lights flicked off, but came on again before I reached the top corridor and charged into the labour ward far more frightened of what I was about to see than any air raid.

Sister Maternity, masked, gowned, rubber-gloved and bare-headed, was stooping between the two occupied labour beds. She glanced up. 'Get up that mask, girl! Get into a gown and gloves—no time to scrub—get dressed—that trolley back there. Then come here, quick as you can! Now', she stepped a little to one side without altering the position of her right hand, 'put your right hand over mine in the same position. Finger on finger. Right. Now, keep that same grip on the head when I slowly move my hand away. Good. Just keep that grip on the crown—that's junior's crown—and when he moves, don't fight him, or let go. Just widen your grip.' As she spoke she watched both women. Suddenly she muttered, 'Knew it!' and lunged for the other bed. 'Looks like you'll be first, Mrs P!' She had to shout over the renewed violence of the guns, and I only then discovered I was attending young Mrs N. Both women lay on their sides with their legs drawn up and heads turned away from me and sweat had darkened Mrs N's light brown and Mrs P's greying-brown to the same dark shade. Sister shouted, 'You're both doing fine, ladies!' And overhead a plane dived. The sticky, black-haired object under my right hand jerked forward and grew bigger, and I thought I heard Mrs N scream, but was not sure owing to the guns' thunderous answer to that dive.

I risked an apprehensive glance over my shoulder. Mrs P had turned onto her back, had her legs crooked, the long operation stockings in concertinas round her ankles, and the whole head of a baby between her thighs. The head was small, bald, round, and in the small round face were two placidly blinking eyes. Whilst I glanced, the rest of the baby slid as placidly into Sister's waiting brown hands. 'You've got your daughter, my dear! Well done, Mrs P!'

Mrs P's answer was drowned by what sounded like a plane just skimming our roof. Instantly, the worst hell of that, or any other night for me that summer, was let loose. Impossible to differentiate between ack-ack shells, tracers, aircraft engines and explosions, but we all heard the small shrill whistle of one falling bomb. Every instinct I possessed demanded that I dived under Mrs N's labour bed, but her baby's whole head had shot out and with the bomb's explosion he catapulted from the vagina into my hands trailing a long silver-blue veined cord. He was so covered in grease and so furiously flaying the air with minute arms that I was too busy trying not to drop him to be more than semi-conscious that medicine and lotion bottles, metal kidney dishes, enamel bowls, jugs, and blackout screens were dropping around us.

Sister dodged back from the other bed to tie the baby boy's cord in two places and cut between the ties. He lay on the bed in the curve of his mother's legs, bellowing with more strength than I ever heard from a new baby. Sister told me to wrap him in towels and blankets, tie round his wrist the waiting name-tape, put him in the waiting cot. 'Then get that large kidney dish in position for the placenta.' She shouted, but not as loudly as before. 'You've got a son, Mrs N, with good lungs. Just the afterbirth, dear!' She noticed the blackout screens. 'Andrews! Get those screens up, fast! I must have the lights on.'

Two screens merely needed replacing. A third had been blown out of its frame and torn in half. I stuck it together with rolls of three-inch adhesive strapping, and then noticed the raid seemed over. The guns were firing only spasmodically and the sound of engines had gone. I looked properly at the patients' faces for the first time. Mrs P had her baby in her arms, her eyes closed, and looked exhausted. Mrs N did not even look tired. She was smiling to herself, but breathing as if she had been running hard. Sister told me to go back to my shelter family. 'I can cope here. Thanks.' She held the baby boy, and as I left the labour ward I saw her put him in Mrs N's arms, 'Meet your son, my dear,' she said.

I heard the ringing of the duty-room telephone through a haze of delayed-action shock. 'Families ?' echoed an irate male voice. 'About time, too! I've been trying to get through to you for the last fifteen minutes! I am ringing for the Garrison P.A.D. Officer to complain about the lights you have been showing on the upper floor. . . .' I stopped listening and when he stopped for breath I apologized mechanically and rang off. I heard the telephone ringing again from the stairs but did not go back. I had to get back to the shelter because Sister Maternity had said so and suddenly I was incapable of thinking for myself. The stairs had become strangely steep. I had to hang on to the bannisters to keep my balance and there seemed many more stairs than usual. The All Clear went as I reached the ground floor and then all the lights went out. One ATS girl, a post-appendicectomy, lit the hurricane lamps for me as my hands shook out the matches. 'Always worst when it's over, isn't it, nurse ?' I nodded in the darkness. A nod was easier than speech.

The Sisters had come down to help back their patients. Sister Maternity, still capless, gowned, masked, but with her gloves off, told me to wait a few minutes before bringing back the babies as all were asleep and she wanted the lift for the maternity patients and herself. 'I don't want to leave my two in the labour ward alone longer than I have to. Neither have lost much, or need stitching, but after producing at that speed anything can, though probably won't, happen, as both babes are fine and wanted.' In the lamplights her mask and forehead were jaundiced. 'Have a quick tidy in here, we may have to use it again tonight, but I doubt it. Dawn soon.'

'Yes, Sister. Oh, Sister—.' I told her about the irate telephone call.

'Narked, eh? H'mmm.'

It was peaceful alone in the shelter with the babies. It took me much longer than usual to tidy all round. I could only move slowly, carefully, as if suddenly very old. The babies did not wake when I re-stacked them and then plunged us in darkness by turning off all the shelter lamps before I remembered to light the one for my trolley. The seventh match stayed alight long enough to start the lamp. I held it in one hand, as I was forbidden to hang a lighted lamp to a pole of a baby-laden trolley, slowly pushed out of the theatre corridor into the main and hit something soft. A torch was switched on. I held up my lamp. The yellow rays illuminated men in uniform. I counted the faces mentally, one by one. Five faces. One face was vaguely familiar and after a second or two my slow-motion brain identified it was the R.S.M.'s. He was a square-shouldered, very straight little man and at his side was a taller, thinner, man wearing a major's crown and belligerent expression. Someone, I thought the R.S.M., announced the Major as the Garrison P.A.D. Officer. Someone else, probably the Major, cleared his throat purposefully and began a long spiel about the lights we had been showing. When he stopped for breath, as before, I apologized mechanically, adding, 'I'm afraid when the blackout screen in the labour ward fell down. . . .'

'When any blackout screen falls, all lights must be extinguished, forthwith! Is Sister-in-charge available as I wish. . . .'

Sister Maternity's stage whisper from the darkness above, cut him short. 'Andrews, what you doing down there with those babes? Want to give them all pneumonia? And who've you got down there with you?'

I hissed back, 'Sister, it's about the labour ward lights. The Garrison P.A.D. Officer has—'

'Sent someone to tear us off another strip? Huh! Please send my compliments to the Garrison P.A.D. Officer and add

—if he wants two women delivered simultaneously in the dark he can come and do the job himself—with tin hat and respirator at the alert! Being only a qualified midwife, when my patients are giving birth I have to see what's happening and until I'm sure neither mums nor babes are going to die on me I've no time for coping with ruddy blackout screens! Now get those babes back up here at the double!' The landing floor above creaked as she stormed back into her department.

The posse were silent. Then the Major again cleared his throat, but less purposefully, and rounded on the R.S.M. 'All screens should be in good order, S'arnt-Major! Can't have these good ladies distressed in this fashion! Mustn't delay this charming young lady in her excellent work! Nurses—what would we chaps do without 'em, eh?' He stepped back, saluted me, smartly. The R.S.M. shouted in whispers, 'Yessir! Rightaway, sir!' and escorted my trolley and self to the lift. In the lamplight his face was solid teak and when he opened the gates for me his left profile was to the posse. Very deliberately, he lowered and raised his right eyelid. It was the only time in my life that I was winked at by a Regimental Sergeant-Major and, as my shock was beginning to wear off, going up in the lift I wished I could have told the men I nursed in my first weeks in N.D.K. But I knew none would have believed it.

The following night I arrived on-duty to find many of our patients had vanished to hospitals further inland. Those that remained were still discussing the new craters outside. 'Nearly got us last night, Jerry did. Still—nearly never killed a man.'

A few nights later I came off night-duty. It was my last night in the camp. The next day, with Betty and ten other VADs I was posted to a new, specialized, military hospital, in a semi-industrial city approximately sixty miles inland from London. I neither saw nor heard anything of those two Sisters again. On my final shift in Families I moaned to both, and the babies and the cockroaches, about being ordered to travel on my sleeping day.

'Typical of the Army to forget you're just off nights,' said the Sisters. 'Don't forget to ask for your four nights off as soon as you arrive or you'll never get them.'

I took their advice when reporting to our new Commandant the following evening. She looked considerably younger than the Commandant we had left behind and addressed us not as 'Members!' but as 'Gels!'

'Just off night-duty?' She smoothed her pale hair and pursed her pale lips. 'Well, I'll try and have a word with Matron and see if we can sort this out, but as the hospital is so short-handed I don't see how Sister can spare you from your new ward tomorrow. Report at the usual time in the morning and I'll see what can be done. Only try and remember—' she smiled palely, 'there is a war on!'

The Battle of Britain had ended, but London was still being blitzed. I did not argue the point. I was far too tired. When the Blitz ended the battered Londoners must have been even more tired. I only worked twenty-eight consecutive nights, but for fifty-seven consecutive nights London was under attack by an average of two hundred enemy bombers every night.

As with our initial posting, the war ended, and I had long left the Army, with the Army still owing me four, un-sorted-out nights off.

Chapter Six

THE Government posters urged us to DIG FOR VICTORY, DO YOUR BIT, BE LIKE DAD—KEEP MUM, remember CARELESS TALK COSTS LIVES, IT ALL DEPENDS ON YOU and to ask ourselves IS YOUR JOURNEY REALLY NECESSARY? And every other person I met reminded me THERE'S A WAR ON and none more fervently than those without personal experience of air raids.

In the new, specialized military hospital housed in a former women's college, the medical and senior nursing staff were almost exclusively civilians in new uniforms. 'Nicer for the patients as they're treated as civvy patients,' explained an older VAD, 'that's the only way our civvy M.O.s and QAs know how to treat patients. But apart from the rare old hag like myself who was in the last show, none of them have the faintest idea how to treat VADs or what we're supposed to do. To be fair, last time we used to say only God Almighty knew what a VAD was, but as we worked hard, were damned useful—as we knew and the Army just occasionally reluctantly admitted—we had roughly officer-ranking and quite a bit of respect.'

'Rather like our last posting.'

'Then you girls were lucky. Don't expect that here. Not on days. Nights aren't too bad as on nights we actually do some nursing. On days, my dears, you won't need lamps, you'll need scrubbing-kneelers and strong muscles. You'll spend most of your days scrubbing floors, baths, lavatories, sinks, sluices, lighting fires, toting coal bins, emptying dustbins. Don't waste breath lodging official complaints. You'll only be told we're here to take the place of men—and there's a war on.'

Shortly after our arrival another contingent of VADs arrived from another large permanent military hospital in southern England. A girl from the second contingent, nicknamed Ollie, was sent on day duty to the same officers' ward as myself. When we discovered that our work did indeed consist of nearly non-stop skivvying, we were as shocked as our fellow VADs in the ward were shocked by our reaction.

'If the army wants us to lug those dirty great galvanized iron bins down two flights, out to the yard, fill them with coal and heave 'em back up, why aren't we issued with fatigues (boiler suits)?'

'Don't bind! We can cope!'

'But it's daft as we've got orderlies!'

'Ours not to reason why, Andrews!'

'Why not? When it'll wreck our aprons and backs for the day and the orderlies do it better as even if they are C3s they've still got stronger arm and back muscles than we have. Look how they shift loaded stretchers and if you think that's easy let me tell you I once had to carry stretchers and. . . .'

'For goodness sake! No line shooting! We've far too much to do. If you want to be on a mutiny charge, I don't!'

'If the Army could put me on a charge for binding, it would have to put the whole flipping British Army on one. If a soldier wants to mutiny, he's got to fling down his rifle on parade and say, "Do what you will, I will soldier no more!" Says so in K.R.R.s.' I did not in fact know if this were true, having only learnt it from a barrack-room lawyer in N.D.K. 'When I mutiny—and it'll be any day now unless someone lets me stop skivvying and do some nursing—I'll march into Matron's office with bucket and scrubbing brush, fling down both and say, "Do what you will, I will skivvy no more!"'

'I hope you don't mind my saying this, Andrews,' she announced as people do when about to say something they hope one will mind like hell, 'but you lot from the south aren't making yourselves too popular. You seem to think having worked down south sort of makes you different to the rest of us. Can't imagine why.'

I did not attempt to explain. It was impossible to convince

anyone without first-hand experience of enemy action of the cathartic effect of that experience and its subsequent legacy of blazing impatience with we'll-cope-ers and muddlers-through still under the illusion that the war was a game to be played and won with a scrubbing-brush and amateur enthusiasm. I had seen that the war was an ugly and serious business and experienced the utter helplessness of the amateur, no matter how willing, when confronted with situations only the trained professional could handle. I remained haunted by that afternoon in 'A'; that night in the labour ward; and the icy fear I had dared not acknowledge until the raid was over, that Sister Maternity would be killed and I left alive with those women and they and their babies would die because I would not know how to save them. I could not discuss this, even with Betty or other VADs with similar experiences, but I had written these experiences down in great detail in the hope of writing them out, as on occasions I could write out disturbing scenes and emotions. Not those. In bed at night I longed for time to hurry up and erase them, as if time were some handy indiarubber. I had yet to learn the only reliable antidote to old sorrow is new sorrow and to old pain, new pain.

It was in those weeks spent on my knees that I began seriously to consider the idea of a general nursing training. Pre-Families, when I found I liked nursing, I had thought this was mainly because I liked the troops. In Families I had liked the women and babies, but at the same time become increasingly interested in the profession of nursing, particularly as practised by the two Sisters. In retrospect more than in the event, I was amazed how successfully those two young women ran that entire hospital at night with no more medical help than the Major's brief nightly rounds. But to acquire their skill would take roughly four years. I could not—would not—believe the war could last so long. I wanted to be a nurse only as long as the war lasted, and then, as ever, a writer. The day the war ended, so would my nursing life, and as that day must come before I finished a general training, it seemed pointless to start something I must leave unfinished.

'You—VAD—whatsyename?'

'Andrews, Sister.'

'NURSE Andrews, when talking to a Sister, girl! How much longer are you going to moon over this floor? Stop day-dreaming over ye boy-friend and put some guts into it!'

'Yes, Sister. Sorry, Sister.'

'Not half as sorry as ye'll be, my girl, if I catch you dawdling again! Do that and I'll have ye guts for garters!'

Ollie's seat and bucket backed out of a bathroom door a few feet away. She sat back on her heels and jerked up two fingers at our Senior Sister's ample back retreating down the long, ward corridor.

'Ollie, is that really a masonic sign?'

'Come again?'

'Well, Peter, Dick and Sammy keep making it at each other and when I asked why they said it was a secret masonic sign and I mustn't do it as I'm a girl and girls can't be masons.'

When she stopped spluttering she explained. Peter and Dick were Spitfire pilots injured during the Battle of Britain, Sammy was a subaltern injured in the first days of the still continuing London blitz. 'Don't let on to them that you know, Lu. Their language may be worse than any trooper, taste in girl-friends restricted to dumb bosomy blondes with necklines to the waist and skirts two sizes too tight, but underneath they're nice types. Shock the living daylights out of them to know you know.' She took another look down the corridor. Sister had vanished into her duty-room. 'Old bitch out for your blood again?'

'And me guts. She wants to wear 'em for garters.'

In that moment, Sister Blood-and-Guts was christened.

She had only recently joined our ward and the Army after working for many years as a senior ward sister in one of London's Big Five. (St Thomas's, St Bartholomew's, Guy's, St George's, and the London Hospital.)

Ollie said, 'If you do decide to train, for God's sake don't go to Blood-and-Guts's alma mater.'

'Over my dead body! Rather than risk meeting more like her, I'll stay a VAD on me benders for the duration.'

'Benders' was another of Sister Blood-and-Guts's favourite

expressions. 'Get down on ye benders, girl, and give that floor a good scrub and I mean scrub! Put some guts into it!'

She was a large lady with an outsize jaw, no lips, a loud voice, shoes that could have doubled as army boots, and according to Peter, Dick and Sammy, they had only survived her nursing because they were too bloody terrified of her to die.

Peter and Dick had beds on one side of their three-bedded ward. Dick's bed was turned the wrong way round to let him face Sammy and see out of the window as he had to lie on his stomach until the grafted skin on his flayed back healed. Peter watched room and view through the two mirrors suspended at special angles over his head, as he had to lie on his back immobilized in a spinal plaster. Sammy, the illest of the three, was only allowed to lie down at night. The car in which he had been driven with a senior officer had been buried by a falling building. The two other occupants had been killed outright and Sammy thought dead when he was dug out of the wrecked car. 'M-m-m-moved in the m-m-m-morgue, n-n-n-nurse.'

I liked all three but especially Sammy with his gentle, stuttering and sometimes faintly slurred voice, unfailing good humour, and extraordinarily sweet smile. He no longer had to wear a cranial cap bandage as the hair was starting to grow again over the long puckered and still bright pink seams in his scalp. Sister Blood-and-Guts never gave us medical reports on the patients, but one afternoon a junior, temporary, relief Sister on loan from the operating theatre told me beneath the skin of Sammy's scalp was more metal than skull bone. 'Sure to God, we'd to build him a new skull. It's a wonder the poor boy's alive at all.'

'He'll be all right now, won't he, Sister?' She just looked at me. 'He seems to be so much better.'

'Is that a fact?'

'That's how he seems.'

'It's glad I am to hear it. There's no doubt at all it was a grand job the Colonel did on him, but seeing himself had to pick up the poor boy's brains and pack them back in, as himself would say, there's no telling at all. Too early for that. Maybe this rally's a good sign. I've known it happen. The once or twice. How long've you been here? Was it in the south you were before? Working now in the city must make a great change for yourself.'

'Makes a change, Sister.'

The biggest changes were in the atmospheres in the crowded hotel restaurants, pubs, shops, 'buses and the local citizens' attitudes to service uniforms and specifically women in uniform. The form of conscription for young women between 19 and 23, unless exempt as the mothers of young children, or five or more months pregnant, or for other stringent physical or compassionate reasons, that later obtained throughout the country, had only just started. Later in the war it often looked as if the entire population under fifty was in uniform, but not where women were concerned in an English inland city in late 1940. We were still a minority group and my few friends in the ATS and WAAF said VADs were dead lucky to have small red crosses on the gold badges on the front of our porkpie outdoor uniform caps, 'Takes a right bastard to accuse anyone wearing a red cross of being a tart, but we get it all the time. "Know why you're in uniform, don't we...."'

My red cross notwithstanding, often when shopping or with other girls in uniform trying to find a table in restaurant or cafe, I recalled with a new empathy Tommy Atkins.

> For it's Tommy this, an' Tommy that, an'
>   'Chuck him out, the brute!'
> But it's 'Saviour of 'is country' when the
>   guns begin to shoot;
> An' it's Tommy this, an' Tommy that, an'
>   anything you please;
> An' Tommy ain't a bloomin' fool—you bet
>   that Tommy sees!

The city had never been raided, and whilst on clear nights the firework display in the southern sky provided a continuing reminder of the London blitz, as the threat of invasion was already forgotten history, aside from the tradesmen enjoying unprecedented prosperity from the thousands of service men and women either billeted in their midst or stationed in nearby camps and airfields, the local civilians seemed to me to see the war as a cross between an impertinent imposition and personal insult.

'Too awful, my dear! We just have to have these two nurses. Of course, we fought against it, but as it was either them or evacuee kids—anything rather than kids. Have you heard about poor Susan? My dear, four cockney guttersnipes—wet beds every night—and what she says about their table manners I daren't repeat over this 'phone! .... Our Two? No, not too ghastly as they don't have to eat with us, thank God, and aren't in much. ... I simply had to put my foot down about baths! Well, I said, if you both insist on one every day, I'm afraid five nights a week you'll have to make do with cold. I can't provide hot water for more than two a week each. Frankly, I don't believe these girls have any idea what we're all having to put up with. Take this morning! I was positively exhausted after queuing in every shop—and dropped into the Copper Kettle dying for a coffee. Not a table? Not a SEAT! Whole place packed out by the RAF and WAAF. Really, I should have thought they'd have some work to do in the mornings. ...'

Several other VADs were billeted in private houses and from their accounts, Betty and I had one of the best land-ladies. 'Doesn't go through your drawers when you're out, read your letters, and never comes in without knocking? God, are you lucky! My old bitch is always on the hunt, never remembers to put things or even letters back in the right places. I used to lock my writing case, but from the scratches she's tried to force the lock so often I now leave it open as I don't want it busted. I think she thought I kept the gin in there.'

'Where do you keep it?'

'In a half-open packet of STs, of course. She never scrabbles amongst the STs. She's got a nice mind. She's always telling me so when she binds about my language. Would it soften-up old Blood-and-Guts if I took the gin on-duty and gave her a slug in her tea? With my bosom I could easily camouflage a half-bottle in the billows under my apron bib.'

'The only thing that just might soften up Blood-and-Guts is a Panzer Division. Why can't they post her to Africa? The whole ruddy British Army's out there, rows of Sisters who arrived since her have gone out—but she stays on.'

'Maybe Mr Churchill has decided to keep her to defend the UK?'

'Then, God help Jerry—and us.'

A new VAD was listening. It was her first week after call-up. 'What puzzles me is the way all the Sisters tell one to do things in different ways. They even make beds differently. Is there any way of coping with them?'

'Sure! Just do things the way they do, even if that's three different ways for three beds in a row with different Sisters. Only two things hold for the lot; cups of tea and M.O.s. At every opportunity present them with the former and avoid the latter, on-duty—and off, unless you go for married men.'

'Are all ours married?'

'Ninety-nine per cent as they were specialists in civvy street and civvy patients like their specialists to have wives.'

Ollie asked, 'Mummy tell you never to go out with married men, Lu?'

'Yes, and wasn't she right. All dripping wet. They all get me in a corner at parties, tell me I'm different and that's what they like about me and their wives don't understand them.'

The new girl was still puzzled. 'Surely, decent married men don't make passes?' She was shocked when Ollie and I begged her to tell us stat. when she met a decent married man.

'Stat.', we explained helpfully, 'is short for the Latin statim, and is the medical term for "at once".'

That same evening she and I were making Sammy's bed together when the closed door was suddenly flung open by a very large Pilot Officer who glared round the room, then for a couple of seconds at Sammy, muttered 'Christ!' and vanished slamming the door without explanation. The new girl blushed, 'I just detest blasphemy!'

'D-d-don't f-f-f-flap, n-n-n-nurse. N-n-n-not b-b-blasphemy. M-m-merely m-m-mistaken i-i-identity.'

Sammy was the first very ill patient with whom I became emotionally involved. I found that first experience of the full strength of the patient-nurse bond acutely disturbing. Later

I experienced it with dozens, if not scores, of other equally ill patients, women and children as well as men. Whilst this continued to disturb me, by then I had realized that it was impossible for me to nurse certain patients with the professional detachment that, in general, was essential if the nursing and medical staff were not to crack under the constant mental strain of working amongst the sick and moribund.

Sammy was transferred to a local civilian hospital especially equipped to provide some new treatment I did not understand, but gathered might help him. He asked me to visit him. 'L-l-love t-t-to s-s-see—i-i-in—p-p-pretty d-d-dress.'

We were forbidden to wear mufti off duty and I had none with me. I bought a sky-blue dress with a frilly collar and blue glass ear-rings shaped as large daisies to match, having long discovered that the average young Englishman's idea of a 'pretty dress' was blue and frilly. One half-day I booked a taxi, and in it removed the greatcoat and cap camouflaging my dress and donned the ear-rings. It was a cold day. The sympathetic taximan thought I would get pneumonia.

Sammy had a single side-ward on the private floor. The youngish, muscular, Sister looked me over. 'Are you a relative, Miss Andrews?'

'No. Just a friend. He asked me to come and see him.'

Her eyes gave me another X-ray. 'Is your name Lucinda?'

'Lucilla.'

'All right. For a few minutes.' At Sammy's door, she hesitated. 'He's not too well.'

Sammy had so shrunk that his cheek and wrist bones looked in danger of breaking through the shiny surface. His speech was almost unintelligible, but eyes and smile remained coherent. I was glad I had bought the blue dress and ear-rings.

The Sister returned and said brightly, 'You must come again after his op. I can see you've done him good. Time to say goodbye now, Mr. . . .'

I waved and smiled from his doorway. Sammy smiled and tried to wave back. The Sister closed the door. 'If you care to ring me tomorrow evening I'll be here on-duty and will be able to tell you how he's got on after the theatre.'

The next evening she said over the telephone, 'Yes, we're all very sorry. Three o'clock this afternoon. Very peaceful. He didn't suffer.'

Betty was on-duty. I raged round to Ollie's billets. 'He didn't suffer! What about all these weeks? My God, I'll never train if it means turning into a callous block of ice!'

Ollie was only slightly older than myself, but much more mature. 'Stop taking everything at face value! She only meant, he didn't die in agony. She can't be a callous bitch or she wouldn't have busted red tape and let you see him. You're not his next-of-kin, a relative, or fiancée and I'll bet she spotted your greatcoat in that carrier bag and that he'd told her you'd nursed him. You know damn well hospital etiquette forbids nurses to call on their patients once they've been transferred to other wards, and I'll bet that goes for other hospitals too.' She handed me a gin and lime. 'Knock that back and use your loaf. Would you really like to have seen poor old Sammy lingering on and weeping over the biscuits and cheese like Johnny?'

'No. No!'

Johnny, who was warded in one of our single rooms, was another Battle of Britain casualty. He was in the late twenties. The only one of his former girl-friends who still visited him, occasionally, told me he had looked like a younger Gary Cooper. The face under the white cranial cap was a pink, pinkly seamed, mask. The eyes in that mask were the eyes of a confused child.

He was now able to feed himself. One lunch, after collecting his barely touched soup, then the shepherd's pie, I took in biscuits and cheese. 'You haven't eaten much. Would you like some biscuits and cheese?'

'Yea.' Pause. 'Like cheese.'

Fifteen minutes later I returned for his tray. He was sitting staring at the tray on the bedtable. The biscuits and cheese were untouched, the former on the side plate, latter in a small dish. 'Didn't feel like any after all?'

He looked up and his eyes filled with tears. 'Yea. Can't remember—how to eat 'em?'

'Shall I show you?'

'Yea.' The tears poured down the pink mask. 'Want to eat 'em.'

'You will. Like this.' I put the cheese on the biscuit plate, cut the lump in tiny pieces, snapped the biscuits, put a bit of cheese on each bit of biscuit. 'Now, pick up two bits together with your hand and put them in your mouth. Then eat it. That's right. Then again.' I dried his eyes. 'See?'

'Yea.' A very long pause. 'Thanks.'

I had only told this to the senior relief Sister on that day and to Ollie, as she cleaned his room daily and had grown as fond of him as I had of Sammy. The relief Sister said in view of his gross injuries it was only to be expected but the fact that he had managed to finish the biscuits and cheese by himself was a hopeful sign. Ollie had nearly wept. 'I'll bet he was polite! He's so damned nice!'

'Didn't he get a gong for it?'

'He did!' She retorted savagely. 'And isn't that bloody nice of them?'

I handed her some of her own gin.

In December Betty and I were moved from the hospital to work in the VAD Mess, there known as the Hostel. Our Commandant called us Home VADs; we called ourselves Hostel Skivvies. In the Hostel we cleaned all the rooms but the kitchen and scullery—the VAD cooks' prerogative—set, served, cleared, washed-up all the day staff's meals and night staff's breakfast and suppers. As the day staff needed breakfast before going on-duty at 7.30 a.m. and supper after coming off at 8 p.m., our working day started at 6.30 a.m. and with luck was finished by 10 p.m. We had the usual three hours off daily, generally in mid-afternoon, and, as we were often reminded, the added bonus of two extra days off when our four weeks ended.

On Christmas Eve, turkeys, sausages, puddings, sacks of potatoes and brussels sprouts jammed kitchen and scullery and gallons of bread sauce simmered on the Aga cookers. That night, as Betty and I were about to return to our billets, we noticed a light still on under the scullery door. In the scullery two junior cooks were struggling to open two huge sacks.

'Sprouts, and we've got to finish 'em now as there'll be no time in the morning.' We hung our greatcoats, tin hats and respirators on the empty plate-racks, found knives, buckets, stools and settled down with them. One cook had a good voice. She sang us *The Folks That Live On The Hill* as a solo, then re-arranged it as a part song. Our Commandant's head came round the door, 'You all sound very happy in here, gels!' When we judged her shut in her own room on the other side of the front hall, I taught the others the words Ollie and I had composed to the tune and refrain of *You'll Be Far Better Off In A Home*. (Several weeks later in a staff concert for the patients, Ollie and I, dressed in hospital 'blues', sang in duet a somewhat less bawdy version and, for the only time in my life, stopped the show.)

When we finished we made cocoa and sat on the kitchen table to drink it. One of the cooks recalled it was Christmas Day. 'Happy Christmas, girls! And when the kids ask—and what did you do in the Big War, Mummy? And you say— peeled ruddy sprouts till one on Christmas morning—they'll never ruddy believe you!'

When our four weeks ended, we were granted our first week of 'privilege' leave since call-up. Our parents had been back in St Leonards for about two months, we were given free travel warrants and so able to go home for the first time since February. Had we lived in the Hostel and not in billets, almost certainly our warrants would have been cancelled before we could use them. Being billeted, we collected the signed warrants the evening before our leave started on the following morning.

All that intervening night the southern sky was red. Sixty miles away the City of London was burning again. We watched the sky anxiously, set our alarms for five-thirty, by six were cycling furtively for the railway station and praying none of our authorities were yet awake or near telephones. We guessed, rightly, that with daylight all travel warrants that involved journeys to or through London would be cancelled or post-poned. 'Won't matter which to the Army. It'll end up for-getting our leave like my four nights off.'

The R.T.O. at the station looked too sleepy to care if our warrants were written in German and signed by Hitler. 'Yes, there's a train waiting. Been waiting hours. Don't ask me when it will get to London, but if it does, ask again about trains to the coast.' He opened a carriage door, shone his torchlight over sleeping soldiers. 'Shift up, chaps—there's good chaps—shift up. In you get, ladies!' He pushed us in, slammed the door, the sleepers groaned but obligingly moved aside to give us the last two seats.

It was just light and the whole carriage was awake when to our combined relief, our train pulled out. We were all in uniform, on leave, and convinced any minute we would be recalled to our units. During the just-under six-hour, sixty-mile journey, we swopped sandwiches, chocolates, cigarettes, bomb—service-horrors—and life stories, and were equally astounded to find we had reached Charing Cross. 'Give over! Jerry's got to be slipping! Why hasn't he flattened it, eh? He's had the time! Losing his grip, I reckon.'

The next R.T.O. said someone had told him a few trains might be running down to the Sussex coast from Victoria that evening. 'Not before 18.00 hours, I gather. Give you time to have a look round. Last night? Oh yes. Jerry put on quite a show. Got the City. Not clear yet how much is still standing, apart from St Paul's. Didn't get St Paul's. Got a small one in through the roof, that's all. Dome's intact. Transport? You take my tip, ladies, and footslog it. Get around much quicker.'

A little traffic was moving again in the Strand and up Fleet Street. A great pall of dark smoke still overhung the City and as we walked closer the acrid air hurt the eyes, nostrils and throat. There were ropes right across the foot of Ludgate Hill and one of the many policemen told us most of the City was roped off. 'Can we get a little closer to look at St Paul's, please?'

The police looked at our uniforms, and as we were back in the war, we were back to wearing armour, and passports. The police held up the ropes for us to duck under, and one walked with us. 'Didn't get St Paul's, did he?' he said.

We walked slowly up Ludgate Hill in the middle of the road.

On either side the blackened smouldering shells of buildings belched black smoke, and down side streets and narrow alleys tongues of yellow flames licked and spat into the thickening grey air. An army of firemen and A.R.P. rescue squads were still working. 'Got a right job on here.' The policeman stopped walking. 'No nearer, nurses, and can't hang about long. No telling what'll come down next and what hasn't yet gone off.'

In silence we stood and looked up at the great dome of the cathedral built to replace the old St Paul's destroyed in that other Fire of London. There were other buildings standing, but in those moments Wren's St Paul's, smeared and blurred by smoke, surrounded by devastation, seemed the only intact building in the City, and because it was intact seemed of far more than aesthetic importance. Turning away, we said, as everyone we spoke to said in London that day, 'Didn't get St Paul's, did he?'

Beyond the ropes and just round the corner in Farringdon Street, a WVS mobile canteen was parked. Three middle-aged women were serving mugs of tea and sandwiches to relays of firemen and A.R.P. workers. The men pushed their black tin hats back on their heads whilst they drank, and mopped their blackened faces with engrimed handkerchiefs that left more streaks of dirt than they removed. (In notes made the following day, 'Those men looked like badly made-up clowns.') They all moved slowly, heavily, under the weight of fatigue, and one noticed us, and called softly, 'Wotcher, nurses!' Then others turned, smiled and jerked up thumbs and we smiled and jerked up ours in return. We were still talking to the police by the ropes when one by one the men drained their mugs, ducked under the ropes, and walked back up Ludgate Hill. The police asked if we had seen Piccadilly Circus. 'One or two changes there.'

On our way back along Fleet Street an elderly woman wearing a dirty floral apron appeared in a doorway, folded her arms and nodded at us. 'Seen St Paul's, ducks? Didn't get it, did he? Not for want of trying, either. Makes you think, don't it?'

There were ropes around Piccadilly Circus, but again we were allowed through. Again there were still men working amongst the rubble, again black, jagged roofless buildings, again street craters. The men worked silently, carefully, in case a sudden sound, or too much force, brought down a wall or roof on those undiscovered and still buried alive. The silence accentuated the sounds; the steady clink of rubble being moved by hand, the chorus of smoke-induced coughs, the slow footsteps on pavements and the wooden planks laid across some of the craters. The slow footsteps belonged to the handful of other sightseers in service uniforms, probably, like ourselves, waiting for trains they hoped would be running later. Their expressions were as stunned as our own. All of us walked and gazed around as if sleepwalking.

We stopped on one wooden plank over a crater not yards from the front entrance of Swan and Edgar's and looked down at the exposed morass of pipes, paving stones, and chunks of tarmac. Betty whispered, 'I wonder if we'll really believe we've actually done this later. This is Piccadilly Circus, Lucy.'

'I know. I'm glad Daddy can't see it.'

We moved on and I kept repeating those words in my mind, and then, absurdly, remembering the old London music hall songs father always sang when shaving in the morning. Through my illness in 1938, I knew all the words of *Any Old Iron, Boiled Beef And Carrots, My Old Man Said Follow The Van, Knocked 'Em In The Old Kent Road* and others.

We heard no songs in London on that bleak, cold, charcoal-coloured afternoon. Everything and everyone reeked of smoke. Most of the faces were dirty and exhausted, and some were annoyed, some angry, and some, incredibly, cheerful. Everywhere were tatty little chalked or scribbled notices: 'Open for business round the back—if you can find the back let me know. Signed. Prop.' 'Chestnuts roasted while you wait. Ta for the free heat Jerry!' And variations on the words already (unknown to me) pasted on St Thomas's collecting boxes, 'Down but not out. Open for business as usual.'

Here and there a cheap, bedraggled little Union Jack fluttered from the top of a pile of rubble. And again and again, scrawled on walls, painted over battened shop windows and across blistered front doors, 'London can take it'.

Slang when used in its right time has one advantage over good English since everyone of that time knows precisely what it means. Being of that time, on that afternoon of 30th December 1940, we knew those last four words contained neither false bravado nor arrogance, but merely a plain statement of fact.

Chapter Seven

IT was only in 1941 that I properly appreciated how the war had my immediate generation by the throat, and this sensation of being trapped by circumstances was shared by millions of my fellow-civilians in uniform, whose lives were equally organized, steam-rollered, and for some ended, by invisible, all-powerful authority.

Every day in the papers maps of North Africa decorated with arrows. One day the arrows pointed left, the next right, then left again, as the opposing armies in the desert swayed backwards and forwards with the restlessness of the sand. In the post, news of schoolfriends in the WAAF, WRNS, ATS and so many St Leonards boys in the armies overseas that not one in my home circle remained in the UK.

Sister Blood-and-Guts vanished to Africa. Betty back to St Leonards for a few months before joining the WAAF for the duration. In late January she heard through the International Red Cross that Tony had died in France in June 1940 and, being just clear of the conscripted age, she resigned from the VADs. A note dated: 2nd March 1941: 'This morning I sewed on my first War Service stripe. It looks like an enormous D.F.C. ribbon worn high on the left sleeve and signifies that Andrews L. M., W/640714, BRCS, Sussex 14, has nursed the Army on active service for one year—actually it's nearly thirteen months but like everything else in the Army my stripe was late in arriving.'

I had then been moved into a single billet in another private house. Through my new landlady I met G, a Flying Officer in the RAF and former newly qualified architect. I only knew him for seven weeks, but as he was the first man I loved and wanted to marry, I remembered those weeks for years. Those seven were the last weeks of G's short life. He was twenty-seven when his aircraft was shot down somewhere off The Wash. It was never recovered.

Afterwards, I had from his best friend on the station the kind of letter received by thousands of other women from other men's best friends in our war—and I imagine in all wars since men could write and women read.

'. . . I am sorry to have to tell you this but I promised him I would let you know if anything like this happened. I'm afraid it will be a great shock and I'm sorry. I'm afraid I don't know what else to say, but I'm very sorry. . . .'

My landlady and Ollie, the only other person to whom I had talked of G in his lifetime, made me tea. Pot after pot of tea. I wondered numbly, as I was to wonder on other occasions of intense personal grief, what had been the automatic English reaction to bereavement before tea was first introduced into England. Years had to pass before I dared wonder what might have happened in the life G and I had just begun to plan together, had our youth not chanced to coincide with an holocaust.

Eventually, Ollie asked, 'What now? Try for a transfer?'

'No. I've had standing still. I'll train. The Army'll let me out to do general. I'll try for one of the London hospitals, only not B.-and-G.'s.'

'When did you make up your mind?'

'I dunno. Made itself up. All I've got to do now is fix on a hospital then see if it'll take me. Do you know the form for applying?'

'Not sure. Ask around in this new bunch of Sisters. Most look quite young and almost human.'

I took her advice. 'What's a goodtime girl like you want to train for—and don't kid me you're not having a good time with your looks! What's that—? You really want to be a—oh, no! Sorry to laugh, Andrews, but it's so funny—you—a writer! You can't even spell! Remember asking me yesterday if "dose" had a "z"? Not to worry! You'll get married and forget all about this nonsense before you're much older!'

I never understood that reaction, and particularly not in the period following G.'s death when I felt as I imagined it felt to bleed internally. I overlooked the fact that I possessed both the tremendous physical resilience of healthy youth, and the kind of blank chocolate-box prettiness that can so often be an obstacle to the understanding of others, and much more often to other women than to men. That reaction left me confused, angry, and hurt.

One week a new senior Sister took temporary charge of my ward. She was a tallish, slender young woman with a cheerful smile who seemed so young that initially I thought her fresh from training-school. Then I heard from others that she had worked in battle zones and on a hospital ship that had been sunk.

In that week she transformed our working life by reducing floor-scrubbing to the necessary minimum and giving us classes in all slack periods. In one class she told us she had been a ward sister in her training hospital before the war. She did not name her hospital until one evening when she and I were alone in the ward kitchens and about to serve the patients' suppers. The first course was soup. At the last moment I discovered our soup ladle was missing. I apologized and braced myself for the inevitable blast. Sister Blood-and-Guts, and others, would have blown me through the roof. The newcomer smiled, 'Have to manage without.' She helped herself to a one-pint china jug, removed her cuffs, pushed up her sleeves, dug the jug into the simmering white soup. 'I dread to think what my Sister PTS would say could she see me dishing up with my sleeves up.'

'Where did you train, Sister?'

'St Thomas's. The Nightingale Training-School.'

'Hasn't St Thomas's been blitzed, Sister?'

'On and off.' She filled the bowls on my tray with care. 'Off you go and I'll get on with the next batch.'

On my return, 'Is St Thomas's still working, Sister?'

She looked amused. 'My child, as St Thomas's has been working since 1153 the habit is a little old to break.'

'I didn't know it was that old! Oldest in London?'

'Bart's is fifty years older.' She glanced at my stripe. 'Thinking of training?'

'Yes, Sister.'

'Take those round and I'll investigate this fish pie.' When I got back with my empty tray, 'Why are you still only thinking about training? I know it'll take a long time, but I'm afraid we're in for a long war.'

I hesitated before answering. Then I thought, as so often, what does anything really matter now G's dead? I explained and waited tensely for her to laugh.

She gave me a long, thoughtful look. 'Yes, I see your problem. How much writing have you done in the Army?'

'Lots of notes. Not much else. No time.'

'There wouldn't be. Nor can I pretend you'll have any more if you do train in St Thomas's—in fact, you'll have less as you'll have lectures to write up in your free time. But you will learn how to nurse and I think you should. And in the process, if you really want to learn about people—and if you are going to be a writer you certainly should—you'll learn a tremendous amount. Won't that help you when you stop nursing and become a writer? Can any writer know too much about human nature? Then why not get yourself the double training simultaneously at St Thomas's?'

Momentarily, I just stared in astounded relief. 'How do I apply, Sister? Just write to the Matron of St Thomas's?'

'That's right. London, SE1.'

She had left our ward, and I think the hospital, before I wrote my application on my next half-day. I was sorry I could not tell her I had taken her advice and for once broke my defensive rule of avoiding full names in my always unlocked notes, to record, 'her name is Theodora Turner'. (In retrospect I suspect Miss T. Turner, O.B.E., A.R.R.C., would have been as surprised as myself when I made that entry, if then told I was recording the name of a future Matron of St Thomas's.)

'Thomas's, Lucy? You haven't a hope in hell of being accepted. It's the most difficult hospital in the country to get

into—you need the Matric. and you've only got School
Cert. . . .'

'Thomas's, Andrews? Why not go into a convent and have
done?'

'Thomas's, eh? Oh well, as they say—

> Guy's to flirt,
> Bart's to work,
> Thomas's if you're a lady.

Enjoy yourself amongst all the toffee-noses!'

'Naturally, St Thomas's has to be careful only to admit the
right type, Lucilla. As Matron explained when she accepted
me, the Nightingale Training-School was founded by Miss
Nightingale herself and was the first nurses' training-school
in the world. That's why St Thomas's nurses are called
Nightingales—frankly, one's rather looking forward to being a
Nightingale. . . .'

'So you want to enter my training-school, nurse? Far be it
from me to put you off, but I think it only fair to tell you
nothing would persuade this Old Nightingale to endure her
training again! Four years of sheer slavery.'

Mother said, 'You won't last three months in St Thomas's.'

And Father, 'If this is what you really want, you'll get in.
Let me know what I have to sign and underwrite.'

It was traditional at St Thomas's that on Tuesday mornings
the Matron, who was also Lady Superintendent of The
Nightingale Training School, should interview in her private
office in St Thomas's, London, applicants to her School. One
Tuesday in May 1941, with two other VADs who had applied
in the same week as myself, I was summoned for interview by
the incumbent Matron. (The late Miss G. V. Hillyers.)

We travelled to London by train, in outdoor uniform, with
buttons and cap badges unnaturally gleaming, and the starch
in my clean shirt collar slicing my neck. Our train deposited us
at Waterloo on time, more to the surprise of our fellow-
passengers than ourselves, as in our pre-interview nervousness
we had overlooked the fact that in the last couple of days
London had had another major air raid. 'Third big 'un this

spring,' said a passenger. 'Ah well, summer soon. Maybe Jerry'll go on his summer holidays.'

We walked from Waterloo to the hospital. It was only a short walk down the Waterloo Road, over the crossing at the southern end of Westminster Bridge then into the Lambeth Palace Road with the hospital sprawling for as far as I could see on the river side. It was the first time I had seen St Thomas's. At first sight that morning it did not look like a hospital. It looked like parts of the City after the fire.

I did not then know St Thomas's had started the war with eight individual blocks and the mortuary a ninth and smaller building at the Lambeth Palace end of the line that ranged from Westminster Bridge, so I did not recognize the extent of the damage since last September. I saw a jumble of three blocks standing close together and one of these looked less than intact. All three had bricks instead of glass in the upper windows and their ground floors were hidden by anti-blast walls and stacks of sandbags. On either side of the standing blocks were the now omnipresent in London blackened roofless buildings, jagged walls, gaping glassless windows, piles of rubble and grime, and one semi-ruined block (4) was still smouldering. A crowd of begrimed men were busy clearing the chaos, and there was a line of ambulances outside a heavily sandbagged entrance marked 'Casualty Department'.

A porter directed us. 'You don't want Cas., nurses, you want Central Hall. Old main entrance. Just along there then up those stone steps. You go on in through the Hall, turn right past Miss Nightingale—you can't miss her—then a mite down the main corridor to your right and you'll see the alcove to the Matron's Office on your left. Can't miss it and when you get there an Office Sister will be waiting to look after you.'

The stone steps led up to tall, heavily battened doors guarded on either side by little stone figures of nineteenth-century cripples. There was no electric light on in the empty Hall. It was so darkened by the bricked-in windows and the battens that it was a few seconds before I saw the cracked plaster on walls and ceilings, the plaster and dust on the floor, and the duckboards laid across a gap in the corridor floor a few feet from the larger-than-life stone statue of Florence Night-ingale holding her lamp.

One of the other girls said, 'Did you notice that porter called her "Miss Nightingale?" '

I vaguely recalled someone, probably one of the VADs already accepted by St Thomas's, telling me to say 'Miss' and not 'Florence' if the name came up in my interview. 'Simply not done to call her "Florence" in St Thomas's.' And with that thought in mind, for the first time on a duckboard I crossed the long ground floor main corridor that had once connected all the blocks.

And crossed into an alcove of orderly calm presided over by a trim figure in a navy blue-and-white-spotted Sister's dress, impeccable white apron and befrilled cap with a lace bow under her chin. 'Good morning! Matron will see you in alphabetical order. Now, which is Miss Andrews? Come with me. Will you two others just sit here.'

It was an extraordinary sensation to walk through devast-ation, step off duckboards and be ushered through one large neat office to a slightly smaller but slightly more luxurious office smelling of polish and normality. 'How do you do, Miss Andrews. Please sit down. Now. Tell me a little about yourself. . . .'

I was offered a place in the set of new probationers due to enter the Preliminary Training School on the 21st September. 'In a large country house we have taken in the village of Shamley Green in Surrey. Very lovely country. I'm sure you will enjoy it.'

Back over the duckboards and whilst I waited for the others, back for a closer look at the stone figure with the lamp, and at the rough wooden wall that ran for a considerable length and narrowed the main corridor. I wondered why it was there, but lacked the courage to ask until an elderly porter stopped to ask if I had lost my way. 'No, thanks. Just waiting. Excuse me, but why is this wall here?'

'Had to put it up, miss. Didn't want to have us all falling down the hole that's the other side, did they? Seventy foot wide it is. Not surprising, mind, seeing the dispensary was down there. Jerry got one slap on it, he did.'

'When?'

'Back at the start—Sunday night, last September. And a proper night it was. Lost two of the doctors that night we did and it's a wonder we didn't lose more seeing as he got Medical Out-Patients and most of College House—that'll be the doctors' house, miss. Proper night it was! Come the morning —oh dear me—what a morning! No water, no gas, no light. And patients coming in all the time—every time you looked round there was a new lot waiting. So we had to start shifting 'em out down the country. Quite nice down there they says.'

He was a small man with grey hair, glasses and a worried expression. 'You don't like the country?'

'All right for some. Too quiet, I reckon. Give me London every time, I say. Mind you, I'm not saying I'd not fancy a bit more quiet here. Noisy week we've had. Still, we got our water this time. Not like last month when Jerry dropped one slap atween the two blocks, busted the water-pipes and gives all the patients in the basement wards a good wash down. Proper shower-bath they had. But we shifted 'em out into the corridors and dried 'em off. No harm done, seemly. Got good basements we have.'

Despite the visible evidence, I thought he had spun me an old soldiers' tale. I later learnt he had understated, and all he had said was true. One of the facts he left out was that the raid on that Sunday night in September 1940 caused three members of the hospital staff to be awarded George Medals. (Dr H. R. B. Norman, resident assistant physician, Mr P. B. Maling, medical student, Mr H. E. Frewer, assistant Clerk of the Works.)

To quote from part of the official intimation: 'After St Thomas's Hospital had been hit by a H.E. bomb it was found that two of the staff were trapped. Mr Frewer formed a rescue party and was joined by Dr Norman and Mr Maling. The débris had crashed through the ground floor into the basement. The dispensary stores had been destroyed and the alcohol and acids caught fire. Gas was escaping and masonry continually falling. Mr Frewer led the rescue party. Dr

Norman, assisted by Mr Maling, burrowed into the débris and gave morphia injections. They succeeded in extricating the casualties.'

I only learnt this when training and only by asking innumerable questions. This was no reflection on brave men, but simply because old air raids became old hospital history within days of the event. During the periods when air raids were part of the normal hospital routine, as in the many, very long intervals without raids, everyone was too busy continuing with the normal routine of caring for the sick, of teaching or being taught, to recall yesterday.

'Once you get in the wards, nurses,' said Sister P.T.S., 'before you have had time to draw breath your training will be over. And please remember you will work IN and not ON the wards.'

The old P.T.S. in London had been destroyed. In that Surrey country house the spirit lived on, as did the lifesize dolls on which decades of young Nightingale nurses had learnt to blanket bath. Mrs Mackintosh, Lady Chase, and George, a baby boy of convenient physique to allow him to double as a baby girl. In the absence of an adult male doll, the technique for blanket-bathing men was explained with ambiguous exactitude. At a precise point after the second change of washing water, the freshly soaped 'back' flannel and 'back' towel were to be handed the patient with the words, 'I am sure you would like to finish yourself off now, Mr Blank, whilst I fetch your mouthwash.'

Straight back to school; to sitting up straight at our desks, no talking in class; morning and evening prayers; lights out at ten-thirty; Grace before meals; cocoa at mid-morning break.

The conversations at break were different.

'Think Jerry will get to Moscow?'

'Don't ask me. I still haven't got over the shock of his attacking the Russians last summer (22nd June 1941). I thought they were terrific buddies.'

'I wish to God they'd stayed buddies. My boy-friend's freezing to death ferrying the Russians goodies to Murmansk. This paper says Jerry's taking same route as Napoleon.'

'I thought the Russians were holding him up at Leningrad—or do I mean Stalingrad?'

'Both. Leningrad's north, Moscow in the middle, Stalingrad south.'

Many of my set were ex-VADs also training because of the war, others had first done other full-time jobs, a few more were straight from school. The minimum entry age was nineteen.

'Do me a favour, Lu. Cut the nails on my right hand.'

'Sure. Hurt your left?'

'No. I just can't manage. Mummy's always cut my right-hand nails.'

'What happened at school?'

'I didn't go away. Mummy thinks boarding-schools make girls too independent.'

'How does she feel about your coming here?'

'Well, She says since I've got to do war-work at least nursing is a ladylike occupation.'

One night near the end of the two months' term:

'Will someone please tell me WHAT that lecture was all about?'

'My God, Lu, are you another who didn't catch on? Bloody funny! Don't know what a lesbian or a homosexual is? Gather round, chickies, and aunty will elucidate. . . .'

'You may read your papers now, nurses . . . last five minutes, nurses . . . stop writing now, please, nurses.'

P.T.S. finals, the first of the many written, viva voce and practical examinations ahead.

At the end of the first year, Hospital Nursing; in the second, Hospital Anatomy and Physiology, the Preliminary State Examination, Hospital Gynaecology; in the third, Hospital Surgery, Hospital Medicine, and at the year's end, State Finals followed shortly by the most vital and difficult of all, Hospital Finals. Beyond—S.R.N.s with Nightingale Certificates and Nightingale Badges.

When we were training, 1941–45, all our lectures, with the very rare isolated exception, had to be attended in our daily three hours off, or on our days off; all academic studying done in our free time, and generally after working a full day or night. For the benefit of the night nurses who had to be in bed by noon, after the first year (no first years did night-duty) our lectures all began at 9.30 a.m. The night nurses were easily identifiable as the sleepers in the back rows.

First year day hours were similar to those I had worked in military hospitals, but only for six days a week. St Thomas's had recently introduced the previously undreamed of luxury to ex-VADs, of a weekly day off for all student nurses. From the second year onwards our day hours were extended to finish at 9 p.m. On night-duty we worked from 9 p.m. to 8 a.m. and, as in the Army, ate our night meals in our ward kitchens or duty-rooms as time and work permitted. Each spell of night-duty lasted for three months; after each shift of twenty-one consecutive working nights we had three nights off.

In my first year we were paid £7 per quarter. The second, again £28 per annum, but as this was paid monthly and superannuation removed, the total was about £25. Third year, £36 per annum. Fourth, once an S.R.N., £60 per annum.

To the best of my knowledge, these rates of pay and working hours applied generally to student nurses in the UK, as did the custom of providing nurses with full board, lodging, indoor uniforms—not stockings and shoes—and indoor uniform laundry allowances. Being civilian nurses, when we travelled from our parent hospitals to work in the various Sectors—blanket terms for the many Emergency Medical Services hospitals opened by the Government—we travelled at our own expense. The E.M.S. hospitals catered for service and civilian patients, and were staffed by civilian doctors and nurses borrowed from civilian medical teaching and nurses' training hospitals. Without these large, loaned, and in the main regularly changing contingents of staff, the E.M.S. hospitals could not have functioned. The last free travel warrant I received as a nurse in the Second World War was in late August 1941, to go home to St Leonards after being released from the VADs.

After the P.T.S. and a week's holiday, back to Hampshire and another great red-brick, former mental now general hospital on an isolated hilltop and resembling not army barracks but a prison camp. The high water-tower looming over the ugly cluster of red-brick gave the immediate impression of sheltering guards with machine-guns. An impression enhanced by the barbed wire surrounding extensive grounds largely devoted to regimental ranks of unattractive cabbages, the many old notices, PATIENTS WILL NOT ADVANCE BEYOND THIS POINT, the miles of green-tiled corridors smelling of carbolic and excreta, the omnipresent sash windows that could only be opened for a few inches at top or bottom and were so often additionally barred, and the huge brass locks and heavy keys on all the doors.

The hospital had about two thousand beds and, as usually obtained in E.M.S. hospitals, each of the several hospitals contributing staff was allotted its own wards and departments and tended to keep itself to itself. Arguably, none more zealously than St Thomas's. My set as Nightingale pros (only St Thomas's first-year student nurses were 'pros'), worked under Nightingale Sisters, were taught by a Nightingale Sister Tutor, and lived together in a former patients' dormitory converted with curtains into two- and three-bedded cubicles in the care of a Nightingale Home Sister. We shared the vast nursing staff's dining-room with all the other hospitals, but by the time of our arrival unwritten law had been written and every hospital had its own block of tables. The only personal contact I ever had with non-Nightingale nurses was in the long queues at the serving-counters in the dining-room when we groaned in unison, 'Not tinned pilchards and Yellow Peril again!' Yellow Peril was bright yellow unsweetened blancmange.

There were no inter-staff canteens, nor communal restrooms, but in the library I discovered D. H. Lawrence, Hardy, Sinclair Lewis, Tolstoy, Emily Brontë, and that Charlotte Brontë had written more than *Jane Eyre*. On-duty I discovered sailors made even better patients than soldiers.

I was sent with two others from my set to be junior pros (the lowest form of hospital life) in a men's medical ward filled with sailors suffering from peptic ulcers, diabetes and a type of jaundice that, according to the sailors, was decimating the Royal Navy. 'Whole ship's company come out yellow, nurse. Reckoned I'd berthed with a load of Chinks!'

The ward had forty beds divided between three largish former epileptic patients' dormitories. The bedsprings were roughly eighteen inches from the floor. This worried the sailors. 'Enough to break your backs after making beds all round this low, nurse.'

Neither my aching back nor the perpetual fire in my feet worried me nearly so much as the junior pros' personal domain, the sluice. 'Why didn't whoever converted this from the housemaid's pantry, or whatever it was, realize medical patients are mostly bed-patients, bed-patients need bedpans and to empty bedpans properly without machines, you need some power behind these water-jets. Can't even clean a bottle (urinal) properly with this swine.'

Having to ask the pros for bedpans worried the sailors. They were great worriers on our behalf, amazingly undemanding, appreciative patients, and clean. Once any sailor was fit to stagger out of bed, he staggered to the nearest bathroom hand-basin and began washing his smalls and festooning radiators with cap, collar linings, lanyards, vests, and the innumerable other bits of white incorporated in Leading, Able, and Ordinary Seamen's uniforms. Like the soldiers, the sailors had mates, but called them 'oppos'.

On my birthday, 20th November, I worked the duty we called 'long trot'. 7.30–10 a.m., 3 hours off, 1–8 p.m. Just after seven that evening I re-cleaned the sluice in a very bad temper having been told it was a disgrace. 'Hve you looked down your bedpan handles, N. Andrews? Have you examined the insides of your bottles?'

I slammed shut the sluice door, tied a long rubber apron round my waist and demanded aloud of the stacks of bedpans and bottles if I looked the kind of girl who went round peering into handles and bottles. 'Either I have to empty you with my eyes shut and holding my breath or I can't empty you at all.'

Another senior head came round the door, 'N. Andrews,

what do you think you're doing?' The question was clearly rhetorical as she vanished swiftly. To cheer myself, I answered to the bedpans and bottles with an adaption of one of Jack Warner's enormously popular monologues on the BBC wireless programme Garrison Theatre:

'I'm a girl what washes bottles in a sluice room,
But a bottle washer-upper's what I yearns,
Still as long as there are bottles there'll be washers-up of
  bottles,
So it looks as though I got the job for years.'

One of my set came in, leant against the door and gazed at the sink as if seeing the Holy Grail. 'Do you realize if Jerry hadn't bombed STH, London, we'd be junior pros in wards with mechanical bedpan and bottle washers?'

I slung more enamel bottles into a solution of carbolic. 'I can forgive Jerry a lot—not this!'

'Think there'll be anything of STH, London, left by the time we're senior enough to get there?'

'Maybe the war'll be over by then. Much quieter now Jerry's so busy in Russia.'

On 7th December 1941, the Japanese attacked the US Navy in Pearl Harbour. I was in the ward when the news came over the wireless. The sailors lowered newspapers, magazines, books, and listened with bemused incredulity or derisive grins. 'Stone me! Whole ship's company taken the liberty-boat?'

The jaundiced congratulated each other and themselves. 'Couldn't be more yellow if we was Japs could we, nurse? Interned for the duration—that's us!'

No grins, no jokes, nor for a while any talking at all when we heard the Japanese had sunk the battleship *Prince of Wales* and the battle-cruiser *Repulse*. (Off the coast of S.E. Asia on 10th December 1941). The stunned reaction of those sick sailors was unlike any ward reaction to national disaster I had yet encountered. It seemed not national but personal. Until then I had assumed the Navy to be as divided into units and loyalties as the Army. In that ward were men from the RN, RNR, RNVR, but suddenly it was as if all were members of the same ship's company and the men who had gone down with those great ships were literally their shipmates.

Normally, the high spot of the patients' day was Vera Lynn's fifteen-minute evening broadcast. I heard a senior nurse quietly ask a Chief Petty Officer, 'Rather not, this evening?'

He looked round the silent ward. 'I think we'll have Vera, please, nurse.'

Normally, whilst Vera Lynn sang, the patients smiled to themselves, or hummed with her. That evening they listened without expression, in silence. At that period '*We'll meet again*' still made me want to cry for G. That evening I had to duck into my sluice sanctuary to weep for two unknown ships' companies, the tears my sick sailors were trying not to shed.

The short winter days and the war news darkened together. New maps headed the war reports. Maps of Hong Kong, Malaya, Singapore, Burma, that temporarily drove our new, mighty US Allies from the headlines.

'Say that again!'

'Hong Kong's surrendered to the Japs. On the news just now.'

'Oh, no! I say—Mary's fiancé's there. Does she know?'

'Yes. She heard the news with me. She's gone out on her bike. She doesn't want to talk.'

'That figures. I say—er—your brother?'

'Far as I know in Singapore, thank God. Hope he stays there.'

'Good morning, nurses. In today's lecture we will discuss barrier-nursing. Barrier-nursing is required when a patient with a communicable infection is nursed in a general ward. To take a very common example; pulmonary tuberculosis. You will meet a great many tuberculosis patients in the course of your training so it is essential for you to learn and observe the stringent precautions that must be taken to prevent the infection being transmitted to the other patients and yourselves. Only too frequently do young doctors, nurses and medical students succumb to the tubercle bacilli. . . .'

The hospital was too far for me to go home for my days off. When lecture-free I usually slept till first lunch at noon and in the afternoons or evenings typed with two fingers on the elderly Remington portable father had loaned me since my last holiday at home. My set endured the irritation with amused tolerance. Home Sister was intrigued and her white-haired, white-befrilled head regularly appeared between my cubicle curtains, 'Still hard at it, nurse? Ah well, there's no doubt you look to be enjoying yourself, but don't forget to take some fresh air on your day off. A good nurse must take care of her own health for her patients' sake as much as herself.'

One day off in mid-February, 1942; 'Wake up, Lu! Wake up!'

I squinted at my watch. 'Why the hell? It's only just after eleven.'

'I know, but I'm on-duty, I've only got permission to nip back for a clean apron and if you haven't heard you'll probably drop bricks at lunch. The Japs have taken Singapore.'

'They can't have! Everyone says Singapore's our greatest base in the Far East and absolutely impregnable!'

'The Japs have got it. BBC news.'

'God Almighty,' I whispered.

So many times when all I could say or write was—'I am so sorry'. All I could do—put on kettles and hand out tea, but in old jam jars not cups as my set's private store of crockery had run out, the hospital had none to spare on loan to the nurses' dormitories, and in the nearest shops in the small town four miles away the crockery shelves were empty.

One afternoon in March: 'Still hard at it, N. Andrews? I fear your wee book's to be interrupted. Hydestile are short of probationers. You'll be away with the first alphabetical six tomorrow. The rest of your set will follow next month.'

After the bombing in September 1940 and the evacuation of patients from St Thomas's, London, to various hospitals in Surrey, the main body of the hospital had finally found sanctuary in a row of long wooden huts left behind by the Australian Imperial Force in a clearing on the side of a wooded hill in the hamlet of Hydestile, near Godalming. On 17th April 1941, St Thomas's-in-the-country (Hydestile) opened with seventy-two patients in two hut wards. When the six of us reached Hydestile just under a year later, the long wooden, Nissen and brick huts held two hundred and seventy beds and had been transformed into a modern general teaching and training hospital. Within days of our arrival the hut wards lost their identifying numbers. Once the old names were added to the already traditional St Thomas's ward interiors, the bombed wards lived again. Christian, Victoria, Beatrice, George Makins, Arthur Stanley, George, in a row on the higher side of the long, sloping, covered, connecting ramp that at the far end beyond George Ward ran into the woods. In small Nissen huts at the wood end, the surgical stores, the mortuary, the chapel. At the lower side of the ramp, Nightingale, Lilian (the children's ward shortly re-named America to mark the hospital's gratitude for the great generosity shown by US citizens), the Theatre, Casualty in a Nissen hut, and directly opposite Christian, Adelaide. In the rash of other single-storey new buildings; pathological laboratories, staff dining-rooms, canteens, classrooms, administration, College House, and at the main gates a small glass-fronted porter's lodge. And already the wallflowers and first small rose bushes had been planted against the hut walls.

About six miles away in a large country house on a hill near Hascombe, the bombed Nightingale Home was re-born to house, as of old, the first year pros. A special coach ferried us to and fro, leaving the Home every morning at 7 a.m., the hospital every evening at 8.15 p.m. As Hydestile pros we had one day and a half free each week, and on all other weekdays were only off-duty from 10 a.m. to 1 p.m. Late leave, only permitted on half-days or days off, ended at 10.30 p.m. and only in very exceptional circumstances extended to midnight. On full working days we were not allowed to miss supper after duty, or go out at night. We shared varying-sized bedrooms; I always shared with six other girls. When off-duty in the Home, unless in mufti, we had to wear our uniform dresses correctly buttoned and belted, and our caps.

Every day we progressed another day up the first-year ladder and since the year was 1942, so progressed the war disasters. When we drove through country lanes with banks alight with primroses, cowslips, bluebells, pale mauve milk-maidens, the may was out in all the hedges, and every cottage garden golden with daffodils and forsythia, the British retreat from Rangoon to Mandalay was over. All Malaya, all Burma, all the Philippines, all the Dutch East Indies had fallen to the Japanese. No dawn coming up like thunder out of China across the bay for the British Raj. Only the flag showing the rising sun.

When reading the newspaper war reports, I wished I had never nursed soldiers and could think impersonally of armies as fighting machines labelled with numbers, or initials. When I read of 'remnants of the Fourteenth Army fighting gallantly in retreat', of 'a magnificent rearguard action defended to the last by a force of Australians and New Zealanders', I saw the faces of the soldiers I had nursed, met, seen marching; faces that belonged not to 'soldiers' but to men in soldiers' uniforms. I remembered how men looked when wounded, the feel and smell of fresh-spilled blood on skin and khaki, the sounds men made when in pain, the cold, stiffening silence when men died. I remembered the dry heat of Suez. No difficulty to imagine how much more unbearable the dripping festering heat of East Asian jungles.

I had only met a few sailors professionally and whilst still too junior properly to have nursed any. But those sailors in men's medical transformed into reality the dreadful, monthly increasing losses of British ships in the Atlantic. One look at the figures and in my mind the faces of Dusty, Shorty, Lofty, Hooky, the C.P.O. and the boy the whole ward called Half-Pint.

In the North African war reports, two names dominating—General Rommel and the Afrika Korps.

'Too bad we haven't a Rommel. If his Afrika Korps don't slow down the poor old Eighth Army'll be paddling in your Suez Canal.'

'Where's Rommel now? No, thanks, don't want the paper. I'm browned off with reading gloom. Just tell me.'

'Now he's shoved us out of Tobruk they think next stop Alexandria. Go there as a kid?'

'No. Parents were there before I was born.'

'How's your father after his pneumonia?'

'Fine. M. and B. knocked it on the head. He's now raising the best spuds in Sussex on our back lawn. Did I tell you Betty was home on my day off last week? She's posted to Gatwick, driving RAF staff cars and having a wow of a time.'

'So's my sister in Oban. Maybe we should have joined the WAAF and WRNS when we left the VADs. Only snag—I just don't see me square-bashing.'

'Nor me, nor my poor feet.' I was lying on my bed with both legs propped horizontally against my bedside wall. 'Poor feet. You thought you had it tough in the Army. Little did you know how civvy pros footslog.'

My life as a pro was a running battle with the clock. A battle punctuated by extra-breathless skirmishes throughout the day at the appointed hours when the screen across the entrance to the ward itself had either to be put up, or taken down. An open screen across the entrance signified the ward as 'closed' and thereby if a women's ward, out-of-bounds to all men, including consultants. In the men's wards the open screen kept out the teaching rounds but not the steady trickle of itinerant long and short white coats and the tweed jackets with leather patches at elbows and cuffs favoured by the medical students.

'N. Andrews! Is one of my patients suffering a major haemorrhage?'

'No, Sister.'

'I presume the sluice is on fire?'

'No, Sister.'

'Then why have I just seen you run from the sluice into this ward? Please remember a nurse may only run for haemorrhage or fire. In future, walk, nurse. With dignity.'

I learnt to compromise between walking and running by jog-trotting, but never with dignity.

Nearly all the patients were civilians and Lambetheans who were driven down from London in the large ambulance convoys that usually arrived between 1 and 2 p.m. on Mondays and Thursdays. The emergency convoys arrived at irregular hours in the intervals with much the same regularity.

In the men's wards I was surprised by the number of London policemen.

'Didn't you know you're the hospital for the Metropolitan Police? New are you? Then you'll not mind my giving you a tip. When you tidy down your side of the ward of an evening, nurse, make sure you get all the used newspapers, all the ash out the ashtrays, and the feet of your bedcastors nice and straight and facing inwards. Sister gets a bit fussed if she sees a paper forgotten and she doesn't like the castors crooked.'

My ward's Senior Pro (a member of the senior set in the first-year) gave me another tip. 'You can tell the cops on the beat from the C.I.D. as the cops wear the red and blue hospital dressing-gowns and the C.I.D. bring in their own spotted silks.'

The consultants' teaching rounds were near-daily events. Often two rounds went on simultaneously at different parts of the ward. One morning I counted and noted on my apron hem the standing posses on either side. On the left, the senior consultant, chaperoned by Sister, escorted by, the Resident Assistant Physician (the senior resident), a medical registrar, a house-physician and twenty-two students. On the right, another consultant, the Charge Nurse, another registrar, houseman, and eighteen students. For the two hours both rounds lasted, the only sounds in the ward were the consultants flattened voices droning on like overworked bees.

Once, in another ward, a large single teaching round lingered on to the patients' tea-time. I sought the Senior Pro. 'Sister told me to do teas and they're all ready. Do I just wheel in the trolley quietly?'

'No, no, Andrews! Not when the Professor's teaching!'

I had still only mentally sorted the Medical Faculty by their coats, jackets, and my personal impression of their importance. If well tailored, and in black or other sober hue—pundits (Consultants). Very important. Long white coats if covering the R.A.P., or his opposite number the R.A.S.;—pretty important. Short white coats, housemen;—of no importance. Scruffy tweed jackets, medical students;—dead bores and wasters of my precious time in chaperoning when I was late with my work routine. 'I didn't know that pundit was the Professor.'

'If you're going to stay in this ward, you'll learn who's who fast. Sister's got a thing about teas, so we can always tell who's big stuff and who's not by the way we can or can't feed the patients' tea. For the Prof., no teas until he's finished. For Mr ABC, we can take the teas round on trays so long as we're very quiet. But when Mr XYZ is teaching, we're allowed to push in the big wooden trolley, urn, cups, jangling teaspoons and all!'

'What does Mr XYZ look like?'

'Look at his feet. He's the one with brothel-creepers.'

From 10 a.m. to 1 p.m. only the pro due for the half-day before the day off remained on-duty. On one of my solitary mid-mornings, a large, unboned fish was the main luncheon dish for the patients. Sister surveyed it with antagonism. 'Is this an infant whale? Am I to nourish my patients on that most endearing mammal? No, no—wrong vertebral structure!' She dissected neatly, thrust at me the carving dish laden with bones. 'Country needs aircraft. Aircraft need glue. Do something constructive with those, nurse. Off! Off!'

I retreated to the ward kitchen and washed the bones under running water with the ward maid glowering at my elbow, hands on hips. 'You're not drying them bones nor boiling 'em into glue on me stove, nurse! Can't abide the pong. You try it on and I'm asking for me cards.'

'Not to worry. Sun's shining. I'll dry them outside.'

The ward maid stopped glowering and burst into her favourite song, *You Are My Sunshine, My Only Sunshine*. '. . . You'll never know, dear, how much I love you . . .' floated out as I arranged the bones in line on an open newspaper spread on the grass verge between the huts and a few feet from the kitchen window. As on fine days, one side of the ramp was lined with beds mostly occupied by tubercular patients. In the nearest bed was a patient newly admitted to my present ward. He was a medical student and had the sturdy build and bulky shoulders of the ardent rugger player he had been up to his illness. When in bed on the ramp he wore a black beret and dark glasses. He took off the glasses to watch me. 'What the devil do you think you're doing, nurse?'

'Drying bones to make glue for a new Spit.'

He was still laughing when Sister charged out to investigate. 'Splendid! Sensible girl! Plenty of good glue there. From now on, N. Andrews, you are responsible for my fishbone salvage.'

Those particular fishbones transformed me into Sister's pin-up pro for the remainder of my time in her ward and began what has become (in 1976) one of the longest friendships of my life with that former student, Charles. In its early years our friendship was as much interrupted by the war as by Charles's illness. A week or so after that morning he was transferred to a sanatorium in Sussex and it was over a year before we next met. And whilst we both then continued to work, technically, in the same hospital, it was never in the same branch of St Thomas's.

The days grew cooler, shorter; the beds out on the ramp disappeared by mid-afternoon; on our early morning drives the hedges were bright with the yellow and red hips of the dog rose, laced with the silver of Old Man's Beard, and the hawthorn was a dense mass of flaming red berries. In the wood above the hospital the copper beeches were on fire, the oaks turning bronze and the chestnut leaves poised to fall silently with the first sharp frost.

'Where's the Senior Pro? Why hasn't that box been returned to the surgical stores by the pro on this morning before her half-day? Take it up now, N. Andrews. You're responsible for your pros. Sit it on a wheelchair and push it up—and don't forget to get a receipt. Shouldn't take a few minutes.'

'Yes, nurse. Sorry, nurse.' I replied, mentally cursing the irate Charge Nurse. Our ward had admitted eleven patients that afternoon, all the pros had heavier than usual evening worklists, and it was one of my new jobs to see we all finished on time and I could ill-afford even a few minutes out of the ward. I trundled the loaded wheelchair at the double up the ramp, and had to wait about twenty minutes for my receipt as the storekeeper was dealing with a more complicated request from another ward nurse.

I started back at the double, then realized it was dusk, after blackout time, all the wards would be at the height of the evening washings, dressings, bed-making rush hour with their blackout screens up, curtains closed, and the downward sloping ramp ahead was empty. I perched on the back of the wheelchair, kicked off and was gaining momentum when a belated teaching round ambled on to the ramp from a ward ahead. A second later, the chair, myself, white coats, tweed jackets and one of ominous black, collided. I toppled with the chair and was picked up by an octopus with two arms in elegant black. 'Terribly sorry—had to get back to my ward—so sorry—' I apologized to disapproving faces. But the consultant smiled indulgently. 'Most understandable. Our fault, nurse.' Instantly the encircling disapproval was replaced by indulgent smiles. The consultant continued to inquire searchingly after my health. 'No degree of shock? No fractures sustained? Good. Gooooood.' He smoothed his greying black hair. I did not recognize him, but in that moment promoted him my pin-up pundit. I glanced covertly at his feet and breathed out. Neat black leather. He bowed the chair and myself off, and I heard him add to his escort, 'Let this be a lesson to you, gentlemen. St Thomas's may have found sanctuary from the path of Hitler's bombs, but there is no sanctuary for any Thomas's man who rashly stands in the determined path of a Nightingale.'

'You may read your papers now, nurses. . . .'

After our first holiday of the year, back to Hydestile, to new blue-and-white instead of purple-and-white striped dresses, to living in one of the long residential huts on the banks by the hospital's main gates. On-duty a new standing, and new responsibilities; in the classrooms, new lectures, all our own consultants; and, as they were all men, always we were chaperoned in lectures by one of our own Sister Tutors.

'Your careers have taken a new course, nurses,' said our Senior Sister Tutor in November.

The Second World War had changed course.

In North Africa the Eighth Army had a new commander, General Montgomery, and General Rommel was still determined to reach Alexandria, Suez and the rich oilfields of the Middle East. On the 23rd October 1942, the British attacked the Afrika Korps at El Alamein.

'Where on earth is that?'

'You should know. You were born in Egypt.'

'Never heard of it!'

The battle at El Alamein went on for twelve days.

'Girls! Get this! We've done it! The Eighth Army have beaten the living daylights out of Jerry! What price Rommel and his Afrika Korps now?'

A few days after the overwhelming victory at El Alamein an Anglo–American force under General Eisenhower landed at the other end of North Africa. Before the stiffness had been washed out of our new uniform dresses, on the 19th November, the Russians started the counter-attack on the long-besieged Stalingrad that resulted in the surrender by Field-Marshal Paulus of the German Sixth Army on 31st January 1943. In those three months the Eighth Army advanced fourteen hundred miles across North Africa and when they ended my set were on night-duty at Hydestile as 'night juniors'.

A note dated Thursday 11th February 1943, and headed; 'Eating my night meal alone in Victoria (ward) duty-room'.

'Daddy 'phoned me this evening just before I came on-duty to let me hear for myself he really is all right before I get his letter explaining what happened at home this afternoon. He was in the garden when a tip-and-run (enemy plane) dived in from the Channel and dropped his load of bombs on either side of our row of houses. Daddy said he found himself flying through the air like the daring young man on the flying trapeze and landed on his chest against a downstairs wall of our house. He says he hasn't broken anything, but I said he must see our doc. and have a check and an X-ray and he promised he would. He said the house is "a bit of a mess'. The parents' bedroom and kitchen seems to have got it worst, but Daddy kept repeating, "By a miracle, your mother, Dopey (our dog) and myself are in one piece and even if that's more than we can say for the house, isn't that all that matters?"'

Chapter Eight

ANOTHER wartime summer, another move, another great E.M.S. former mental hospital now crammed with soldiers wounded in the North African campaigns and injured and sick civilians from London. Botley's Park, Surrey. I never discovered the origin of 'Botley', but the 'Park' was apt. The old independent villa wards and ward blocks, the new ubiquitous hut wards and hut staff's homes were dotted around with carefully tended little beds of flowers and shrubs, joined by concrete paths that were small roads and surrounded not by barbed wire but luxuriant hedges and tall trees alive with the clapping of the wood pigeons' wings. On the small roads, small armies of nurses on bicycles and on foot; of soldiers limping on walking-plasters, artificial limbs, walking sticks, low hand-crutches, swinging on high-armpit crutches with one empty trousers leg pinned up, propelling themselves in wheelchairs, being pushed in spinal carriages. Amongst the khaki, civilians on the same plasters, tin legs, sticks, crutches, with the same missing limbs, wheelchairs, spinal carriages. The hospital was only twenty-odd miles from London. Near enough for the ambulances from the London hospitals to whisk down in just under an hour; far enough for the London patients to sleep mostly undisturbed nights.

The war in the desert was over. On 13th May 1943, all the Axis (German and Italian) troops in North Africa surrendered to the Allies. A few weeks later in July the Allies invaded Sicily and in another few weeks, on 3rd September, southern Italy. After each and all the subsequent Allied invasions of Italy, as the hospital ships returned home, the convoys of wounded arrived with the regularity of the ambulances at Hydestile, but instead of in early afternoon, most seemed to arrive at around eleven o'clock at night.

Shortly after the Allies landed in Italy, the Italian Army surrendered to the Allies and became our 'co-belligerents'. A term that evoked hilarious laughter from the men in the beds lining the long hut ward where I then worked as senior Second Year—on the rare occasions when they remembered it. The war in Italy was far from over as the strong German force there was fighting on, fiercely. 'Ah well,' said the soldier-patients, as other soldiers in other wards four years earlier, 'Jerry's a fighting man as knows how to fight and he don't pack it in easy.'

Two-thirds of those patients were soldiers, chiefly guardsmen or commandos, and the remainder were London air-raid casualties.

One row of commandos with extensive flesh wounds also had near-identical knee injuries caused, so they insisted, by their habit of leaping down from thirty-foot walls.

'Must you always leap? Couldn't you just climb down?'

The row looked shocked. 'Sorry, nurse, just not done,' explained one ex-public schoolboy commando with a fair, smooth boy's face, but not a boy's mouth or jaw. 'Dashed bad form. Bad as leaving a knot in your bit of string.'

'What bit of string?'

'The bit with which one strangles chaps. Very bad form to get it knotted. Show you mine.' He lunged sideways into his locker and inadvertently twisted his sandbagged injured knee. Knee injuries were (and are) excruciatingly painful. 'Damn the bastard!' he exclaimed, wincing.

An Irish guardsman some beds down, with both legs strung up on traction-splints, hauled himself up on his lifting straps and bellowed up the ward, 'Mother of God, man! Have you no bloody manners at all to use such language in front of the nurse?'

After the arrival of a new convoy I nursed my first ex-prisoners-of-war, repatriated from prison camp hospitals in one of the new exchanges of severely wounded prisoners between the opposing armies in Italy. All I nursed had been in camps run by the Italian Army. Only initially was I surprised to hear individually from all that they would have much preferred to have been imprisoned by the German Army. 'It's like this, nurse—if there's any rations or medical stores going, Jerry'll have 'em—or know how to get 'em.'

From the thinness and physical weakness of all, no need to ask if they had been kept on short rations, but as all were too badly wounded ever to fight again—which was why they had been exchanged—I asked about the conditions in the prison 'hospitals'.

'Couldn't rightly blame the Eyetye M.O.s, N. Andrews.' A regular sergeant watched me put a fresh dressing on the flap of skin over the newly-trimmed stump of his amputated left leg. The original amputation had been at mid-thigh. 'Reckon they did their best with what they had, only like the lads were saying, they didn't have what you might call much. So when it's me turn for the chopper, the M.O. as spoke the best English he says to me, your leg no good, sergeant, you understand? Must remove, yes? But have no medicine to make you sleep. Understand?'

My mask suddenly stifled me. 'You mean no anaesthetic?' I glanced up from the dressing. His face was beginning to glisten and his neat light brown moustache looked black. 'I'm sorry, sergeant, I shouldn't have reminded you.'

'Not sure it wouldn't be best off me chest, nurse. Couldn't tell the wife when she come, but it's different with you being a nurse.' He took a few long breaths. 'The Eyetye M.O. got to use what he got, see, and what he got was ice and cotton-wool. He packs me leg with ice to freeze it good, signals his lads to stand-by to hold me down, bungs the roll of cotton-wool in me mouth and gets on with the job.' He mopped his face with his pyjama sleeve. 'Not just me, nurse. Same for a lot of our lads.'

And from a lot of our lads: 'That's straight up, nurse. Ice and cotton-wool.'

For the setting of bones, removal of bullets and shrapnel and other amputations.

Despite the ward windows open all day, the reek of damp

plaster, mingled with the sickly smell of pus, hung in the ward air. The time was still pre-penicillin and the antibiotics, and beneath many of the long plasters immobilizing limbs or whole bodies from necks to toes, deep-rooted old wound abscesses still suppurated. To encourage the pus to drain out, windows (small openings) were cut in the plasters over the infected areas, and the rubber drains in the wounds (either corrugated or narrow tubes of rubber) were covered with surgical dressings changed three, four, or eight hourly. Sometimes the dressings were enough to contain the seepage; at other times the flow suffused dressings and large patches of plaster. Sometimes the effluvium could be muffled by encasing the whole plaster in a kind of unstitched, felt carpet-bag. When gangrene set in, the only available way of drowning the smell was by burning strong incense cones in small enamel bowls under the bed. Almost invariably, after gangrene appeared, another amputation.

'Sister or Charge Nurse around, nurse?'

'No, Mr X. Sister's still at lunch and it's the Charge Nurse's weekend off.'

'Never mind. Just want a private word with that chap in 24. I don't want you, nurse. Oh—Sister tell you I was coming back?'

'Yes, Mr X.'

Another second-year some months my junior drew me aside. 'What's our pundit doing coming back without his registrar and houseman and why's he looking so haemadementic (bloodyminded)? He's usually a cheerful bod.'

'He's come to tell Tom (in Bed 24) his leg's got to come off. He always tells the patients in private before he has to amputate and amputating always makes him haemadementic. Sister says it does all good orthopod surgeons and none'll pick up their saws until they've tried everything else on God's earth to save the limb. But now Tom's gone gangrenous it's got to come off fast and high.'

When Sister returned; 'Now he's been told, N. Andrews, do the first two skin preparations this afternoon and evening. The night nurse can do the third early tomorrow morning.'

Always three skin preps. before orthopaedic operations whether major or minor and all body hair in the specific area shaved. 'You're not going to shave me with that, nurse! Wouldn't you like to borrow my safety?'

'If this really worries you, I'll get a ward safety, but I'm much safer with a cut-throat as we're all first taught shaving with cut-throats.'

'If you're handy with your Sweeney Todd, nurse, you use it! You'll not mind if I close my eyes and say my prayers?'

So often so little cause for laughter, yet always the most frequent sound in that, as so many other wards, was the sound of the patients' laughter. When the theatre porters arrived with the theatre trolleys, the patients for operation were wheeled out to shouts of 'Good luck, mate!' 'Oy, mate—swap your left boot for my right when they fetch you back and we'll both have two good-half-pairs.' Later, when the anaesthetic and shock had worn off, the ward followed with interested empathy the slow, progressive disappearance of the 'phantom' (amputated) limb.

'How's it today, Tom?'

'Stump's comfortable and much better in meself, nurse, but me phantom's playing up Old Harry. Feels to be sticking straight up in the air through me bed-cradle and the toes are tickling shocking. Can't get it comfortable.'

And later, 'Me phantom's settled lovely to the knee, nurse. Just the knee giving me gyp.'

Slowly, as the pain in the nerves faded, the phantoms faded to the stumps, and invariably from the extremities first.

Occasionally at night either a solitary or several German bomber pilots mistook the hospital for a war factory. I never heard of their bombs doing any real damage to the hospital, aside from breaking a few windows, displacing roof tiles, or the metal sheets roofing the huts, but the raids made a great deal of noise. This only annoyed me for the sake of the patients, as, after every working day, once in bed I was asleep. It took more than an air-raid siren sounding the Alert to wake me. A number of the other girls in my cubicled hut slept as soundly, to the irritation of the one very light sleeper. 'Girls, girls! The Alert's gone!'

'So what? If Jerry does drop a few it's just to show willing. He doesn't really want us. Go back to sleep!'

'Don't be so dumb! Listen to those planes! Right overhead!'

'Phoeey! Miles away! Shut up and let us sleep—' the voices were cut off by a barrage of explosions that rattled our hut like a tin can.

I shared a cubicle with another ex-VAD. We reacted identically, rolled out of our beds and onto the floor beneath. In the next slight lull, we pulled down blankets and pillows and slept out the raid and night on the floor. I dropped off to the sounds of growling aircraft and the light sleeper's triumphant 'Didn't I say they were overhead? I'll bet they hit our roof!'

We slept several nights on the floor under our beds. I slept very well mainly because I was so tired, and probably also because I was subconsciously aware I had taken the only shelter available, was off-duty, had to be back on-duty at 7.30 a.m. and tomorrow's expected busy day could be made still busier by the bombers above. My attitude seemed pretty general in our hut. If any girl was frightened, none showed it, and our light sleeper's running commentary always seemed more prompted by her pleasure in being hut Cassandra than from personal apprehension.

'Girls, girls! Something's hit the bathrooms' roof!'

'Shut up, get under your bed, and let us sleep! You're worse than Jerry—'

'I am under my bed!' An ear-splitting clank of tin. 'That was our roof—just above me!'

A chorus, 'Are you hurt?'

'Of course I'm not! I'm under my bed! But I'm sure my roof's come in!'

'If you're not hurt, shove a pillow over your head and go to sleep!'

In the morning we were woken by yells of laughter further down the hut. 'My God, she was right! The roof's caved in onto her bed and she's sleeping like a baby underneath. Give us a hand shifting her clear!'

The light sleeper awoke, unhurt, unshocked, torn between fury and complacence. 'Didn't I say this would happen?'

The patients worried for us. 'You nurses got no air-raid shelter? Not even tin lids?'

'Not us. We're civvy nurses. Sorry you've all had such a rough night.'

'We did all right, nurse. The night nurses gave us all extra mugs of tea. Always kip lovely after a good cuppa.'

At home on one day off in early autumn father asked, 'Have you any idea of the number of really difficult and demanding patients you have now met?'

'Yes. Since 1940, three. Two men, one woman.'

The roof of our house had long been repaired, the windows were now all intact and in my parents' bedroom and the kitchen, temporary battens held up the temporary ceilings. Mother was in WVS uniform, working full-time at the local WVS centre and two nights a week as a Civil Defence fire-watcher. John had joined the RAF. Father's age, 67, exempted him from all National Service. 'The only member of my family presently minus a uniform.'

His appearance disturbed me. For the first time I thought he looked his age, but his medical check after being blown across the garden by the blast had apparently been satisfactory. I knew he was very anxious about John's flying training in particular and the war in general. John was a few months past his seventeenth birthday. When father with Dopey saw me off at the station, he glanced at the huge poster on the wall. MEN OF SEVENTEEN AND A QUARTER TO THIRTY THREE CAN FLY WITH THE RAF. 'If this war lasts much longer,' he observed dryly, 'His Majesty's Government will be calling boys of fifteen, men.'

In the train I reminded myself it was not surprising father should be showing his age after the long dragging weariness of a war that still seemed endless. Also I knew he had never wholly recovered from deep sense of personal shock he had suffered from the British surrenders in the Far East in 1942. It might be 1943, but father remained a Victorian Englishman and held fast to his Victorian attitudes, convictions and loves. He had loved and taken pride in the Empire in which he had worked for so many years, and felt the same emotions towards his own country. In many ways he was a very simple man, despite, or possibly because of, his subtlety of intellect. It was not merely that the word 'surrender' had no place in his personal vocabulary; he did not understand its meaning. Any battle was an event that for him could have only two ends; victory or death.

In another day off in 1943—and in that year we talked together more than at any other time in my life—we discussed the personal and professional battles that occur in private lives. He said, 'Never fight for the sake of fighting. But once your intelligence is convinced you have no alternative to putting up a fight, fight hard, keep on fighting hard, and only stop fighting hard when you've won.' Then he laughed. 'You can then enjoy the breathing space until the next round.'

Before 1943 was out my set were prematurely back on night-duty and owing to the shortage of more senior third and fourth years, instead of, as normally, working as 'reliefs'—i.e., nurses who moved between wards relieving the nights off of both seniors and juniors and gaining gradual experience of the senior position—most of us went straight into the senior job. At that point of the war the continuing need of the Forces Medical Services for newly qualified doctors and S.R.N.s was stretching increasingly thinly the medical and trained nursing staffs in civilian hospitals. The EMS came into this category.

The night senior's position in my training was probably the most responsible, and in my view the most interesting, of our student years. Briefly, the senior was in sole charge of her ward at night, assisted by seldom more than one junior, and supervised, mostly if only for geographical reasons at a distance, by the Night Sister (not yet re-named Night Superintendent), her one, or at the most two, deputies, and the resident medical staff. In Botley's, as in all large general hospitals of my experience, the Night Sister and her deputies were responsible for the whole hospital at night, based in the Matron's office from whence they made constant sorties round the wide-spread wards. Every ward, every night, received three official 'Night Sister's rounds'; every ward in an emergency immediately contacted Night Sister's office. Usually each round lasted about twenty minutes. The residents all did night rounds of all their respective wards, generally between 10 p.m. and 12.30 a.m., and when in bed for the night were on-call, and often called-up more than once each night. Their rounds could last from five minutes to an hour or more, depending on the particular situation in the ward. During the many hours between rounds, the night senior had to rely on her training herself, and the speed with which the hospital switchboard operator could contact more experienced help when emergencies arose, or looked about to do so. 'Bleepers' for medical staff were only just coming into use; walkie-talkies non-existent. The telephone was the ward's lifeline.

In the three and a half months I was on nights in an acute orthopaedic villa, not infrequently, owing to the scarcity of registrars and housemen a consultant orthopaedic surgeon did the night medical rounds on his own. 'Makes me feel quite young again to be walking the wards, nurse, but By God, it's even harder on the feet than I remembered. Right! Let's take a look at the chaps and then their notes.' (For some inexplicable reason, all consultant surgeons said 'Right!' and all consultant physicians 'Good' pronounced 'Goooood!').

Once familiarity lessened awe, for a man of renowned talents both as an orthopaedic surgeon and lecturer, I regarded his rounds as a godsend. Though some nights he looked an old and not just middle-aged man, he was always willing to spare time for explaining in detail the patients' case histories, his operative and post-operative techniques, modern advances in orthopaedic surgery in general, and as he had been for years a general surgical registrar before specializing, general surgery in general. My Hospital Surgery examination was fast approaching, but every morning in bed I fell asleep before I read half a page of my general surgical textbook and as always on nights did not waken until shaken in the evening in time to get into uniform. Being a night nurse throughout all our surgical lectures, I slept through most. That later I passed Surgery rather well was solely due to that consultant.

Neither he nor our registrar and houseman—when we had either—were Thomas's men, and nor was the Night Sister a Nightingale. They came from another London voluntary hospital, but their methods and attitude varied little from those to which I had become accustomed. 'We chaps may wear different ties and you nurses different caps,' said that consultant, 'but we're all much the same under the white starch just as we're all much the same people we were before we put on the starch. Surgery, medicine, nursing—don't change people. All they do is turn people into caricatures of themselves when young. Ergo, the callous young grow more callous, the kind, kinder, the wise, wiser—and the born bunglers bungle on to their eternal salvation and patients' damnation.'

My night junior was a VAD with two War Service stripes up who could jog-trot as fast as any Nightingale, was one of the hardest workers I ever met, and whatever the hour or the rush, invariably able to provide mugs of hot strong tea in seconds.

In Italy, Rome was still in German hands, the Allied landing at Salerno had met with formidable German resistance, and the still mounting British casualties were continuing to fill the homeward-bound hospital ships. In that villa (it was an officers' ward), as in my hut ward, were men wounded in Italy, North Africa, ex-P.O.W.s, and a very few who had been in hospital beds since Dunkirk.

It was a single-storey villa with two longish wards set either side of a small reception hall used as a night duty-room. By long-established tradition in 1943, the senior officers' ward was known to patients and staff as 'the west end', and the junior (captains and under) as 'the east end'. At the far end of both wards were two padded cells mainly reserved, in the absence of other side wards, for very senior officers—to the constant joy of the east end. One night after the casualty porters had removed themselves and their trolley from a padded cell and I helped into an operation gown a wounded

Brigadier, he surveyed the padded walls and grinned weakly, 'Pity my Brigade can't see me now, nurse. Always said I'd come to this! If you don't mind my asking—where precisely am I?'

I kept being reminded of my hut ward. The blackout screens accentuated the reek of damp plaster and pus, entrapped the clouds of cigarette smoke and anaesthetic fumes lingering over the beds of the newly post-operative patients. There was the same intangible atmosphere of gaiety, the same outbursts of laughter, the same tolerance of each other, the same high proportion of the special courage required to withstand not short periods of acute pain, but long periods of acute and exhausting discomfort. And as in all servicemen's wards, every officer had his special friend from his own unit who visited him whenever possible, but instead of these friends being called mates or oppos, most seemed to be called Nigel.

The only thing I disliked was the tiredness. I infinitely preferred night to day work, and being able to nurse the same patients continuously for three months. It took less than the first month to develop the relationship with the whole ward that resulted in what was one of the most delightful sounds for any nurse to hear. It was the sound of a ward hauling itself up on its lifting straps, elbows, or feebly raising its head from a pillow to smile and chorus, 'Here they are! Here come "our" night nurses!' Often on day-duty a patient would label a nurse 'my' N. So-and-So. On night-duty it was always 'Our night nurses'!

Just as more babies were born at night, so did more patients die at night. In sickness and in health in the small pre-dawn hours the human body is at its lowest ebb, and so, very often, is the human spirit. None of my patients died during that night-duty, but several at different times were on the D.I.L., and more for longer periods on the S.I.L. In those small hours when every broken bone, every wound abscess, every heel, ankle, elbow, and back muscle ached beyond bearing, a hospital bed could be the loneliest place on earth. The lonely, everywhere, need to talk. In the darkness and in whispers, the British talk more easily. Talk of home, wives, children, girl-friends, civilian jobs, and war.

'I thought they'd forgotten me, nurse. Three days and three nights I laid out there on that bloody sand. Got quite fond of the stuff by the end, only wanted to turn over and couldn't. Some of the time I was a bit off my rocker, but all of the time I was bloody thirsty. Got hellish confusing. Chaps kept bending over me, heaving up my head, pouring water down my throat, and talking in different languages. English, Yank, German, English, German—lost count. Hellish confusing. Only realized later the bloody battle had been swaying backwards and forwards over yours truly.'

'Tea'll be great, but no sugar, thanks, nurse. Lost my taste for it in the bag. Had a bit of luck when they picked me up just outside Tobruk—when—oh—July '42—as they picked up one of our M.O.s. Decent chap—brooded over us like dear old mum. Be in Germany now. Jerry shifted him out with the rest before my lot were swopped. Hope the war doesn't last too long.'

'Maybe your M.O. chum'll escape?'

'God, no, nurse! M.O.s can't escape. They can't leave the chaps. He'll only get out of the bag when someone else unties the string.'

Washing at dawn a young captain who had won a Military Cross and been badly wounded on the final day of the battle at El Alamein. 'What was Alamein really like?'

He thought this over with closed eyes whilst I dried his face. 'Noisy, N. Andrews. Dead noisy.'

We always washed the men unable to wash themselves before starting the general round of early morning teas, temperatures, dressings, washing and shaving bowls, rubbing of backs, heels, elbows, skin preps. and bed-making at 6 a.m. We were allowed to leave six of the twenty-eight beds to the day nurses. It took roughly twenty minutes to wash and re-make the bed of a man on traction or in heavy plasters and longer if surgical dressings were involved, and as we usually had ten to fourteen men to wash, never started later than 4 a.m. and often at three-thirty. The patients never objected. On the contrary.

'Thank God for the rose-coloured dawn.' A man in his mid-twenties who had last stood on his feet at Dunkirk thankfully sipped his pre-wash tea whilst I tied a red shade-cover over his bedhead lamp then screened his bed. The screens were red and he lay outstretched in a hip plaster in the red glow. 'Heaven'll reward you even if I don't. Praying you'd do me first,' he whispered. 'In a muck sweat am I. How did you know I was awake? I had my eyes closed.'

'You stopped snoring, Mr. . . .'

'I never snore!'

'Shush—please.'

'Sorry. Just listen. I've a new quote for your collection—with apologies to *The Burial Of Sir John Moore*:

> She washed them softly at dead of night,
> The sods with her cold hands turning,
> By her ailing torch's misty light,
> And the bedlamp dimly burning.'

Every night when they were all asleep or trying to sleep, every twenty minutes round all the beds and from time to time stopping in the middle of either ward with my hand over my torchlight, listening to the varying rhythms of sleep. Mr A, quick and shallow; Captain B, a short snort every five or six breaths; Captain C, only a snore when about to wake up; Mr D, the heaviest snorer in both wards; Messrs E, F, G, H, I, all sleeping the soundless sleep of the boys they were only in age; Major J clicking his false teeth; Col K, muttering in sleep as always when his temperature was up. And woven amongst the snores, snorts, clicks, mutters, the occasional jangle of the lead weights as a patient on traction moved in sleep, the creaking of the leather straps under the mattress of the high orthopaedic beds; the distant chink of a glass on wood that meant the Major-General had woken in his padded cell.

'Tea, nurse? Nectar! Busy night?'

'Quite quiet. No convoys in tonight.'

On the next convoy night: 'Night Sister speaking, nurse. Five officers on their way to you. Yes, in emergency beds until your ward Sister rearranges her bedstate in the morning. The registrar will be round to see them directly he's free. And your other patients ? Very well. I'll be round shortly.'

Neither the registrar nor Night Sister had arrived when the VAD and I met briefly in our ward kitchen nearly two hours later. Her normally cheerful face was creased with distress. 'I didn't realize our admissions were more ex-P.O.W.s.'

'Nor did I till I read their notes. Thanks for laying on the special cocoa and scrambled eggs. I know they've been trying to feed them up on the hospital ship, but they still look as if they haven't had a square meal in years.'

'Two of them wept all over their scrambled eggs. I felt so awful for them, and both, after I had mopped their faces, said they were only crying because they were so happy to be home. Happy. With legs and arms blown off.'

'I know.' I had to lean against the kitchen table. 'You know that one I've been with this last hour ? The commando captain ? Shrapnel sliced his spine. Paraplegic. When I got him undressed he said he thought he'd better warn me he had a bit of a bedsore on his back and they seemed rather worried about it on the ship, but it hasn't bothered him as he can't feel anything. When I turned him over and took off the dressing, I couldn't believe my eyes.' I linked my fingers as if in prayer and held out my hands (size 6½ in theatre gloves). 'The sore has made a hole deep enough for both my hands to go in like this up to the wrists without touching him. I had to measure as I didn't think anyone would believe me if I just described it. I've never seen anything like it. Never wish to. Packing it used a new whole tin of tulle gras. (Medicated vaseline gauze). I've settled him propped on one hip and we'll have to keep turning him or he'll get hip sores.'

'He can't feel anything ?'

'No feeling, no control from the waist down.'

She leant against the table. 'He looks quite young.'

'He's younger than he looks. Twenty-nine.'

I was very upset about the captain and the other admissions. Being very upset and very tired, I spoke aloud the words that had been running through my head since I admitted the five men.

' "But things like that, you know, must be,
   After a famous victory." '

'Come again?'

We had worked together for two months.

'Just the end of a verse I'm stuck with.'

'Say it.'

> 'They say it was a shocking sight
> After the field was won;
> For many thousand bodies here
> Lay rotting in the sun;
> But things like that, you know, must be,
> After a famous victory.'

And other things and other victories.

One cold, wet afternoon in March, 1944, I was back on day-duty, off from two to five, and riding back through the main gates at about four o'clock with my head down against the driving rain that had emptied the small roads of all but one khaki figure lumbering awkwardly and more sideways than forwards, towards me.

'Don't you know one of your old soldiers, N. Andrews?'

I leapt off my still brakeless bicycle and recognized the man in the greatcoat, with collar upturned and jammed down service cap, with astonishment. 'Sergeant! It's you—' I waved at his legs 'no crutches and two legs!'

It was the Regular Sergeant who had first told me about ice and cotton-wool. His face was still very thin, but a much better colour and beaming. 'Bit of all right, eh, nurse?' We shook hands. 'Just giving me new tin leg another practice run.'

'Doing fine, but isn't it a bit damp and chilly?'

'Don't bother me, nurse, and like as I says to the Sister before I come out—I'd rather get in a bit more practice on me todd. Folk mean kindly wanting to offer a hand like, but I got to fend for meself.' He looked down at his feet, and the rain poured down the inside of his coat collar. 'Now I got the two, it's meself as got to stand on 'em, isn't it? Do a bit more each day like and this afternoon I've promised meself I'll get to the gates and back to the ward. And how you been keeping, nurse?'

We talked a little then I rode on and not to hurt his feelings did not risk looking back until well away. The rain was heavier. Through the curtain of water I watched the solitary khaki figure lumbering on, awkwardly, crabwise, up to the gates and a couple of steps beyond. As he began to turn, I got back on my bicycle.

Chapter Nine

MAY 1944, Hydestile. On the calendar, early summer. Outside the ward windows, a sky the pale parchment of February. Against that sky, the trees in the wood above the hospital looked artificially lush and painted into a landscape by an artist who had never lived in the country.

The Allied Invasion of Europe was daily expected. Hydestile, as hospitals all over the country, awaited the sea of British casualties that must sweep back over the Channel as surely as our retreating army had swept back four years earlier. As May ended and June opened, every evening the whole sky was blackened with Allied bombers flying east. Looking up on those evenings was just like looking up into a series of giant, black, open umbrellas. Directly one droned slowly away, it was replaced by another, and another. Often it seemed even the wealthy United States could not possibly afford one more plane, yet still the evening umbrellas reappeared and moved on eastwards, black and inexorable as death.

After Dunkirk and perhaps to the end of 1942, I might have found those umbrellas exciting, gratifying. The war had lasted too long for those trivial emotions. I had seen too much human mutilation, too many ruined homes, too many tears, to feel anything but sick at heart and stomach when watching those air armadas. Only my intellect could accept the death and destruction they were about to cause to so many, including so many of themselves, were necessary to save the life of civilization, just as in the operating theatre I had had to accept it was necessary to cut off a breast, cut out a stomach, uterus, rectum, or amputate a limb to save an individual life. Never once in any operating theatre was I able to watch, or assist in, a major operation without that same sickening of the heart and stomach. (The only aspect of my general training that I abhorred, from first day to last, was my theatre-training.)

Throughout the first half of that year my training had forced my intellectual, but not emotional, acceptance of the inevitable approach of the greatest personal disaster of my life to that point. Father, though still living at home a near-normal life, was dying on his feet of an inoperable carcinoma of the lung. 'I can understand your desire to rush him into St Thomas's for operation,' said the specialist I consulted in private during nights-off just after Christmas, 'and I know your thoracic surgeons are now successfully removing certain lungs. Unfortunately, your father's growth is far too extensive—and you must remember his age.' He showed me father's X-rays, read my thoughts. 'Yes. A wonder he's still with us.' He switched off the X-ray screen light. 'He wants to remain at home and on his feet as long as he can, and I'm not stopping him. I'll do what I can to help him with the symptoms as they arise. I only wish there was more—'

There was only one thing to say, 'Thank you, Doctor.'

4th June 1944. 'Hey, Lu, have you heard? General Alexander's taken Rome at last.'

'Jolly good.'

6th June 1944. 'D-day, eh, nurse? Can't say I envy that General Eisenhower and the lads if they've had the gales we've had here. Still, I reckon they'll have too much on their minds to be sea-sick.'

'I expect so.'

A week later, 'What's all this about Hitler's launching a Secret Weapon on London?'

'Doesn't sound much cop from today's papers. Sort of little robot-planes. Flying bombs, or something. Says the RAF are having a party shooting them down.'

I listened without interest. On the following day I was due to start a week's holiday and all my thoughts were concentrated on getting home. Great anxiety, as great grief, is a very isolating emotion, and always in my particular case it shutters my outward mental vision as successfully as it does my physical vision.

Betty and John had managed to have the same week on leave as myself. Betty was now a WAAF sergeant plotter in the operations room of a Pathfinder (RAF) station in the Midlands and engaged to a Squadron Leader on bombers. John was a RAF student at the University of St Andrews. The next evening we had all reached home and had our first look at the V1s. 'Ugly little things,' we agreed, as two more small robot-planes with square-tipped wings and flames spurting from their tails streaked jerkily inland, high in the sky. I thought they sounded like revving motor-bikes. John disagreed. 'More like a Ford Model T.' We were all glad our parents now had the Morrison shelter father had bought last year as the 'tip-and-runs' had continued to harass the Channel coast towns since 1940.

The shelter stood against an inside wall of our ground floor sitting-room which was emptied of most of its normal furniture. The shelter (6ft 6in long, 4ft wide, 2ft 9in high) looked like a large, square, squat steel table with stout meshing between the legs. Inside there was room for two adults in reasonable comfort, four if squeezed like sardines. Father could lie in the shelter propped up, which was essential for his cough, but not sitting up. From the second week in June 1944 to all but the last night of his life, father and mother slept in our Morrison every night. In those early weeks of the attacks the V1s were launched on England from sites in France, Belgium and Holland, it seemed incessantly; some were shot down into the sea by the coastal guns, others over open country by the RAF, but many others got through to London, and Kent and East Sussex earned a new nickname: Doodlebug Alley.

On our final Sunday afternoon, sitting over tea at our dining-room table, we watched two RAF fighters, one Spitfire, one Mosquito, shoot down five flying bombs over The Ridge—the long fold of hills backing Hastings and St Leonards. 'Five down between first and third cups,' observed father. 'Unusual

Sunday teatime entertainment. I must say it is very pleasant to have my whole family round the table again. When was the last occasion ? '41, as I recall.'

Three weeks later, on the afternoon of 13th July, after surviving sixty bombing operations over Germany, Betty's fiancé was killed in a mid-air collision over their station. The following morning Betty went home on forty-eight hours' compassionate leave. She had to be back in her ops. room by the evening of Monday 17th. At 1 a.m. on the 18th July 1944, father's long, gallant fight with terminal cancer ended in seconds and without pain, in a major internal haemorrhage.

A few days later his body was buried in the small, very beautiful country graveyard of the rightly named Church in the Wood, at Hollington, on the inland outskirts of St Leonards. The summer had at last arrived, the sunshine was brilliant, every rose in Sussex seemed in bloom, and the trees in full summer glory hung over our heads and father's open grave. High above the trees the flying bombs spat fire from their tails as they raced jerkily towards London, the RAF fighters wheeled, screamed and spat machine-gun bullets; and the massive battery of anti-aircraft guns then ranging the coast roared out a requiem.

Chapter Ten

THE expected sea of Allied casualties flowed elsewhere. Into the London hospitals, on to Hydestile and other hospitals, flowed the sea of civilian flying-bomb casualties.

The first flying bomb landed on Kent on 13th June 1944 (Swanscombe); the last to arrive over Britain was destroyed over Kent (near Sittingbourne), on 29th March 1945. In those nine and a half months over 9 000 flying bombs were launched on England. In the first three weeks of the attack, alone, as the Prime Minister, Mr Churchill, told the House of Commons on 6th July 1944, 2 754 flying bombs had been launched and had killed 2 752 people. The number of people injured by the flying bombs and detained in hospital on that day was about 8 000. This figure did not include those who had suffered minor injuries and were treated in first-aid posts and hospital out-patients' departments. (The final figures for flying bomb casualties were 6 139 killed, 17 239 seriously injured.)

London, more battered, burning, bleeding, grimly angry, grimly humorous, grimly indomitable than I had ever seen before. 'If it's not them blitzes it's them doodles, nurse. You pays ye money and you takes ye choice.'

The worst agony of grief had to wait. A victory slid by barely noticed. On 23rd August 1944, Paris re-captured by the Allies. In the newspaper reports and under the pictures of the Free French troops decked with flowers and kisses entering their capital for the first time in four years, a new word, 'Liberation'. Time only for momentarily recalling one French baker, wondering if he had survived, and if so, if he remembered enough to feel ashamed; or if, as I had noticed happened to patients after bad illnesses and myself after personal agony, in self-defence he had developed those patches of amnesia without which life can be unliveable.

In September 1944 the V2 rocket attacks on London began. (The first landed in Chiswick on 8th September.) Interwoven with the impression of being bombarded by some elemental force too swift, too silent until arrival, and too destructive for human comprehension or even fear, the news of yet another British Thermopylae.

A patient hitched up his headphones. 'Seems our lads are still hanging on at this Arnhem, nurse.'

'That's great!' But we both knew it was not and that our lads were being slaughtered. Yet 'great' applied. The men who had dropped from planes and gliders to try and establish a bridgehead over the lower Rhine and so cut off the German Army in Holland fought, and many died, with great courage.

No time for dwelling on courage. In a very few weeks, State Finals.

Before our results arrived I developed a septic right forefinger, had the nail off under an anaesthetic and for two days was the only patient in the sick nurses' ward on the ground floor of Riddle House. Our Home Sister could not have nursed me with more care had I been on the D.I.L. I then returned to work on 'dry-duty' with my right arm in a sling. The hospital was too busy to spare even a one-handed nurse. Being 'dry' meant I could not get my right-hand wet—i.e., scrub-up—which ruled out all ward work. I spent my time (just under three weeks) chaperoning, mostly in the ante-natal clinics in Mothercraft, in one of the innumerable caverns in the hospital basement. 'Dry' hours, 9.30 a.m. to 5.30 p.m., I regarded as a sinecure, and standing all day in the airless basement was compensated for by the comforting thought that overhead was the thick basement ceiling and remains of the hospital. I was frequently very frightened during those months, but never when in the hospital basement. It had been built to withstand the pressure of the Thames for long years before anyone thought of world wars, and it was always my secret conviction that it would withstand a rocket, though almost certainly there

I was wrong. Luckily the only enemy weapon from the air that did not fall on St Thomas's, London, in the Second World War, was a rocket. (Had one done so it is highly unlikely this writer would be recording these moments.)

Our main Maternity Unit had long been evacuated to Surrey, but, as the distance was too far for the ante-natal clinics, these continued in Mothercraft. Most of the women I chaperoned were having their first babies. A number were unmarried girls uniformly appalled by the diagnosis. 'Oh, no, doctor, no! I can't be! It was just the once!'

Endlessly repeated, there and later when I was a pupil-midwife, 'Just the once!'

And, in private, from experienced obstetricians: 'When will the human race learn it only has to be once? If I had my way, nurse, every mother in this country would hang framed over her every infant daughter's cot, ONCE IS ENOUGH TO MAKE A BABY.'

I was in a sling the morning the letters arrived from the General Nursing Council for England and Wales. A friend opened mine. 'You and me, both, Lu. S.R.N.s.'

My main reaction was relief as it meant more pay and on £5 a month I could afford the train fare home more often on my days off. Father's pension had died with him, and as he had neither savings nor insurance, and mother only a small widow's pension, from his death his children, as millions of others, had to support themselves on their own earnings.

Off 'dry' duty, back to an upstairs bricked-in ward, and the sweating shirt-sleeved students with the stretchers came back to the ward doorway.

'My, God, Christmas again! I thought the war'd be over by now. Why aren't we in Berlin?'

'Field-Marshal von Rundstedt.'

'Why the hell has he got to hold-up the Yanks in the Ardennes? He must know he hasn't a prayer—and if you give me your spiel about Jerry being a fighting man once more, Lu, so-help me, I'll bloody crown you! I'm fed to the back teeth with fighting men who won't pack it in not because they're so bloody brave but because they bloody enjoy fighting and can't bear life unless there's a war on. If it weren't for men we wouldn't have wars. If you ask me, most men love wars—until they get chewed up in the machinery. Let me have men about me who are not only fat but cowards! I want to live in peace!'

'So do the rest of us who are trying to catch up before Hospital Finals! If you and Lu want to start a private war, get up to your rooms and stop yak-yak-yaking down here!'

'Well, nurses, I hope you found your Final results quite pleasing and will enjoy the remainder of your fourth year and the insight it will provide into the full responsibilities of the ward Sister and hospital administration. Unfortunately I must warn you that this new ruling from the Minister of Labour (Mr Ernest Bevin) applies specifically to newly trained State Registered Nurses as yourselves. I presume you have all read the official directive on the notice board.'

'Sister, please, does this mean we have got to do either mid-wifery or a tuberculosis training even if the war with Germany ends before our fourth years ?'

'According to the new ruling, nurse, yes. Were the war to end tomorrow, the country will remain very short of midwives and nurses with the T.B. certificate. Once you have acquired the certificate of your choice, as I understand the ruling, you will then be free to join the Armed Forces Nursing Services or take other civilian nursing posts, but nurses are unlikely to be released from the nursing profession for some considerable time to come.'

I seethed with inner fury at the Government's arbitrary treatment of a profession that in my growing opinion was over-worked, under-paid, and arguably one of the most valuable in the country. My fury was accentuated by a recent event at home. Our rector of the now long-bombed St John's had called round to see mother on one of my days off, to ask for Betty and John's official RAF numbers and ranks for inclusion in the Roll Of Honour he was drawing up for the serving members in his parish. He had with him the Government's official list of all occupations regarded as National Service. 'I'm sorry, my dear Lucy, but I'm afraid I can't include your name, as civilian student nurses are not listed as doing National Service. Of course you were a VAD. Your name can be entered as a VAD.'

'No, thanks, rector. I'm a civvy nurse. Leave me out, please.'

After being woken by a flying bomb switching off overhead for the last time in late March 1945, it took me a very long time to accept so much was all over. Only then, when nights were undisturbed, could I afford the luxury of nightmares, and regularly woke soaked in sweat, or leapt instinctively out of bed when an early tram turned sharply off Westminster Bridge. For over a year I could only sleep flat on my face with a pillow over the back of my head and neck.

At last, daily off-duty was free time. Time to write; time for thought, friends, and even more than I had been stealing since the autumn, for the theatre. The flying bombs and rockets had near-emptied the London theatres. Through the generosity of the managers who daily sent free tickets to the London hospitals for the nurses' use, in those months I think I saw every play in London, and British theatrical history in the making at the New Theatre, St Martin's Lane.

The New was the temporary home of the bombed-out Old Vic Company that included Laurence Olivier, Ralph Richardson and Margaret Leighton. That season they put on four plays. *Arms And The Man*, *Peer Gynt*, *Uncle Vanya*, and *Richard III*. I saw the first three twice, and the fourth, thrice. No need for notes to recall the memory of the Margaret Leighton silver and slender as a young moon in the darkness of the hall of the Mountain King; Ralph Richardson musing dreamily on the swing as Uncle Vanya; the magic of Laurence Olivier's voice, heard in person for the first time. Towering over all other memories, Olivier as Richard III, moving about the stage with the evil grace of a scarlet spider; standing at the right corner up front by King Henry's coffin, his black head and mournful face bent piously over an open prayer book and glancing languidly sideways at the audience with eyes alight with mockery and triumph.

With another girl who shared my passion for the theatre and the co-operation of our ward Sisters, whenever possible on matinees we were off 2 to 5 and sent to last lunch at 1.30, which added an extra half-hour to our off-duty. Wartime matinees and evening performances started earlier because of the blackout. By missing lunch, racing over to Riddle, leaving our caps and aprons in the ground floor cloakroom, donning waiting coats and scarves to camouflage uniform dresses, running over the bridge, up the embankment, Northumberland Avenue and St Martin's Lane, we could drop into our front stalls as the curtain rose. (Always our free tickets were for the best seats.) Richard III ran a little longer than the other plays, and as we had to be back on-duty as Big Ben struck five, Richard's final, desperate 'A horse! a horse! my kingdom for a horse!' signalled our urgent need to creep silently from our seats and back up the nearest aisle as Richmond (Richardson) sprang forward in blue and gold from upstage centre: 'God and your arms be praised, victorious friends; The day is ours, the bloody dog is dead.'

In those and other performances in other theatres, at varying moments the voices of the cast were drowned by the chugging above or the explosions nearby. I never saw one actor or actress hesitate more than the seconds necessary for a hearing, duck, wince, or pay any other visible attention to the dangers obvious to all. But when a low flying bomb or an explosion ripped the eardrums a few seconds before some line such as 'Did you hear that gentle tapping on the window?' cast and audience collapsed with laughter. Then the play went on, and the audience went back into the dream world that provided the short, blessed, escape from reality so desperately needed.

After father's death my now old friend Charles, recovered from his illness and qualified, insisted on taking me to the Prince of Wales Theatre to see Sid Field. I had never before seen Sid Field and when we sat down was in no mind for laughter. Sid Field golfing, Sid Field in long black overcoat, black homburg hat, trailing white scarf as the prototype of all blackmarket spivs, Slasher Green from the Elephant and Castle, reduced me to helpless laughter. I had never (and have never) seen any comic to reach his brilliance. The packed audience rocked, writhed, bellowed with laughter. That was the only time I saw Sid Field on the stage and I never forget the occasion or his genius. The Old Vic Company gave me hours of enchanted escape. Sid Field gave me one evening of pure joy at a time when I had forgotten the word 'joy' existed.

By March 1945 the Allies had crossed the Rhine, the Russians, advancing even more swiftly into Germany from the east, had crossed the Oder. I had moved to Casualty and in my first month there had personal contact with British nursing history. It was the last month before the retirement of the Sister Casualty (the late Miss Annie Beale) who had held that post unbroken since 1909, and been a Nightingale probationer while Miss Nightingale was still alive and in close contact with her School.

As I saw that legendary (in St Thomas's) Sister Casualty, she was a small, stoutish, be-spectacled elderly lady with grey-white hair, a brisk manner, and no equal in the speed at which she could diagnose at sight and allot to the correct place on either the rows of long wooden benches or in one of the many small examination clinic and dressing-rooms that lined both sides of her department, the non-stop flow of incoming patients. With equal speed and efficiency she dealt with the equally non-stop incoming and outgoing long and short white coats, white aprons, blue-coated porters, tweedy and shirt-sleeved students, stretcher-trolleys and wheelchairs. Amongst my many mental pictures imprinted for life is the one of Sister Casualty on my first Saturday afternoon in her domain, when the solitary flying bomb of the afternoon switched off its engine overhead. Sister Casualty, standing straight as a guardsman with her be-frilled cap and the starched lace bow under her venerable chin in impeccable order, announcing with calm firmness, 'Will all patients and staff please get down on the floor,' to a department already crouched on its knees with its head under the nearest bench. The bomb exploded on ruins and brought down every medicine and lotion bottle on every shelf in Casualty, but otherwise did no serious damage. Before getting off the floor, I squinted up at Sister. She was still upright and briskly polishing her spectacles.

The next night one of my friends arrived back at Riddle House from her weekend at home, white and breathless. She had forgotten to ask for late leave and a key to our front door locked at eleven, and her train had been late in at Waterloo. 'To save time I thought I'd nip back through The Cut (Lambeth). I knew I was daft and soon as I got into The Cut I was scared stiff. I could feel I was being watched from the darkness and nearly screamed when two shadows suddenly loomed up on either side of me. Two spivs—black coats—black hats—the lot. And they gave me hell. "Nurse ain't you? Going back to old Thomas's? What you think you're doing then. Don't you know no better than to come along of here this time of night? Ain't you got no sense, gal? We'll see you back but don't you never try this on again, see? Don't you never!" They practically frog-marched me all the way back to our front steps still narking, then vanished in the blackout before I could thank them.'

Someone said she was lucky they had not been GIs; someone else thought the Poles were the worst; then by common consent that particular accolade was awarded the French Canadians. Those views were only based on academic observations. London had for years been filled with alien Allied servicemen and British servicemen, had the normal hazards of any great city, and was under a constant blackout that in winter transformed the early evenings into pitch darkness. But never in my training, as in the Army, did I know or hear of one nurse even mildly assaulted when walking in the streets of London alone or with another girl, in the blacked-out nights. When away from the hospital, we wore not protecting uniforms but civilian clothes. Nevertheless, to say 'I'm a nurse' produced seats on the most crowded buses, trams, tubes, trains, and more free taxi-rides from London taxi-drivers than I could possibly recall.

To our St Thomas's patients, we were 'The poor nurses. Lovely girls. It's not right.' And the residents were, 'The poor doctors. Lovely young men. It's not right.'

The war with Germany was nearly over when another rocket

landed in our zone. I was loaned to a ward for the afternoon and evening. Just after nine that night I pushed a metal trolley out of the ward entrance as a young couple charged up the stairs and up the short outer ward corridor. 'Nurse, have you got our Doreen? Age, nine—short fair hair—brown eyes, tall like. That old Sister below reckons as you might—oh, nurse!' The young mother grabbed from the lower shelf of my trolley a pair of dusty blue child's sandals. 'Them's our Doreen's! See, Frank, see—that's the buckle come off down the Tube last night and I mended it afore we come back home this morning —oh, thank Gawd! You got her—you got her—how is she, nurse? All right, is she? Can we see her—be with her?'

That was the most terrible professional moment of my nursing life. A few minutes earlier I had closed the eyes and straightened the limbs of the unknown dead child who had worn those sandals.

I thought that night that I had seen the worst of man's inhumanity to man. About three months later I discovered I was wrong when I heard the first-hand accounts from some of the twelve senior medical students from St Thomas's who were amongst the first Allied contingent to arrive in Belsen Concentration Camp. 'The pong was beyond belief or description. Faeces everywhere. Right up the walls, thick on the floor and all over the kind of wire pigeon-holes they had for beds. No bedding, pigeon-holes full of skeletons, only some of the skeletons were alive and they all had diarrhoea and were starving and too weak to lift themselves. On our first morning when we walked into our first hut—it wasn't like walking into hell. Hell, in comparison must be clean and decent. And there was this extraordinary thin wail going round. We couldn't understand it—we were working in pairs—and neither of us spoke German. One of the skeletons, I think he was a Pole, spoke English and told us the wail was their way of trying to cheer us. He died the next day. Rows died. Everywhere outside the huts were bloody great mounds of dead. All unburied.'

When they reached Belsen, on 2nd May 1945, the unburied dead numbered 12 000. In the first few weeks after the Allies' arrival, 12 800 former political prisoners beyond saving also died. Quite near Belsen Camp was a German Army Panzer Training School with sturdy barracks, a cinema, a swimming pool and just beyond the gates, a German Army Hospital. Roughly three miles away was a country village called Bergen. After Belsen Camp was finally evacuated and with flame-throwers the Allies burnt down all the original prison huts, some of the Bergen villagers, I was told, helped tidy away the ashes.

On 1st May Hitler killed himself in his Berlin air-raid shelter. One evening in the last week of the European war, an old VAD friend now in her fourth year at the London Hospital, asked me to a party at her parents' home in Hampstead. At one point she and I and some young men were chided for laughing by a newcomer, a young woman of about twenty-seven with lank dark hair and a darkly intense manner. 'The trouble with all of you', she said, 'is that you haven't the faintest notion what's really been happening in this war!'

One of the men, a newly returned civilian with an artificial foot in his left shoe, had known her at University. 'Where did you get your great insight into the recent hostilities, darling? I thought you'd wangled a nice cushy Ph.D. after your degree in Eng.Lit.?'

'My dear man! Let me tell you I have spent the last three months working in a hospital as a nurse! Once one has nursed, one knows what real suffering is and one can't be expected to enjoy or approve frivolity.'

My friend and I exchanged glances. A middle-aged man, standing near, looked up from his pin-striped legs. 'Personally, I subscribe to Aristophanes' view that only those who have known great grief are really cheerful.'

I had a day off on the last day of the European war and spent it at home. All day we waited for the official announcement from General Eisenhower and were still waiting when I had to return to London. In the outer suburbs the bonfires were being lit, and my carriage shouted from the windows to the porters as we drew into Victoria. 'Old Ike made up his mind yet?'

'Not yet, mate. War's still on, seemly.'

In Riddle House I went out on our roof with one of my set. Her only brother had been missing since the fall of Singapore. John was in Texas training as a pilot on one of the Lease–Lend inter-services training schemes. 'I don't feel all that victorious, Lu. Do you?'

'No.' We leant on the roof wall and looked down with the same dazed detachment learnt from the same years of bad news. Having for so long been braced against the bad, the defences needed time to relax enough to accept the good. 'Doesn't look that victorious. Doesn't look much different, aside from those few lights in windows and the bonfires.'

Very few lights visible from that roof that night. Nearly everywhere windows as lifeless as those bricked-in across the road. The hospital looked unchanged. The blast and sandbag walls outside the entrance to Casualty, Out-Patients, the many side ramps running down into the basement, were merging as usual into the shadows. The crumbled blocks, the roofless windowless wards, the heaps of rubble, the empty uneven patches, belonged to the pigeons and the inquisitive gulls wheeling in from the black river. Below in the Lambeth Palace Road a few of the private cars had the black paint half-scraped from their headlamps, but one tram had both heads clear and as it swept round from the bridge with the half-roar, half-scream that so uncannily resembled the sound of a diving plane, the whole road was illuminated by twin searchlights.

When the light faded, more bonfires blazed on old bomb-sites and in cul-de-sacs, and as a red glow rose over Lambeth I shivered in memory. In a clearing a few hundred yards off a little group of people lit another bonfire, dragged an upright piano from a half-ruined empty house and against one jagged outer wall. A man began playing *Roll Out The Barrel*, some children started dancing round the fire, and their strangely elongated shadows danced on the high, jagged wall behind the piano.

Voices floated up. 'When is Ike going to make up his mind about stopping the war?' Girls' voices from the windows below; men's voices from the Two Sawyers, the pub on the nearest corner; student's voices from the hospital terraces. All sounded packed with false excitement. Good news was not to be trusted and who could be sure the news was good until General Eisenhower officially accepted the Germans' unconditional surrender and told the Allied armies in Europe to stop fighting?

The students on the terrace let off a few tatty fireworks. One of the tugs on the river sounded her siren, other tugs followed and then all the ships in the docks. We went inside. 'Has it come, girls?'

'Not yet.'

The sirens' chorus continued until quenched by a tremendous thunderstorm that seemed to last all night. I fell asleep to the comforting uproar and knowledge that it was only thunder. In the morning I woke with a start, sweating, as an early tram turned down from the bridge, and discovered General Eisenhower had ordered 'the cessation of hostilities at one minute past midnight' whilst I had been asleep.

I was on at 7.30 a.m. and free from 2 p.m. for the now official Victory half-day given to the whole Casualty medical and nursing staff. Half of us had that first day of peace, the other half, the second. We had expected an empty department. Lambeth had other views. Now the war was over the time had come to nip up to old Thomas's and let the doctor take a good look at that old trouble in the tonsils, stomach, knee, back, big toe, little finger. All day our benches were packed.

One woman had a headache. 'Torment, doctor, that's what. Torment. I tell you no lie. Started up the day the war started and not given me no peace, not the once. If you was to ask me, doctor, I'd say as I got a geezer up there with a hammer and he's been a-banging away, bang bang bang, since it started.'

It was 4.15 p.m. and the house-physician attending her had the same half-day as myself. 'Not to worry, madam. War's over. That chap with the hammer'll ask for his ticket. You'll have no more headaches.' Filling in her blue Casualty card at the standing desk, he murmured to me, 'Chap needs a Long Service Medal. How long's he been on the job?'

I could not remember, either. We used our fingers to calculate from 3rd September 1939, to 8th May 1945. He wrote in to the hour, the exact time-span of the headache.

Charles was working as a houseman in the Sector, had the same Victory half-day but less-active patients and reached London by 3.30. He came into Casualty and sat in an unwanted wheelchair. When asked by other members of the staff if he needed attention, he replied truthfully, 'No, thanks, I've been discharged. Just waiting for someone.'

I eventually got off just before five, and having changed quickly out of uniform, with Charles and a temporary escort of three Thomas's housemen, joined the crowds streaming west over the bridge into Parliament Square. All traffic in that area had stopped, and pavements, roads, islands, lamp-posts and railings were massed with people. We managed to squeeze onto an island at the foot of Whitehall towards the end of Mr Churchill's speech to the crowd from a Ministry of Health balcony, but I could not hear a word he said for the laughter. 'Pity you missed most,' said the man jammed against Charles's left side, 'old Winnie was in top form. Spicey!' We joined in the wild cheering after the speech. The crowd cheered everything and everyone from the Prime Minister to the inevitable policeman who lost his helmet. A little later we were swept back with the one crowd, the three housemen swept away by another. Charles and I found ourselves in the front row of the parted ranks through which the ubiquitous Mr Churchill with permanent beam, cigar in mouth and two fingers raised in the V-sign, was driven into the House of Commons. 'Mind your backs, please,' coaxed the police, to allow through two more cars. I recognized the occupant in the back of the first as Mr Hore-Belisha, but not the man in the next car, though I cheered him with the crowd.

'Realize who you're cheering, Lucy?' Charles yelled into my ear. 'Ernie Bevin!'

'My God! No!' Most of my set had already been directed by the Government into midwifery or T.B. nursing. I had chosen the former and signed to start a midwifery course in August, before inquiring the pay for this enforced project. It had never occurred to me this would involve losing money as well as time. The pay for pupil-midwives was £4 per month.

The moment was too good to be shadowed by anger. I forgot the Minister of Labour within seconds of his car's disappearance into the House of Commons yard.

We decided to visit the King and Queen, along with, apparently, half a million others. It took us so long to squeeze through Birdcage Walk, that again our ranks were parted for Mr Churchill's car. More wild cheers, beams, and V-signs from the cigar-smoker. The crowd outside Buckingham Palace was the thickest yet, the cheers were not so much wild as affectionate. 'Didn't catch him nor his good lady turning no evacuees, did you,' observed the Londoners clinging with ourselves to footholds on the Victoria Memorial. 'Stuck it out here same as we had to and when a bomb's got your moniker on it you can't say as it makes no difference if you got a crown on your napper or a titfer. Took his chances, he did—and his good lady—and when they says to her as she best scarpa to Canada with the two young 'uns, she tells 'em straight out—politely like, mind—as she can't leave her old man and the young 'uns can't go without their mum can they, so ta very much but the lot'll be staying put. Here they comes—and with old Winnie this time!'

The atmosphere grew more euphoric. We greeted and were greeted by total strangers, exchanged life, war histories, and bad jokes that we assured each other were good enough for ITMA. We saw very few drunks, and heard from the crowds and discovered most pubs in that area had long run dry of their meagre supplies.

In the last pub we visted, the landlord offered us his remaining stock. A siphon of soda and small bottle of what looked like purple syrup. The landlord said he would tell us straight he'd not fancy it himself. 'Alright, mind, if you're partial to a drop of linctus.'

Charles sipped his mixture. 'Nothing against a good linctus, but I wouldn't call this vintage. Bit hard,' he added, 'here we've been singing for ages about getting lit up when the lights go on in London. How in hell do you get lit up on linctus? I thought this would be like Armistice Night. My father said that was a riot.'

The landlord was elderly. 'Your old man's dead right, boy.

Different, this do. Mind you, this do's been a different do and it's not really all over bar the shouting yet seeing as we still got to finish off the Japs. But nice to have the lights back on. Fetching them back ten-thirty, won't it be? Reckon they'll be having quite a time fixing all the fuses seeing they've not been needed for six years.' He stacked away glasses, wiped his counter. 'When you've done I'll shut up and nip out to watch 'em fetch 'em back on.'

We thought, again with about half-a-million others, that we would get the best view of the switch-on from the middle of Westminster Bridge as from there we could see the north and south banks and up and down the river. By more squeezing, pushing, apologizing, joking and swapping life histories, we managed to reach our chosen spot with roughly half an hour to spare. Never before, or since, had I been in a crowd of the magnitude of the one now swamping every inch of London discernible through the deepening darkness. A man just behind us had squeezed his way from the Bayswater Road. 'Not standing room this side of Hyde Park. Case of father turns, we all turn.'

In theory I would have expected to find a crowd that size terrifying. In fact I found it neither frightening nor even mildly claustrophobic. As all the crowds all evening, it was too good-natured, and above all, too relieved even for minor intolerance. If feet were squashed, glasses knocked off, elbows jammed in ribs, well, all part of the bit of fun wasn't it and a lot better than a poke in the eye from a sharp stick. 'Or them doodles. Can't rightly credit there'll be no more of them doodles.'

The chatter, the laughter, the snatches of songs from hundreds of thousands of throats, rolled to and fro over our heads like the rolling roaring waves of a great amiably growling sea. Suddenly, silence. Suddenly, unbelievably, the lights of London came on again and when they came on, for a second or more, the whole crowd around us, stayed silent. It was as if none of us dared trust our eyes or even risk breathing in case the mirage disappeared. When it did not, at first almost hesitantly, the cheering started again, and then the cheers rose and rose in crescendo after crescendo.

Maybe not every bulb in every street, embankment and bridge light was working properly and not every public building a triumphant tower of light. But that was how it looked. Tears were pouring down my face, and when I looked around, down the faces of all the women and more than a few of the men in my sight. And when my eyes were clear of tears and acclimatized to the new lighting, the whole city seemed blazing with light and most wonderful of all, still there. There, the Houses of Parliament and Big Ben, there Millbank, there Vauxhall Bridge, there New Scotland Yard, there, just visible, the dome of St Paul's, and there, on both sides, north and south of the Thames, the jagged roofless walls and the great stretches of empty bomb-sites, with the scars softened by the darkness enhancing the glory of that glorious moment in London's history.

Chapter Eleven

JULY 1945 and the first General Election in Britain for ten years.

'The department's having a quiet moment, N. Andrews,' said the new young Sister Casualty, 'nip over to the polling booth and cast your first vote.'

I slung my cloak over my indoor uniform, slightly adjusted the Nightingale bonnet on my head, crossed the Lambeth Palace Road and, with so many of my fellow-citizens voting for the first time, used my first democratic opportunity to record my objection to having been deprived of my youth.

The Election results changed British political and social history. The Labour Party was returned with 392 seats (211 gains), the Conservatives and other Parties, 189 seats (194 losses), and Mr Clement Attlee replaced Mr Churchill as Prime Minister.

On the 6th August one small atom bomb was dropped on and extinguished the city of Hiroshima in Japan. Two days later I started training as a pupil-midwife and the following day, with the mind still numbed with the horrifying reports of Hiroshima, the news of a second atom bomb on Nagasaki. 'For God's sake—why another?'

'Presumably those in high places don't think burning one city to a crisp is enough to set the rising sun.'

On 14th August 1945, Japan surrendered unconditionally. At the bottom of St Thomas's long-exiled Midwifery Unit's Surrey garden the midder-clerks built a huge celebration bonfire no-one had time to light. V.J. (Victory in Japan) Day had come and gone before I realized the war had ended and had time to remember my old intention to stop nursing and become a writer when that end came.

Never had I worked so hard. The day pupils' day started at 7 a.m. and finished at 9 p.m., unless one of the twelve maternity patients, which every pupil taking the course required before the examination for Part I of the Central Midwives Board Certificate had to deliver, had gone into labour. Once in labour the pupil stayed with her patient until delivering the baby and giving the first bath. Then, as in 1940, seventy-five per cent of all British babies were born at night. It was not unusual for a day pupil to finish a delivery in the small hours and report back at 7 a.m. Pupils did no delivering during their four consecutive weeks on night-duty; night hours were 9 p.m. to 8 a.m. Once again lecture and study-time had to be fitted in the daily three hours off and weekly day off.

'I can't think why you pupils keep grumbling because you only get four quid a month. When I was a pupil in '38, we had to pay to do midder.'

'I think that was disgraceful too, Sister.'

'Why? I wanted to be a midwife and I love midder! Don't you like it?'

'Yes, Sister, but liking doesn't come into it. I think it disgraceful because I think all forms of slave-labour disgraceful—even if the slaves are happy. There's no war on now—and there was no war on when you did midder.'

'Put the world right tomorrow, Andrews! This water's nothing like hot enough for the babies' baths. Pop down and see what's amiss with Jimmy. The two night pupils on this month are hopeless with the boilers.'

The Unit had neither porters, stokers, nor pros. The midder-clerks (medical students taking their midwifery course) did most of the porter-ing, the solitary gardener dealt daily with the boilers, except on Sunday, when, as at night, they were stoked by the pupils. All the cleaning and bedpan rounds were done by the pupils; and, in the smaller of the two country houses converted into maternity hospitals by the Unit, in the gardener's absence on Sundays the pupils burnt on bonfires the previous twenty-four hours' accumulation of dirty dressings.

When stokers and refuse-burners, we worked in pairs. I was

paired with Joan, a fellow-Nightingale and ex-VAD. Owing to our military past, in either capacity we basked in the sunshine of senior smiles. 'How you two never fail to keep the boilers going or to get a blazing bonfire in pouring rain I can't imagine!'

'Natural talent, Sister,' we simpered and covertly returned the half-empty tins of floor polish to the housemaid's (i.e., pupils') cupboard.

In both houses the labour wards were on the first floor, the lying-in wards on the ground, and there were no lifts. In Ashwood House, the larger of the two, the midder-clerks did all the daytime stretcher-bearing. At night this was shared between the houseman, the clerk on-call, Night Sister and night pupils. As the houseman lived in Ashwood and there were no clerks in the smaller house, there the Sister Midwives and pupils carried all the stretchers. Women, even at full term, were lighter than men. Normal labour has three stages. For any clerk or pupil who trained in St Thomas's bombed out Midwifery Unit there were four. The fourth stage arrived when the newly delivered mother on the collapsible, poleless, canvas stretcher was carried from the labour ward, along the corridor, down the twisting stairs to her bed in a former dining-room, drawing-room, or billiard-room.

Another sideline at Ashwood was the laundry. On occasions the daily laundress did not appear, so Sister Nursery and the pupils took over the washing, boiling and mangling of the daily average of four hundred nappies. (No washing machines.)

Working in that Unit was just like being in a chummy stage crowd. Everyone played several parts, but the inter-staff atmosphere was extraordinarily amiable. Possibly, being a small, tightly enclosed community, we realized we either had to tolerate each other or go mad, or possibly we were all too busy for introspection and blood feuds. Whatever the basic cause, I noted in February 1946: 'Here (at Ashwood) we are on the whole one Big Happy Family and with a few lapses our hearts beat as one.'

The pupils spent their six months' course working between the two houses. The midder-clerks usually had three weeks' residence in Ashwood; the day one set moved out, the next set moved in. Their sets varied between four and eight and were promptly assimilated in the stage crowd. In addition to their midwifery schedule of delivering their allotted patients, watching the more complicated deliveries performed by the houseman, or obstetric consultants, watching the Caesarian operations, attending teaching rounds, taking medical case histories, learning how to bath, feed and change babies, the clerks carried stretchers, heavy laundry baskets, heaved full and empty oxygen cylinders up and down the stairs, washed clean of bloodstains the labour ward sheets used by their respective patients, mopped clean the labour ward floor after their deliveries, transferred from large kidney dishes to newspapers their patients' discarded placentas and burnt the packets in the larger and newer of the two boilers in the cellar.

The older, smaller, boiler was Jimmy, the newcomer, Jimmy's Little Brother. Jimmy was the more likely to choke to death on clinkers in the small hours, with devastating results as the L.B. then wilted in sympathy and the whole hot-water system—and babies' early morning baths—depended on both boilers. When Joan and I went on night-duty we were warned that Jimmy was a temperamental swine to be handled with great gentleness. We decided otherwise. Every night, immediately free of the handing-over report, we raced for the cellar, hung our caps and aprons on the outside of the cellar door, descended the few stairs and amongst the coke and the cockroaches, whatever the boilers' condition, disembowelled both, rebuilt them only with the still glowing coke, opened every vent the gardener had carefully closed down, and raised the cellar temperature to a degree that would have shamed Dante's imagination.

Some nights a nervous new clerk appeared at the top of the stairs gingerly holding out a packet seeping redly. 'Terribly sorry, nurses—er—Sister Labour Ward told me—er—to shove this in something called Jimmy's L.B.'

'Don't you dare damp the bastard down with your placenta, Mr . . .! He's being a worse neuro than Jimmy tonight! Leave it on the top step. We'll bung it in later.'

The Ashwood nursing staff shared bedrooms on the attic floor, the men lived over the garage occupied by the Unit's autoclave. As the obstetric houseman was in residence for from six months to one year, he had a tiny private bedroom. The clerks shared a plywood-partitioned box decorated with charts, diagrams and Medical School wit that ranged from Rabelais to prep school. The autoclave, a massive, silver, cylindrical machine in which was done all the Unit's sterilizing, was directly under their box. I learnt how to work our autoclave but never understood how I did, or why, at intervals, it chose to whistle violently or belch jets of boiling steam. When the steam billowed up the loft stairs in clouds, and wisps came through their floorboards, unwary clerks hurtled from above gasping piteously, 'Where's the fire brigade? Are they coming?'

'Relax. Just part of the system—and do get out of the light. I've turned up taps A, B and C and if I don't turn down taps D, E and F we'll probably all go through the roof.'

The majority of the clerks by 1946 were just too junior to have had personal experience of a hospital under air attacks and it was the first time they had actually worked with nurses, as opposed to standing around wards watching the nurses work. I was frequently surprised by how little even those within a few months of qualifying knew of the actual workings of a hospital and how their knowledge of illness and injuries was almost totally academic. In my general training I had already noticed how swiftly medical attitudes to nurses changed after qualification. Doctors and nurses were, and knew they were, on the same side. Medical students, no matter how individually pleasant, were basically antagonistic to the nursing staff, possibly because until medical students became doctors they needed no professional help from nurses.

Another thing that surprised me was how young they seemed, how similar to the boys I had known before the war and dissimilar to the boys I had known in the war and who, at their same age, had been men. Some of those men I had known, when they died, had been even younger than the clerks— whose ages were roughly twenty-one to twenty-three. One evening in the small sitting-room shared by the whole staff when drinking the tea served when we came off at nine, the conversation centred on 1941. All the five clerks present had then been reading medicine at Oxford or Cambridge. 'Glorious April and May,' said one. 'Lilac everywhere and the college lawns green velvet. Glorious sense of peace—war didn't seem to matter—going on in another world. . . .' I thought of G being shot down in that other world at that same time, left my unfinished tea and walked alone round the darkening garden until my anger cooled. I was not angry with the clerks. Their good fortune was not their responsibility. I was angry for G and for all those thousands of other young men who would never know the scent of another lilac or the sight of another green velvet lawn but had made it possible for millions of others to know both. Are people forgetting them already, I wondered, and then realized that already most of us who had known the war preferred not to talk about it. It was that that cooled my anger. And I remembered a middle-aged patient once saying to me, 'Yesterday's always forgotten. Youth is only interested in today; middle age in tomorrow; old age in the day before yesterday. Nobody bothers with yesterday.'

The next day was the kind of day only a maternity hospital experiences. Seven babies were born. The labour ward door swung to and fro like an hotel foyer. Every half hour the staircase echoed with the grunts and groans of the clerks in the fourth stage and the giggled encouragement of the weary patients, dazed with relief and joy. 'You're doing all right, ducks—doing lovely!' I was working in the nursery crowded with the extra row of portable canvas labour-ward cots identical to those I had used in the shelter at nights for the new-born babies in Families. But in that row of cots, damp-haired, finger-sucking, shouting, blinking, new-born babies only awaiting their first baths and born into peace.

I liked working in the nursery as much as I disliked working in the labour ward. I had neither the temperament nor talent for midwifery and only managed safely to deliver twelve healthy babies through the combined help and advice of my supervising Sister Midwife, the lectures from our Midwife

Tutor and consultant obstetricians, and 'my' twelve mothers. All seemed to me to spend more of their labour comforting and encouraging myself, than vice versa.

'Childbirth, nurses, is, of course, a natural function for women. However, before you are tempted to equate natural with easy, just remember, so is death a natural function for men and women. But—easy?'

March, 1946: 'You may read your papers now, nurses. . . .'

After the written we took the then extant practical and viva voce examination for Part I, C.M.B., at another London teaching hospital. The examination patients were all volunteers from the midwifery department. One of the three male consultant obstetricians asked me to examine a patient hidden by an open screen at the other end of the room. 'I'll join you in a few minutes, nurse.'

Very nervously I walked round the screen and wished the youngish woman, obviously in advanced pregnancy, a good morning. Before I could touch her bed or pick up the waiting foetal stethoscope, she murmured under her breath, 'He's trying to catch you out on me, duck. All do it. I got two in there and one's upside down and lying on top of his mate.'

I was too used to trusting helpful patients to doubt her, and as I knew what to look for, made the correct diagnosis. The examiner grunted 'H'mm, well, yes.' He had a little chat about the weather with the patient then suggested we went and sat down for a small talk. He walked away first and she winked at me behind his back. I did not dare wink back.

Once Part I was obtained, pupils who were not continuing to Part II, and the six months' course in district-midwifery and further examination necessary for the full qualification State Certified Midwife, were required by St Thomas's to work another four months in the Unit as Maternity Staff Nurses. Civilian-trained nurses had still not been released by the Government, and I was given the post of Nursery Staff Nurse. I enjoyed those months more than any in either of my nursing trainings. When paid my first month's salary as a Mat. Staff

Nurse, I thought there had been a mistake. '£8 ? Just for òne month?'

'That's right, nurse. Government's put nurses' pay up. You're in the money now!'

Finally, unbelievably, 'Well, nurses, now you are all free to choose for yourselves—what are you going to do?"

In late July 1946, I had my farewell interview with the Matron of St Thomas's in the same office off the alcove from the main corridor in St Thomas's, London. I was astounded to be offered a post as Sister in an acute surgical ward at Botley's Park with an initial two-year contract. Whilst the offer was being made, I knew instinctively, and regretfully, that I must refuse it. I had grown fond of St Thomas's, but I had signed too many contracts, used up too many years. In November, half-way through the twenties; five years' time, thirty—middle age. As I had to earn my living, nursing was my only means of doing so until I could change to professional writing. So I decided I must only take temporary posts—I knew too well how difficult, if not impossible, it was to combine the two occupations. And as civilian nurses had no demobilization gratuities I had to find another job very quickly.

I was given some helpful advice on temporary nursing posts and wished success in my future career as a writer. 'Thank you, N. Andrews. Goodbye.'

No duckboards across the main corridor, no chips of plaster and thick dust on Miss Nightingale's statue and in Central Hall, no bricks left in any windows, and everywhere giant machines clearing the ground and preparing to build the new hospital on the old Lambeth site.

Chapter Twelve

FOR the remainder of 1946 I worked as a temporary day Staff Nurse in a series of London nursing homes. In one of these, into one of the rooms for which I was responsible, an elderly Jewish gentleman was admitted for ophthalmic surgery. He was special-nursed by ophthalmic-trained nurses, but as he was in one of my rooms I relieved his specials for meals and off-duty enough for him to put a name to my voice. He looked a very fragile figure when propped up in bed with the pillows carefully arranged behind his high-domed bald head, his eyes bandaged and thin, aesthetic face tapering to the point of his little grey imperial, and was a courteous, stoic patient of such unassuming charm that I was astounded to learn, only from his visitors, that he was one of the great figures in Jewish and world history. (Consequently, here only, the full name of one of my ex-patients.) He was Dr Chaim Weizmann, the founder and future first President of the State of Israel. (Inaugurated 15th May 1948).

Sometimes when I was alone with him, Dr Weizmann talked quietly of the country still called Palestine and I listened and remembered the obscenity called Belsen.

'One day, N. Andrews, one day, when we have our new Jewish State of Israel, you must come and visit us. One day.'

One morning I sat at his bedside helping him with his breakfast. 'Please, Dr Weizmann, can I ask you something that I'm afraid may sound rather daft?'

'But, of course, and I'm sure it will not sound daft. It is— ?'

'I've been wondering how it must feel to be you and know you're founding a new State, a new world, for your people. How does it feel?'

Dr Weizmann, his eyes still shaded, reflectively swallowed the final teaspoonful of boiled egg and continued to reflect for some seconds. 'Troublesome, N. Andrews, troublesome.'

(I have not yet been able to visit Israel. In 1968 my daughter Veronica (Vee), between grammar school and Cambridge, was awarded one of the scholarships provided by The Bridge In Britain and spent six months in Israel working first in Kibbutz Kfar Hanassi and then Jerusalem. On her return she said she had never mentioned my having briefly nursed the late Dr Weizmann (1874–1952) until near the end of her stay at a party in Tel Aviv. 'Ma, I could've won the Six-Day War single-handed. I shot top of the pops over Moshe Dayan and I didn't need an eye-patch!' And I remembered the frail propped up figure with bandaged eyes saying, 'One day....')

In the autumn of 1946 instead of, as I had planned, spending all my spare time writing, I spent most of it visiting a patient in the Brompton Chest Hospital. He was a young doctor, J, whom I had known slightly at Hydestile in 1943, and he had a lung abscess. He was a heavy smoker, and on all my visits his single-bedded side-ward was clouded with tobacco. 'Come on, Lucille, try one. I hate smoking alone. No, don't suck it, breathe in.' One of the many lasting consequences of my visits to the Brompton that autumn has been my addiction to nicotine.

Early in 1947, J was well enough to return to full-time work as a junior registrar in a mental hospital and hoped to specialize in psychiatric medicine. I continued in full-time nursing until two days before our marriage on 1st May 1947. On the evening of 30th April, I tore up and burnt the unfinished novel I had begun after leaving St Thomas's. It was dull, pompous, rubbish, and I knew it. I had intended making a fresh start when we returned from our honeymoon but in the event had other matters on my mind. By the second week of our honeymoon I had learnt, with a distress beyond description, that my husband suffered from a condition my training and every professional instinct insisted, must be fatal.

At the first opportunity I consulted privately a certain

medical specialist. 'He doesn't believe it's so serious, Doctor.'

' "Physician, heal thyself." Alas, so seldom.' He talked at length and kindly. Finally, 'I'm afraid all we can do is devoutly hope we'll be proved wrong.'

For over two years hope died slowly and hard. Eventually, the day that had been inevitable from the first week of our honeymoon, arrived. On that day, in August 1949, Vee was four months old, and I had to accept reality and take over as both parents and breadwinner for us both. Our home in a small London flat had to be abandoned and as I had neither income nor savings I had immediately to find work. And a roof. The Welfare State was just over a year old. There were no supplementary benefits, no family allowances for the first child. The allowance for every child after the first was 5s. (25p) per week. State recognition of the existence, much less the problems, of the one-parent family was a quarter-of-a-century ahead. (The Finer Report on *The Problems Of The One-Parent Family*, July 1974).

In 1948 mother had sold our St Leonards' house and moved into a top floor rented flat.

'Of course you and the baby must come for a holiday by the sea. . . .'

'My dear, I've got the perfect answer! There's a cottage down our lane going furnished for only six guineas a week and just a bit more for the daily who's a treasure!'

'Are you not over-dramatizing? Why can't he be cured? Everyone knows doctors are working miracles with this penicillin stuff. . . .'

'Only too happy to advise you, m'dear, having known your late father and all your family these many years. So your sister's got herself a job as a secretary in London? Most enterprising you young ladies these days! We old fogies who think a woman's place is in the home are having to shake up our ideas, eh? And young brother now a medical student? Excellent things these new government grants for the ex-service youngsters. Fine profession for a man, medicine. Now what precisely is your financial situation . . . no savings? Surely, during your nursing years you managed to put by . . .

no, possibly not. Indeed, yes. Regrettably your late father was unable to leave more than the mortgaged house and the small widow's pension. The many years of travel and school-fees took their financial toll of too many of those long-exiled in our now sadly defunct Empire. House had to be sold to pay off the mortgage and provide a small supplement to your mother's slender means. Unfortunately many a pension that appeared adequate in the twenties and thirties is being rendered increasingly inadequate by the rising cost of post-war living. Bluntly, m'dear, the last war cost this country much more money than it could afford. We'll be in the red for years—but I mustn't bother your pretty little head with these sordid financial matters. Leave them to us mere males, eh! However, we should discuss the income you'll doubtless be receiving from your husband . . . oh. Nevertheless m'dear, you mustn't take such a pessimistic view! No cloud without a silver lining! You haven't a bank account? Well, what you must do is put some money in, then you'll be issued with a cheque book and can draw it out as you please. Only don't forget—ha ha—you've to put the money in first!'

'Yes, madam. We can offer you forty pounds for this engagement ring. Sign here, please, madam. Thank you, madam. Good morning.'

'You have an S.R.N. Part I C.M.B., and Nightingale Certificate? Yes, indeed, I am sure I can offer you a junior ward Sister's post . . . oh. Oh, no. I'm afraid we have no crèches—this is a general hospital, you'll remember—and I'm afraid we cannot adjust staff day hours to accommodate domestic responsibilities. Oh, no, we never employ part-time trained staff—but if you can arrange to board out your baby, please come and see me.'

By day the voices in reality; by night, in the mind. The nights were the worst. Anxiety, fear, sadness and the throttling helplessness induced by the growing realization of my limited education and the limited salary and long hours I would have to work if I returned to hospital nursing, gripped the throat and haunted sleep. From our first day alone I remained determined Vee should not lose both parents because she had had to lose one. I knew I was the one figure that provided continuity in her already disturbed life and refused to contemplate breaking that continuity throughout her childhood.

'I think you're right, but I'm afraid you're going to find this very difficult, Mrs. . . . Useless to pretend this isn't a tough world, or, it must be admitted, a man's world. For a young woman to bring up a child alone it can be a very tough world. How are you going to manage?'

'I don't know. But as I have to, I will.'

The stranger from whom I had sought professional advice looked at me over his desk, then nodded. 'Yes. When one's got to do something, one does it.' He avoided my eyes and fiddled with his blotter. 'I don't know if you're aware—that is to say—there is now something called National Assistance. You'd certainly qualify for help in my opinion, but I doubt it would be—at the most—more than ten shillings a week. Would you like me—'

'No thank you. I'll earn the ten bob a week for myself.'

He nodded again. 'So would I.'

The Welfare State was too young for either of us to have outgrown the conviction deeply engrained in all British social classes that all public assistance was charity and existed only to help the physically disabled very poor. As engrained and widespread was the belief that even when an individual was poverty-stricken it remained the fundamental responsibility of that individual to right the situation as best he or she could by his or her own efforts.

'All very well to say you'll manage, but how? How can you ever be financially independent? How can any woman, unless she's had the luck to inherit money or to have had enough education to be something like a doctor, a lawyer, a teacher? Teachers mayn't earn much, but at least they have the long school holidays and weekends free with their kids. How many women doctors and lawyers do you know?'

In 1949, amongst all the girls and women I had known since

boarding-school, two doctors, one lawyer. The last, a war widow with a small son, was the only woman I knew able to support a child and herself in their own home on her earnings. She had qualified as a solicitor just before she married.

In the three weeks I took to find work I formed the two resolutions that pre-set the course of our entire future. The first was that Vee must have a first-class academic education and a university degree, whether she later wanted marriage, a career, or both. The second was that I must be earning enough by writing to be able to work from home by the time she was old enough for school. I had no idea, nor did I attempt to plan, where our home or her school would then be. I made the last future plans of my life, and for the last time escaped temporarily into my fantasy world, in the first week of May 1947.

I knew Vee was far too young for me to assess her intelligence, and that even if she were not, I loved her too much for a balanced judgment. But I knew, had nursed and seen in normal and abnormal circumstances by the hundreds, my fellow-women. I had observed how high was the average intelligence of 'the average woman', and simultaneously, how often this tended to be underrated not so much by 'the average man' as by the more academically educated esoteric minds of both sexes. I had also observed the fact that the old medical maxim 'Commonest things are the most common' was true. I saw no reason why Vee should be a non-average baby girl. If she was an average, I was convinced she could get into a university and that one of the two basic reasons why millions of women (including Betty and myself) when trying to earn livings found themselves surrounded by locked doors and were only able to open those that led into the poorly paid—and usually—blind alleys, was not lack of intelligence but lack of education. The second reason, of course, was—and is—that women bear babies.

From a chance encounter with old friends I heard of the existence of a new babies' residential nursery and rang the Matron to ask if she needed trained staff.

'And what's a young Tommy's lass with midder want with a job here? Can't be a general hospital in the country that'll not snap you up, gladly!'

I braced myself for the eighth time, 'I want to bring my baby to work with me, Matron.'

'Oh aye? With your qualifications, lass, bring five, so long as all are under one year. First birthday law says they've to go. Nought to one for my bairns. Come and see me this afternoon.'

I put down the receiver and wept.

The Matron was a youngish married woman who wore a white overall, a baby under each arm and an astute expression. She looked us over. 'Right, lass, let's get it out the road. No husband or bad husband?' And after, 'Only one end there, lass. Got a problem or two ahead, haven't you? Could be worse. You've a training.' She handed over her babies to a nurse, unhitched and lifted Vee from her borrowed pram, weighed her on flattened hands as if guessing the weight of a cake at a fête. 'You've a right PRO in this little lass. No problems here. Come into office. Hours eight to six, Mondays to Saturdays, Sundays free, non-resident—pay, three-and-a-half guineas a week paid Saturdays, lunches and cups of tea on the house and you can feed the little lass at her usual times.'

The relief of her attitude was almost comparable to the relief of having the job.

The nursery was supervised by the local authorities and a training school for nursery nurses. It was large and airy, well-equipped with fitted baby baths, good cots, prams, playroom, milk-room, central heating and plate-glass windows overlooking the large back lawn. Most of the babies were from London and sent in either by the local authorities or private welfare organizations with whom they had been placed in care. A very few were entered privately by parents or other relatives. No difference at all was made in the care all the babies received.

I worked mainly in the Prem Room. None of the babies there in my time were in fact 'prems'—i.e., newly born and beneath five pounds at birth-weight. In later years the room would probably have been renamed the Intensive Care Unit. It was the smallest nursery and clinically equipped to accommodate the babies admitted grossly underweight and suffering malnutrition caused by parental neglect, ignorance, or poverty.

Some had unmarried mothers who, occasionally, I met.

'I tried, Staff, honest I did. Couldn't even get a room nowhere. Landlady takes one look and slams the door in me face.
"Not having the likes of you here! This is a decent house!"'

Some mothers were married and deserted by their husbands.
'They says to me best go see the National Assistance. So I goes.
Ten bob a week, they says. Be thirty bob most like, they says,
if you wasn't married. You can get maintenance, can't you?
You tell me how, I says, seeing as he's scarpered and don't pay
up. You catch up with him, they says, he'll have to do time if
he don't pay. And what good's that to me? Bunging him in jug
won't pay me rent nor buy the baby's milk. Ten bob. I ask
you! And handed over like I was trying to nick it. You can't
manage, they says, have to put him in care, won't you. I'll
never, I says—but I had to, didn't I? Couldn't get work with
him. Couldn't keep him without working. Had to, didn't I?'

Other babies who first came into the Prem Room had been
found abandoned by the police. Where the parents remained
untraced we called the babies by the first names of their
rescuers. Stevie was found in a carrier bag on the floor of a
telephone booth; Johnny in the lower half of a shoebox left on
the front steps of a police station; Martin in a shopping-
basket in a railway waiting-room; Patrick in another carrier-
bag on a park bench. Very occasionally, as for Patrick, a tragic
little note was safety-pinned to a grubby shawl. 'Please call my
baby Patrick and be kind to him. I am very sorry.' That note,
as all similar that I saw, was unsigned.

I never heard if Patrick's mother was traced but often
thought of her when feeding Vee. On admission, Patrick
looked about three months old and weighed just over six
pounds. He did not look like a baby. He looked a tiny, yellow,
wizened old man with sad, adult eyes. I learnt to recognize
those tragic eyes in babies too young for milk-teeth, but not
for an adult apprehension no infant or child in either a sup-
posedly civilized or a primitive community should possess.
'Seen it all, Staff, and don't fancy owt—and who'll blame the
poor bairns? You ever met the bairn as asked to be born? Me,
neither.'

Slowly, after weeks of regular warmth, sleep, milk, orange juice, cod liver oil, cleanliness, fresh air and a kindness that if sometimes impersonal was invariably kindly, the pale worried crinkled miniatures of old age turned into healthy babies. Patrick progressed with astonishing rapidity.

'No surprise to me, Staff. Maybe his mam hadn't nous or cash to feed him rightly, but she's not starved him of love. Bairns need love as they need milk. Some place now that poor lass is likely still crying herself to sleep. Rum world. Half the lasses are crying as they've not borne bairns and other half are crying as they have.'

The nursery was good for Vee and myself. Vee was born a gregarious extrovert and enjoyed the companionship in the day nursery, playroom and the back lawn. As every baby of my experience, she flourished physically under the fixed daily routine of our lives. Throughout infancy and early childhood she slept unbroken twelve- to fourteen-hour nights. She was a cheerful sturdy baby with curly hair. 'Don't know why you bother to work, Staff—just get Fairy Snow to use the little lass in their advertisements. Dead spit of the one that walks round in a nappy.'

I liked, as always, working with babies. The 'prems', I loved. It was a joy to watch them grow into health and content, turn their heads like a Wimbledon crowd when I moved about the Prem Room, grin toothlessly when talked to, and drop off to sleep when sung lullabyes. I discovered how much they had helped me the evening I heard myself singing in slow time as a lullabye, the waltz 'The Girl That I Marry', from *Annie Get Your Gun*, a show J and I had seen in London early in our marriage when, very briefly, the optimism of the will had triumphed over the pessimism of the intelligence.

'What'll you do now, Staff?'

'Move us in with my sister and brother in Chelsea and work as temporary Night Sister in a pie-factory if the personnel manager approves. One of my old set at Thomas's has the job and wants a longish break. She's been asked to find a temp. Pay and hours are stupendous. Eleven quid for five nights a week, Sundays to Thursdays only nine to seven.'

The woman personnel manager had the well-scrubbed forthright air of a good ATS administration officer. 'And what happens the night your child suddenly gets ill just as you're about to leave for work?'

'First I ring for the nearest G.P. Then I ring the factory to say I'm sorry I won't be in first-aid that night.'

There was a silence. I thought the job lost.

'Fair enough. Now. . . .' Showing me out later, 'Think you'd had it?'

'Yes.'

'No. I've done this job long enough to know good liars and bad mothers make equally lousy employees.'

The first-aid department of the pie-factory was on the ground floor at the back of the packing hall. The department consisted of a small outer office, a large surgical dressing-room equipped as a first-class Casualty Department, and two tiny clinical rooms fitted with examination couches. The only entrance was from the packing hall into the office, and throughout were concealed emergency bells. On my first night the night manager showed me each bell. 'Not that I'm expecting you'll have any trouble, Sister. We've got a very decent type of man on our regular night shift—roughly hundred-and-fifty regulars—but we do have to take on casuals as unskilled workers on the belts. I expect you saw some lads waiting outside the gates to be taken on for the night on your way in.'

'Yes. I wondered why they were there.'

'A night's pay comes in handy for more than a few round these parts, Sister. What with prices the way they are, this austerity, not all that many jobs going. Bread rationing too— I dunno. Managed without that in the war, but now we've got it along with all the other rationed foods. When's it going to end, eh? As I was saying—these bells. Better safe than sorry. You are the only woman in the factory at night, on your own here and—well—you'll not mind my saying, not very old, are you? Just remember, first hint of trouble, or if you're only a mite anxious, you touch one of these bells. All ring in my office and all the night foreman's offices and we'll all be down, pronto!'

That night, between nine and midnight, every few minutes the door from the packing hall was pushed open by some man scattering a fine haze of flour whilst gingerly rubbing stomach, forehead, back, or demonstrating the cough that had kept him awake all day. 'Just a drop of peppermint water . . . just a couple of APCs . . . just a drop of linctus, please, Sister. Ta.'

At midnight my night meal was sent down from the canteen. I ate in the outer office, never in the canteen, an all-male preserve at night. About twenty minutes after the canteen worker removed my tray, the night manager raced in and held open the door. 'Nasty accident down the butchers' shop coming in now, Sister. Lad cut his own leg accidentally.'

The injured butcher was carried in by three of his colleagues with his foreman as escort. All five were soaked in bright arterial blood as the injured man had inadvertently stabbed his right femoral artery. The little I had to do before sending the man to hospital took very few minutes. The factory had an arrangement with the nearest general hospital that allowed the night-shift Sister to send in patients without first calling a doctor. In half an hour an ambulance had removed the injured man and he was in hospital. When I had cleaned the bloodstains from the couch, floor and myself, the night manager and foreman butcher returned with the official forms the three of us had to fill in immediately in each other's presence.

The night manager explained the procedure. 'I've got to ask this question, Sister. You are sure he was wearing his proper protective leather apron?'

'Quite sure, Mr X. I took it off him and handed it to the foreman.'

'That's right, Mr X. That's what the Sister did. Not that I'd let one of my lads pick up a knife in my shop without his protective. . . .'

'Of course you wouldn't, Mr Y, but I have to ask this.'

Mr Y, the foreman Master Butcher in his shop of all qualified butchers, was the exception in build. All the other butchers were gigantic men. Mr Y was a neat little man with the face of a weary poet. Now a distraught poet. 'You got to get used to lads nicking themselves a bit in the butchering trade, Sister, but I never had anything like this in any shop of mine before. Gone in deep, had he?'

'Quite, but cleanly. He hadn't severed the artery. Just opened it. He told me his knife missed the protective apron, went in just below and he was using too much strength to stop in time.'

Both men made notes. Mr Y said some of his young lads didn't know their own strength and when a young lad stood six foot two and weighed fourteen stone he'd got some strength, he had. 'Not but what you got to use your strength when rinding pork as he was, Sister.' He demonstrated with movements graceful as a ballet dancer's. 'You take a hold, and you bring your knife up then you bring it sweeping down like, towards you. Not but what the lads don't get enough practice. Cut up six thousand pounds of pork of an average night we do. How do you reckon he'll do?'

'I'm not a doctor, Mr Y, but I'd say, very well. I think they'll stitch him in the theatre tonight under an anaesthetic and doubt he'll be warded more than a few days or off work more than two or three weeks. He looked a very healthy young man and from his colour, pulse and blood-pressure, he hadn't lost much blood.' (This forecast proved correct.)

The men exchanged nods and glances. The manager asked, 'Do much nursing in the war, Sister?' At my answer he smiled faintly, 'No wonder it didn't give you a turn to see a bit of blood spilled.'

At six that morning he returned alone. 'Never got round to asking—meal suit you? Coffee hot? Good.' He glanced through the log book in which were entered the names, occupations, ailments, treatments and times given of every man I had attended in the night. 'Forty to midnight. Kept you busy.'

'Is that a typical number, Mr X?'

'Varies.' He pushed his glasses to the top of his head and smiled more to himself than at me. 'Numbers'll depend on the weather, how near it is to pay night, Thursdays—always less on pay night—and well, when we've got a new young Sister down here, human nature isn't it to want a look-see. No trouble, I take it ?'

'None, thank you.'

Neither then nor ever during my time in that factory. (My only regret here was that it prevented my seeing the night manager and all the night foremen descending on first-aid, pronto.) Beneath the butchers' blue coats, trousers, striped aprons, 'protectives' and straw boaters; the cooks' dapper white jerkins, cravats, white trousers and chefs or baseball caps; the maintenance staff's boiler-suits; the long-distance van drivers' old service greatcoats, thick scarves, cloth caps; the casuals' dungarees and flapping floury aprons, were men identical with those I had nursed from N.D.K. in 1940 to Casualty in 1945. A very few were ill and needed to be referred to the firm's medical officer; even fewer were malingerers. The vast majority had genuine minor ailments or injuries and wasted neither the firm's, their own, nor my time. Within minutes of swallowing anti-acid mixture, linctus, the peppermint water particularly beloved by the pastry cooks, the APCs beloved by all, or having their nicks dressed, splinters removed, sprains soothed, black eyes camouflaged, all rushed back to their floors leaving me rushing round removing flour with a damp duster.

Every night factory life reminded me more of hospital life. There was the same hierarchical ladder with the same clearly defined rungs and tribal customs. On the top rung were the butchers (consultants) who fraternized only with each other, and talked to the night manager (Matron) and myself (Night Sister in both). The pastry cooks (senior residents) laughed heartily at the butchers' jokes, fraternized cheerfully amongst themselves and with dignity, with the meat cooks (registrars and housemen), and all chatted to the night manager and myself. The maintenance men (medical administrators) kept themselves to themselves. The van drivers (post graduates) were the most individualistic group and ready to exchange yawns with all but the casuals. The casuals (medical students) appeared universally regarded as silent audiences to be endured but neither approved nor encouraged. 'If you ask me, Sister, casuals aren't what they were . . . can't be bothered to learn a trade I reckon . . . now, when I was an apprentice. . . .'

One of the butchers' customs gave me a peculiar pleasure. For some reason I never risked querying for fear of committing a solecism, when moving around the factory to and from work or canteen, they walked in single file headed by their foreman with his towering young chargehand immediately behind. When the file and myself passed each other, invariably first the foreman raised his straw hat "Evening, Sister!' and one by one the file echoed action and words.

The factory was in a reputedly tough area of London that was as bomb-damaged as Lambeth. In 1950, with the country struggling through the years of post-war austerity, much of London was still burnt-out, jagged, roofless and filthy. Every night after leaving my nearest bus stop I had a ten-minute walk down side streets and alleys and passed little groups of men standing aimlessly at corners, in doorways, against alley walls. I walked alone and as safely as in Lambeth in the blackout. Most nights, particularly on Thursdays, larger groups of men waited outside the closed main gates of the van-lined factory yard in the hope of casual work. The nightly number of casuals taken on depended on the number of orders for the following day, and on Thursdays, for Fridays and Saturdays. When the manager's appearance at the gates coincided with my arrival I rushed in as I dreaded seeing the disappointment in the faces lined and prematurely aged by pre-war poverty, when the younger and stronger were picked out. 'You, you, you, you, you . . . that's all for tonight lads. Sorry. No more wanted. No use hanging about.' It was the first time I had seen the sad, ugly sight of men standing waiting for work. It gave me a new, very-belated insight into the term 'unemployed'. I never asked any of the men in the factory their pay but several casuals volunteered the information that they could earn 27s. 6d. for a full night.

Summer arrived early with a heat-wave and into first-aid arrived double the usual number of casuals. The majority were young Irishmen newly over from Ulster or Eire who had spent their days sleeping in the London parks. I used pints of calamine lotion on their shoulders, backs, foreheads and noses.

'How long were you asleep in the sun today ?'

'It's no idea I have of that at all, Sister, but there was I waking to the terrible stiffness and the great burning.'

'Haven't you lodgings ? Even a bed somewhere ?'

'Sister, now this'll be the way of it—and haven't the three of us the one bed and isn't it the grand scheme with Mickeen and myself working nights and Paddy the days and himself having the bed the morn and myself the noon—but what does himself do but get himself a woman ? And it's a grand woman she is, says himself, and she's not the woman at all to be—she's not the woman at all to be—'

'She needs the bed ?'

'Sure to God, Sister, and isn't that a fact ? So it's out to the park you'll be going, says himself, and it's out to the park I'm going and thanking the Blessed Saints for putting in a fine word for myself with the sun shining and the grand smell of the warm grass—and then waking to the terrible stiffness and the great burning—and isn't it a grand cooling you're giving my backside, Sister, and it's a grand woman you are yourself and may the Holy Angels bless you. . . .'

In the heat-wave early morning, London, from the top of a bus, turned into a country village. There were women with spotted handkerchiefs over their heads, legs bare and brown, sturdy arms folded, chatting to each other from open door-ways; newspaper sellers in collarless shirts with sleeve high, caps over eyes, whistling amicably between their teeth as they laid out their stacks or caught them from cruising vans; barrow boys spruce, neatly shaven, lovingly arranging and grading their fruit, turning blemishes from the light, snuggling over-ripe pears in purple tissue paper; flower-women shaking dew from their skirts, shouting to each other across the fast-filling streets as if over country lanes. The voices were clear in the clean young air that later thickened with exhaust, petrol fumes and the sickening smell of overheated tyres. The early sun sparked on pavements, streets, and transformed to black diamonds the tar that before noon had started bubbling up between the flags and was still steaming when I left for work at night. I watched from the top of buses as if I had never seen

London before. It was some time before I realized what I was beginning to see again was life through the slowly opening anxiety-shutters. Not all were opening. When my bus ran along the Fulham Road I never looked at the Brompton Chest Hospital. When pushing Vee along Chelsea Embankment I never looked across the river towards Lambeth.

First-aid, as all Casualty Departments, had its regulars. One of my regular casuals told me he was a poet and his muse (sic) was inspired by nocturnal work on the belts. 'I see all those dear little pies rolling by, and as I brush the spare flour off their dear little faces, I think very beautiful thoughts, Sister.'

His floor foreman told me he was a good worker. 'Stands there all night with his little brush happy as larry brushing every pie like he fancies each one but he'll never buy a 'second' seeing he's a vegetarian.'

After each batch of pies was cooked and checked, any flawed were removed and sold to the staff at a discount as 'seconds'. One morning I bought a 'second'. Vee and I had it for lunch. It was the best pork-pie I had eaten and Vee regarded it as ambrosia. That night one butcher cut his finger deeply and as I stitched and dressed the wound I told him about my 'second'.

'Didn't know you'd a nipper, Sister.' With his free hand he produced a snap of his two small sons. I showed him one of Vee. After we had congratulated each other, he looked woodenly at his feet. 'I—er—heard as your hubby's poorly.'

'Yes. Keep that finger dry, Mr Z.'

'I'll do that, Sister. Much obliged.'

Between three and four that morning in his tea-break he reappeared looking sheepish and clutching a packet wrapped in greaseproof paper. 'They'd to make a special order of fancies (miniature pies) upstairs tonight, Sister. My nippers get real made up when I fetch 'em home fancies and as they always go quick as 'seconds' I got a couple extra as—er—well—er—I reckoned as maybe your nipper might fancy 'em—oh, no Sister! Ta very much, but oh, no! They been paid for.'

First-aid was quiet for some little time after he left. In that time I sat at the desk in the outer office and looked at the wrapped packet beside the blotter. At that time of the night all human defences were low. Mine collapsed. I thought of that butcher's love for his two little sons, I thought of father, I thought of Vee missing all her life the love of a good father, I thought of J missing all his life the love of his child. I thought of the man he had been and I had loved. The pain of those thoughts kept me as numbed and unblinking in my chair as I had seen the pain keep numbed and unblinking patients having coronary thromboses. Whilst the pain ripped through me and I sat and stared at two carefully wrapped tiny pork-pies, the distant clanking of the machinery that went on all night and the revving of the vans about to start their pre-dawn journeys all over southern England and the Midlands sounded louder and more intolerable than the loudest and most intolerable artillery barrage.

'Sorry to bother you, Sister—' a van driver charged in un-winding his muffler—'just a drop of linctus to get her on the road, please! Ta. Lovely!'

It became an unusual night that ended without a wrapped packet on my desk. 'Just thought as the nipper might fancy 'em, Sister. . . .' Not one man would accept repayment of the discount price. All those pies were as good as the first, and made, as I saw, with skill and hygiene.

It was one of my occasional jobs to pay unannounced visits to the various floors, to look inside the pastry-mixing machines that when empty looked like spotless, shining builders' cement-mixers, to watch the butchers butchering, the cooks cooking, the casuals standing working at the long, moving belts, the lines of pies baking slowly on the rollers rolling slowly through the great open-mouthed, open-ended ovens. When each night started the men looked reasonably fresh, as the night unwound the colour left their faces until even the park sleepers' tans turned yellowish. 'Can't wonder, Sister? Takes it out of you, working nights. The women on days— always carrying on they are about wanting to work the night-shift—but I ask you, Sister, how could any woman stand up to regular night work?'

In the following twenty-five months, I spent twenty-one on full-time night-duty in the Buchanan Hospital, St Leonards. The Buchanan was one of the Hastings Group of Hospitals, part of the nursing training school run throughout the Group and a few minutes' walk downhill from mother's flat. I was employed as a Senior Staff Nurse and occasionally acting-Night Sister. Most nights I was in charge of the former private floor, a rambling assembly of eleven rooms, some single, some double, some treble-bedded. The floor still admitted a few private patients, as well as N.H.S. Amenity patients and General Ward Emergencies. The G.W.E.s were either over-spills from the general wards, or in the continuing absence of Intensive Care Units, patients requiring maximum quiet and often on the D.I.L.

The N.H.S. was very slowly improving nurses' working hours and pay. On night-duty in the Buchanan, the whole night staff worked a repeated two-week rota, with the student nurses changing every three months, the Night Super-intendent, Night Sister and any night Staff Nurses as myself, remaining on permanently. In the rota, for the first week, four nights were worked, two off; in the second (8-day week), six on, two off. Night hours were 8.30 p.m. to 8 a.m. and as these were longer than the law then allowed, every night nurse had to have one free hour during the night aside from the night meal-break. Night meals were no longer allowed to be eaten in ward kitchens and duty-rooms at odd moments but were served at fixed times in the staff dining-room. My pay as a Staff Nurse in the top grade was £28 per month (take-home pay approximately £24).

'Let's see how you manage for a month,' said the Matron when I asked her for an interview and advice in late August 1950. 'We'll have another chat at the end of September.'

At the end of September, 'All well with the little one? No disturbed nights? Grandmother enjoying baby-sitting? Splendid! How about you? Getting enough sleep?'

'Yes, thank you, Matron.' I did not specify my sleeping hours as I was uncertain how long I could last on only four hours a day. However, once I grew acclimatized to that schedule, it proved an invaluable bonus to both my careers as without any harm to my health it allowed me twenty-hour instead of the more usual fourteen-hours days.

My job on the private floor was continuously interesting owing to the variety of patients. For the first few months my work worried me more than I dared admit to any but my old friends, our elderly now retired, widowered former G.P. 'The Doc', his daughter Ann, and myself. In the five years since my general training ended the new chemotherapy had revolution-ized so many medical, surgical and post-operative techniques. I borrowed modern medical and surgical textbooks from John, the houseman, and one of the Doc's sons, a senior surgical registrar at a London teaching hospital. All my own were use-less, having been written pre-penicillin and antibiotics.

The most spectacular change I noticed, was in pneumonia. Early one night we admitted a middle-aged woman with double lobar pneumonia. The next night her temperature was only a little over normal and she felt well enough to be annoyed that her husband had forgotten to bring in her hair curlers. Later in the duty-room I voiced my amazement to a houseman and my second-year night junior. 'Incredible! Remember her respirations when she came in last night?'

My colleagues were puzzled. The houseman had been quali-fied a few months. 'Why incredible?'

I explained that I had been accustomed to some pneumonias clearing up in several days on the sulfa drugs, but that I had remembered those I had seen as junior nursed through to the old ninth-day crisis when either the patient's temperature soared fatally, or fell dramatically (by crisis), or dropped in the more gentle fall, rise, fall, rise, fall to normal pattern (by lysis).

From their expressions I had worked in the Crimea with Miss Nightingale. The houseman asked, 'Do you honestly go back pre-sulfa?'

'I go back to M. and B. 693, and as it didn't suit everyone—yes.'

He closed his mouth with an audible snap. The junior was still lost. 'WHAT was M. and B. 693?'

On nights off I pushed Vee round to the Doc's house. 'I'm beginning to feel like a bit of nursing history.'

The Doc's sparse hair and luxuriant walrus moustache were all white, his deafness had increased, but he still wore his glasses on the end of his nose and looked over them with direct blue eyes. 'My Godfathers, Lucy, how do you think I feel? Fifty years since I got m'Fellowship. Started as a houseman with Lister's carbolic spray—ending with Fleming's penicillin. I'm not a bit of surgical history. I'm the history of modern British surgery personified and petrified. Want to borrow some more literature? How's your own coming along? When are we going to read Vol. 1?'

'Still on the first draft I started at the nursery, Doc. Coming along a bit faster now in my free hours at night.'

'That's better. What's it about?'

'Mostly a hospital in wartime London. Think that's a good idea?'

'Why not? You know what you're writing about.'

The ruins of St Johns lay between his house and mother's flat. The ruins had been tidied, the steeple stood alone, looked smaller than I remembered and very forlorn. I avoided looking at the steeple and tidied gap. Never for choice did I walk along our old road past our old house. On most fine days I took Vee onto the beach, but never to our 'tent' beach by the long-destroyed St Leonards' pier. In my personal life, nostalgia appealed to me as little as masochism, and I only accepted the fact that to varying degrees I was enduring both when writing my novel as it seemed I had no alternative. I had not consciously chosen the theme or my characters, but directly I began writing all were released by my subconscious in such a powerful flood that often I had the impression the novel was some private arrangement between my brain and my hands over which I had no control.

Without Vee I would never have gone back to St Leonards. But living there was less expensive than London; there I had old friends and my only roots, and both were of particular importance to any fatherless child. As soon as fatherless children can talk and have friends of the same age, they are asked, 'Where's your daddy?' When the answer is already known to friends and friends of friends, on park swings, roundabouts, pebbles and while digging holes in the sand, the question was generally rephrased, 'When's your daddy going to stop being sick?' (From this experience, ever after, when asked for advice by other young mothers similarly placed, I have answered, 'Go back to your own roots, your own home town or village, and there start again. It'll help your child and so, yourself.')

By November 1951 the Doc and Ann had moved to Small-hythe, near Tenterden, Kent, and my novel was still un-finished. I was no longer able to stay awake when I sat down to write in my free hours at night, or after putting Vee to bed on my nights off. Having saved £30, I resigned temporarily.

In mid-February 1952, a few days after the death of King George VI (6th February), I finished the novel. I had run out of money and needed an additional £10 to pay for the pro-fessional typing of one top and one carbon copy. I went straight back to night-duty. When I sent the novel to be typed I had no clear idea what to do with it when it was returned. I knew nothing about publishing houses, had never heard of literary agents. In that interval, as so often in my nursing life, a patient helped me. She was an elderly lady whom I nursed for a longish period and as we became friends she heard about my novel. One of her regular visitors and great friends, I then learnt, was a distinguished biographer, who said:

'When your book's ready, let me have a look at it.'

When the typing firm returned my copies, I had saved £12 10s. and had nights off. I drew out all but the 10s., paid the firm, used the remainder on postage, and—since Vee and I were temporarily alone—a celebration lunch to mark the start of my professional writing career. It was 17th March.

Vee surveyed the restaurant with approval. 'When you write lots of books, mummy, can we have lots of feasties and can I always have lemonade with two straws and chicken and chips and chocolate ice cream?'

In the glass of dry white wine I had bought myself, I toasted her and our future. 'Next book, Vee, three straws.'

On-duty, in my free hour I began another novel. A month later the biographer rang me from London one night when by sheer good chance I was again off. 'I have shown your book to a friend who is an established writer and we both think our literary agents should see it. If you hear from them, as I think you will, for God's sake listen to what they say and take their advice. They know the book trade.'

In early May the literary agents wrote asking me to visit their London office. Then, 'We're interested in your book, Miss Andrews, but not sure we'll be able to sell it. Worth the try. How about the next? Started? Good girl. Let us see it when it's ready.'

I returned to St Leonards semi-delirious with premature relief and joy. My wartime novel was rejected by six London publishers. It was in the process of collecting its second rejection slip in early June when I asked my Matron for another interview.

'I can't afford time off without working, Matron, but again I can't keep awake in my free hour. I must have some time on days or I'll never get this book written. Is there no part-time day work anywhere in the Group?'

She was a tall slender woman with a long, gentle, face, and a smile that removed at least twenty years from her age. 'I'll ring round and see what can be done.' Later. 'One possibility. That former Home for Retired Professional Women, now being converted into an N.H.S. Geriatric Unit, is so desperately in need of trained staff that they are willing to take day part-timers. I'm afraid the pay isn't good.'

In June 1952, the official N.H.S. pay for an S.R.N., Part I C.M.B., part-time Sister and deputy Matron was 2s. 9d. (14p) an hour. The Unit cleaners were paid 2s. 6d. an hour.

For six weeks I worked five hours a day, seven days a week. I split my hours between two in the early mornings and three in the late evenings after Vee was settled for the night. All those weeks the weather was glorious and every day Vee and I had picnic lunches on the beach. Whilst Vee dug holes, sand castles and tried to empty the Channel with other toddlers, against a breakwater I wrote my second novel.

'Down to the beach again, Sister?' queried my new patients. 'That's nice for you and the little girl.'

Not all were elderly, but all the younger middle-aged were severely disabled by rheumatic conditions. The majority of all were single women who had lost their fiancés, or hopes of marriage, in the First World War and earned their own livings until forced into retirement by age or ill-health. 'I'm afraid I only managed to save very little, Sister. When I was young we didn't enter the teaching—the nursing—profession with any thought of money. But when one isn't as young as one was, money is rather essential—not that I'm complaining! We're most fortunate here and having so much done for us since The Change.'

The older patients all referred to the N.H.S. as The Change. The changes were considerable. The former 'Home' had been renamed 'House'; various inside walls had been knocked down, bedrooms enlarged, renamed 'wards'; the old dark green and dark brown walls had been repainted in pastels, fitted hand-basins installed, old bathrooms converted into modern and some into sluices. The old red-plush furniture and red-plush curtains heavy with bobbles replaced with deal, plastic and chintz.

'All very hygienic and scientific, dear, and, of course, we are allowed visitors three times a week and it is only understandable that we should be asked to keep our locker-tops clear of knick-knacks, but I never did like pink.'

The pink was on the identical shell-patterned quilts now provided for all the beds.

Efforts were made to maintain a homely and not Home atmosphere, and particularly with the arrangement of the small tables in the dining-room and chairs in the communal sitting-room. But hope was missing. The patients knew they were there until death and the knowledge cast a tangible shadow. And yet, though some of their lives seemed to me unliveable, every elderly patient there, as elsewhere in my nursing career, clung to life to the final breath. Never, anywhere, did one such patient in my hearing admit a desire for death.

I have read and been told of the dying protesting, 'Animals

are put to sleep—why not me?' In nine years' bedside nursing I never once heard that. In consequence, though I do not subscribe to the belief that active attempts to prolong life are always morally or humanly justified, nor, in any circumstances, do I subscribe to legal euthanasia.

In those six weeks I heard constantly, 'Don't grow old, Sister. Don't ever wish to grow old—if it means being like us.'

After I left the Unit, several patients wrote to me for years. Their letters were alive with items of Unit interest: the fascinating exchange Miss X had had with Miss Y over the position of an armchair, the really fierce displeasure expressed in the dining-room over the new type of marmalade, the disturbing effects of the new screen covers. 'Modern art it may be, but, personally, I think it looks like a bilious attack in a thunderstorm—I much preferred our daffodils and roses.' For years at Christmas they sent hand-made cards 'To Sister and the little girl'. One by one the cards and letters ceased to arrive until all that remained was the sadness and the wonder at the amount the human spirit can surmount.

At the end of July 1952 I was back on night-duty in the Buchanan and had finished the first draft of Vol. 2. At the end of August my literary agents sent me a copy of a letter written them by the third publisher to reject Vol.1. That latter, dated 21st August 1952, included these words: 'I am quite sure that people could not be induced to read this book now, with its all too graphic and painful reminders of things as they were for those who saw some of the worst of them . . . But', as my readers sympathetically say, 'let her (L.A.) not make it too harrowing a story and let her, above all, leave the past to bury its dead.'

On reading that it struck me that Dr Werner von Braun might agree. I remembered again, 'No-one bothers with yesterday.'

On my next nights off I re-read Vol.2, realized the same objections could apply, and that in my anxiety to portray hospital life as I saw it I had narrowed my focus onto the blood and tears, and ignored the humour, absurdities, temperamental incompatibilities, and inter-staff love affairs that were as much a part of the normal life of any large teaching hospital as the teaching rounds and bedpans. I thought of all the doctors, medical students and nurses I had known and worked with, how seldom any were over thirty or married, and how every other one was either in the throes of, or just recovering from, what he or she regarded as the love of all time. I thought of the laughter I had heard in so many wards and so many places where it would have seemed the angels must have wept. Not humans.

I decided to re-write the whole novel without falsification, but with a much lighter touch, and the inclusion of at least one major love affair. Neither then (nor for some years until informed of this) did it occur to me that I was writing either 'an hospital novel' or 'a romance'. I was merely writing of the world I knew best without any idea that others might find this world interesting. In 1952 the arrival on British television of *Dr Kildare, Doctor At Large, Emergency-Ward 10, Dr Finlay's Casebook, et al.*, were in the future.

One night in my free hour I was sorting the pages into chapters on the floor when a houseman put his head round the door. 'What are you doing, Staff?'

'Organizing Vol.2.'

He crouched and picked up a chapter. 'You've given a blow-by-blow of a breech—' he turned the page 'and why give the baby a spina biff.?'

'Don't ask me. Just happened that way.'

'Is it all midder?'

'First half. Later the girl gets tubercle.'

'But ends up falling into the hero's arms and stepping into the sunset?'

'Ends with her still warded and not sure she loves him.'

He sat back on his heels. 'Who'll want to read this stuff?'

'God knows.'

'What are you calling it?'

'*The Print Petticoat.*'

'Alliteration may help. What does your old man think of Vols. 1 and 2?'

'I don't know as we haven't discussed them.'

He was momentarily silent. 'Actually, what is his prognosis ?'

'Nil.'

We were both silent, then began talking about the patients. 'Got some bad news for you,' he said, 'though it won't surprise you. I've just left Miss Z's latest Path. Report on your desk.' He shook his head. 'Plus, plus, plus.'

'Oh, God, no!'

'Yea. Bloody everywhere. Bloody hell. Bloody nice woman.'

Miss Z was a youngish woman in an Amenity bed. She had been a senior buyer in a large department store until her short, terminal illness. She was a woman of great fortitude and dignity, she did not want to die, and to her final and coherent breath she fought one of the greatest fights I ever witnessed. I was with her when she died and as the night senior performed her Last Offices on what proved to be the last time in my nursing career. It distressed me as much as on the first time when I helped my senior as a night junior in 1942.

(Three months later when Vee and I had moved to Kent, a few days before Christmas, a parcel arrived addressed to Vee in an unknown hand. Inside was a large, exquisitely dressed girl doll with washable golden hair, a voice that said 'Mama' and a card in different handwriting. 'To little Vee with love to you and Mummy for Christmas and 1953 from one of Mummy's sick ladies, Miss Z.'

I rang the department store and was put through to the owner's wife. 'Yes, I sent it as I promised when Miss Z wrote the card and chose the doll before she passed on. I asked the hospital for your new address.')

One night in early September 1952 I was acting-Night Sister and sitting at Matron's desk in her office filling in the bedstate for the whole hospital from the night seniors' returns when the Night Superintendent came back from her free hour. She slapped on the desk a copy of a top-selling woman's magazine. 'Read the short story in your hour. I'm sure even you could do better! Why don't you write a short story for a magazine instead of the books you're always working on ?'

I think it was the first magazine short story I had read. That took about three minutes. I re-read it, noticed it had only two major and two minor characters, a beginning, a middle, an end, and counted the words. Three thousand. I spent the rest of my hour writing on the blank backs of old used temperature charts a love story in that frame and became so engrossed that I over-ran by fifteen minutes. The Night Superintendent was amused. 'I guessed genius was burning and as we're having such a slack night left you to it. Finished it ? Good! Mind you send it up.'

Mainly to appease her I had it typed for 7s. 6d., sent it to my agents, and then forgot it as a major personal crisis had arisen. I learnt belatedly that the lease of mother's flat expired at the end of October, for legal reasons could not be renewed, and mother was convinced we should all move to London.

'The Chelsea flat only has two bedrooms and one's tiny. There isn't room for four adults and one very active small child.'

'It's useless trying to find another flat down here. I've been asking around. That's why I haven't told you. . . .'

Once more the avalanche of unsought advice, 'Go back to Thomas's . . . go into a shop . . . be a model . . . be a receptionist . . . how could you night nurse much longer without getting ill ? . . . . . You'll have to give up nursing. You simply can't afford not to—look how you have to work a whole month for £24!'

As suddenly my working life had become more demanding. A boy suffering from acute tetanus was admitted to one of our rooms and I was relieved of all other duties to be his special night nurse. For several nights he was dangerously ill, but eventually he walked out of hospital with his parents. On the morning before his discharge the wave of sheer joy that swept round the hospital was (and is) one of the reasons why doctors and nurses remain in their professions.

That morning I walked back up the hill smiling foolishly over one of the large boxes of chocolates presented by his parents to all his nurses. Vee greeted the chocolates with unsurprised pleasure. 'Mummy's sick gentlemen always give us sweeties,' she informed John, who was down to help with the domestic crisis. 'Mummy's sick ladies sometimes give us flowers and me toys, but the sick gentlemen just always give us sweeties. Please can I have one ?'

John reminded her she had yet to have breakfast. 'Don't worry, uncle. I can eat sweeties and breakfast. I can eat everything.'

This was true. One of the advantages of a lack of parental ability to afford food fads was the way these had no chance to develop in their children.

I was too tired and pleased about the boy to remember my usual 'Any post ?' until the afternoon.

Vee ambled off to collect from mother's bedroom the letter that had come for me in the first post. She returned with it inside the box of chocolates. John told her she should have been born a few centuries earlier. 'Vee, honey, you could've given the Danes tips on Danegeld.' He noticed my agent's name on the envelope I had opened. 'More news of Vol.1 ?'

I shook my head and in speechless wonder handed him the letter. *Good Housekeeping*, not the magazine I had in mind when writing my first short story, had bought it for 25 guineas.

It was my last night before nights' off. Previously I had decided to reach a decision about our future after tomorrow night's sleep. For two years mother had willingly baby-watched on my working nights, she loved London, and it had already been decided she should move in, if only temporarily, with Betty and John. Walking down the hill that night my mind made itself up. I asked the private floor day Sister to stand-in for me for an extra fifteen minutes and the Matron for an immediate interview. I showed Matron (and later the Night Superintendent, Night Sister, and half the night staff) my agent's letter, and asked to be released from my job at the end of October.

No nurse could have had a more sympathetic and helpful Matron. 'Will you be able to sell more stories to magazines ?'

'What I can do once, I can do again, Matron. Even if this is only beginner's luck, presumably I can learn how to write for magazines much as I learnt how to nurse.'

'That sounds logical.' She smiled. 'I rather think this time we will lose you.' She made some calculations. 'With your nights off, your last night on duty will be 29th October. But don't forget. If you ever want to return to nursing, come and see me. Where will you be living when you leave us ? London ?'

'That I've not settled, Matron. May I let you know ?'

'Of course. And, congratulations, Staff Nurse and—very good luck!'

Next morning I rang the number of a sixteenth-century house in Smallhythe, Kent. 'Ann, when you and the Doc left St Leonards you both said if ever I was really in a spot to let you know. I'm in one now.' I explained briefly, then added, 'With the *Good Housekeeping* money and what I'll have over from next month's pay, I should have thirty-five quid. I've got to re-write *The Print Petticoat* before I send it up. That'll take about two months if I'm not working.'

Ann, as her father, never wasted words in essential moments. 'You and Vee must stay with us whilst you re-write it.'

'Ann, God bless you, but shouldn't you talk to the Doc about this first ? Or rather, I think I should, and as he can't hear me over the 'phone, could Vee and I come out for the day some time in the next four weeks ?'

'Aren't you on nights off ?'

'Yes.'

'Then what', demanded Ann, 'are you both doing to-morrow ?'

A SELECTED LIST OF
FINE AUTOBIOGRAPHIES AND BIOGRAPHIES
AVAILABLE FROM CORGI BOOKS

THE PRICES SHOWN BELOW WERE CORRECT AT THE TIME OF GOING TO
PRESS. HOWEVER TRANSWORLD PUBLISHERS RESERVE THE RIGHT TO SHOW
NEW RETAIL PRICES ON COVERS WHICH MAY DIFFER FROM THOSE
PREVIOUSLY ADVERTISED IN THE TEXT OR ELSEWHERE.

CORGI BIOGRAPHY SERIES

☐ 99271 2	MY HAPPY DAYS IN HELL	George Faludy	£4.95
☐ 12833 3	THE HOUSE BY THE DVINA	Eugenie Fraser	£3.95
☐ 12863 5	THE LONG JOURNEY HOME	Flora Leipman	£3.95
☐ 99247 X	THE FORD OF HEAVEN	Brian Power	£3.50
☐ 99293 3	THE PUPPET EMPEROR	Brian Power	£3.95

GENERAL AUTOBIOGRAPHIES & BIOGRAPHIES

☐ 12851 1	CHILDRENS HOSPITAL	Peggy Anderson	£3.99
☐ 09332 7	GO ASK ALICE	Anonymous	£2.50
☐ 13220 9	THE GENTLE ART: A MIDWIVE'S STORY		
		Penny Armstrong & Sheryl Feldman	£3.95
☐ 99054 X	BORSTAL BOY	Brendan Behan	£3.95
☐ 99307 7	QADDAFI	David Blundy & Andrew Lycett	£4.95
☐ 12889 9	ADRIFT	Steven Callahan	£2.95
☐ 99328 X	THATCHER'S BRITAIN	Terry Coleman	£3.95
☐ 13126 1	CATHERINE COOKSON COUNTRY	Catherine Cookson	£5.95
☐ 09373 4	OUR KATE	Catherine Cookson	£2.95
☐ 11772 2	'H' THE AUTOBIOGRAPHY OF A CHILD PROSTITUTE		
	AND HEROIN ADDICT	Christiane F.	£2.50
☐ 12727 2	MEN	Anna Ford	£2.95
☐ 12501 6	BEYOND THE HIGHLAND LINE	Richard Frere	£1.95
☐ 13070 2	BORN LUCKY: AN AUTOBIOGRAPHY	John Francome	£2.95
☐ 13254 3	ANNE FRANK REMEMBERED	Miep Gies & Alison Leslie Gold	£2.95
☐ 13032 X	NO LAUGHING MATTER	Joseph Heller	£2.95
☐ 99285 2	GETTING HITLER INTO HEAVEN	John Graven Hughes	£4.95
☐ 99098 1	AUTUMN OF FURY	Mohamed Heikal	£3.95
☐ 13248 9	CUTTING THE LIONS' TAIL	Mohamed Heikal	£4.50
☐ 13060 5	KHASHOGGI: THE STORY OF THE WORLD'S		
	RICHEST MAN	Ron Kessler	£3.95
☐ 99294 1	TO HELL AND BACK	Nikki Lauda	£2.95
☐ 11961 X	SHOUT!	Phillip Norman	£2.50
☐ 99158 9	BRENDAN BEHAN	Ulick O'Connor	£2.95
☐ 99143 0	CELTIC DAWN	Ulick O'Connor	£4.95
☐ 13094 X	WISEGUY	Nicholas Pileggi	£2.95
☐ 12577 6	PLACE OF STONES	Ruth Janette Ruck	£2.50
☐ 13058 3	THE MARILYN CONSPIRACY	Milo Speriglio	£2.50
☐ 12589 X	AND I DON'T WANT TO LIVE THIS LIFE	Deborah Spungen	£3.50
☐ 12072 3	KITCHEN IN THE HILLS	Elizabeth West	£2.50
☐ 11707 2	GARDEN IN THE HILLS	Elizabeth West	£2.50
☐ 10907 X	HOVEL IN THE HILLS	Elizabeth West	£1.95

All Corgi/Bantam Books are available at your bookshop or newsagent, or can be ordered from the following address:

Corgi/Bantam Books,
Cash Sales Department,
P.O. Box 11, Falmouth, Cornwall TR10 9EN

Please send a cheque or postal order (no currency) and allow 60p for postage and packing for the first book plus 25p for the second book and 15p for each additional book grdered up to a maximum charge of £1.90 in UK.

B.F.P.O. customers please allow 60p for the first book, 25p for the second book plus 15p per copy for the next 7 books, thereafter 9p per book.

Overseas customers, including Eire, please allow £1.25 for postage and packing for the first book, 75p for the second book, and 28p for each subsequent title ordered.